Ocean Falls and Beyond

Experiences of an Authentic Canadian Guy

By John Forbes

Ocean Falls and Beyond
Experiences of an Authentic Canadian Guy

Library and Archives Canada Cataloguing in Publications

Forbes, J.A. (John Andrew), 1944-, author
Canada Autobiography
BC West Coast, Ocean Falls, Comox Valley
Royal Canadian Air Force (RCAF)
European Travel, North American Travel

Genre/Form - Non-Fiction
ISBN 978-1-77136-568-0

Book cover & layout by Linda Graceffo, The Writer Connection
www.selfpublishingresources.ca

Printed in Victoria, BC, Canada.

Email John Forbes at ejforbes@shaw.ca

Dedicated to the memory

of

Donald Ross Forbes

THE EARLY YEARS

Trail, North Vancouver, Ocean Falls

1944 - 1963

IN THE BEGINNING

I was born in the spring of 1944, in the town of Trail, British Columbia, Canada. My name is John Andrew Forbes, and this book is a compilation of humorous stories and events that I have experienced. I hope you enjoy the trip across Canada with me, learning about life in small towns, the pulp and paper industry, my travels and career with the Royal Canadian Air Force and beyond. My aim is to make you smile as you read about the interesting characters I have met in my journey, and the amazing and crazy things I went through. My life started out in the backwoods from humble beginnings but turned out very rewarding. Welcome to a truly Canadian experience from the viewpoint of an average, authentic, Canadian guy.

Trail is located in the beautiful West Kootenay region of the BC interior. When I think of that region it brings to mind high mountains, swiftly flowing rivers, hot summers and plenty of snow in the winter. The area was home to numerous mines, one in which my father was employed. Trail has the largest non-ferrous lead and zinc smelter in the world and is also famous for being the home of the Trail Smoke Eaters who won the World Ice Hockey Championship in 1939 and 1961.

My mother was born in 1914 in Humboldt, Saskatchewan, one of eleven children of Mike and Ida Lemmerich. Grandfather Mike was born in 1882 in Reynolds, North Dakota, approximately one hundred and sixty miles south of Winnipeg, Manitoba. He was a first-generation North

American whose parents had immigrated from Otterstadt, Germany. In 1903 the Lemmerich family, now with six kids, decided to make their final move to the Humboldt area where cheap, fertile land was available for homesteading. My grandmother, Ida Lang, was born in Iowa and moved with her family to Saskatchewan. There she met Mike and married him in 1907. Mike and Ida started a grain and cattle operation within a few miles of Humboldt, and like good Catholics, they began a sizable family. An interesting footnote here: their firstborn son, Adolf, changed his name to Al when he enlisted in the Canadian Army in WWII. I wonder why? Mom was the only one of eleven children in the family to go beyond high school. She took her nursing training in Macklin and Humboldt and graduated from St. Elizabeth's Hospital School of Nursing in 1935.

My paternal grandfather John, after whom I was named, and his wife Mary had three children by 1911, but tragically the oldest, a girl, died after contracting influenza. My father Andrew, the next oldest, was born at New Kilpatrick, a small village that is now a suburb of Glasgow, Scotland. From what I learned from my uncle Archie, Dad's youngest brother, we believe that my father was born sometime between 1905-07. Dad was very close-mouthed about himself, and even after my Saskatchewan cousins did some research in Scotland, we never did discover what his middle name was or if he even had one. Times were tough during that period in Scotland because of general living conditions and insufficient good jobs.

Shortly after their firstborn died, they looked for a fresh start in a new country with better prospects, and thus immigrated to Canada, settling in Regina, Saskatchewan, in 1912. Grandpa was hired by the school board as a custodian, where one of his main duties was running the coal furnace. No doubt that his experiences and skill acquired while working for British Railroads on their steam engines helped him land the position.

I have a six-by-eight-inch photo taken around the turn of the twentieth century titled "No. 224—Engine of Tay Bridge Disaster." In the picture, there are twenty-five railroad workers posing in front of and on the train engine. My cousin, Barry Forbes, who grew up in Regina and was much more familiar with Grandpa than I was, pointed out where he was standing. He said that he was the ninth person from the left, you can tell by the eyes. Ninth from the left looked like a fifteen-year-old kid, fairly short in statue. During a violent storm in 1879, the Tay Railroad Bridge, spanning the Firth of Tay by Dundee, collapsed as the train was crossing, sending all seventy-five people aboard to their deaths. Surprising enough, No. 224 had only superficial damage, which was later repaired, and saw another forty-five years of service. There are two interesting footnotes to this saga: first, engine No. 224 earned the nickname "The Diver," because it plunged into the drink not once but three times. Once during that fateful night and twice more in botched recovery attempts. The other footnote I learned while holidaying in Sedona, Arizona, of all places. I met a Scottish tourist who related to me an interesting tidbit about this sad affair. The word "botched" came into the English language as a result of the accident. The bridge designer was a well-known English engineer whose name was William Bouch. The Scots pronounced his name as "Botch." Shortly after the bridge was completed, Queen Victoria rode across in a railroad coach, and the Queen was so impressed that she subsequently knighted Mr. Bouch for his great feat of engineering. In the court of inquiry, it was determined that many factors contributed to the collapse, but the main reason was that Sir William didn't make allowances for wind loading. He died within a year, his professional reputation as an engineer in tatters.

Dad had three brothers. Ian was born in Scotland in 1910, Bill and Archie in Canada in 1912 and 1917 respectively. Dad ran away from home at age sixteen. There was a lot of friction between him and his mother, and it was likely because young Andy wasn't too impressed with getting an education. Two of his brothers would go on to university. Ian became a chartered accountant and Bill a mining engineer. Uncle Bill spent most of his working life in British Guyana in Central America where he was a world-renown bauxite mining engineer. When he finally moved back to Canada, he settled in Montreal, but from what I gathered he didn't last too long. He died at age sixty after succumbing to tropical diseases that he'd acquired while living in British Guyana. Another sad story about Bill was that his first wife lost her life during WWII when the ocean liner that was bringing her back from Britain to British Guyana was torpedoed by a German U-boat. The youngest brother, Archie, had his hopes for a higher education interrupted by army duties during the war; however, he did go on to a successful career in the printing business in Regina.

Andy, the black sheep, rode the rails to California. This is quite similar to a like-father-like-son story. Later, you will discover that I also wasn't too fond of school, and although I never rode for free on railroad freight cars, I did my fair share of hitchhiking back and forth across Canada. Dad never did reveal to any of his children what he did on his adventures or even where he travelled. Ten years was more or less unaccounted for with only a few snippets that he told his brothers, when he resurfaced back in Saskatchewan in 1934. I suspect that he didn't want us to experience what he did, but instead to stay in school to get that education that was the "key" to success.

Uncles Bill and Archie filled in some of the blanks for us. Dad worked on a tramp steamer that had two ports of call that they knew of. While in Hawaii he bought a ukulele that he never did master, and in Japan he bought a beautiful set of hand-painted dishes as a gift for his mother to win her over after the abrupt parting of the ways. He wrote grandmother a note saying that these dishes were en route. She waited patiently for months and when they finally arrived, ninety percent of them were broken. At one point in his travels Dad hung around the Monterey Bay area of California, and according to Bill, he knew some of the colourful characters that were eventually portrayed in one of John Steinbeck's early novels, *Tortilla Flat*. From California, he headed over to Arizona and worked in a huge copper mining operation at Bisbee, six miles north of the Mexican border. My wife and I drove there from Sedona in 2013 because I wanted to find traces of Dad's wanderings, but the local museum had no record because he wouldn't have had a phone if he lived in the single men's bunkhouse, thus no recorded phone number. And the mining corporation's policy was to destroy all records of any employees terminated or laid off, in case of any possible lawsuits down the road. Those mines weren't the healthiest of environments. We came up empty-handed but we did enjoy Bisbee. It's built on a hillside, is full of old heritage buildings and quaint little hotels, and has a thriving arts community.

In 1934, because of the low copper prices due to the Great Depression, Dad was laid off, so he had to swallow his pride and have money wired down to Arizona in order to bus it back home. Back in Regina Dad moved in with the family. There were no jobs to be found because of the Depression. Archie told me he spent much of his time in his room practising on his ukulele. To Archie, Dad was like a folk hero, back home after wandering to the ends of the world. I can imagine there was some tension in the household because Grandma was a very strong-willed lady. My cousin Barry was telling me that in the 1940s, she was the first woman in Regina to work as a saleswoman in real estate. Finally, after two years of sitting around, Dad hired on with the railroad in the B&B section—bridges and buildings—where he got his start in carpentry. The B&B crew travelled throughout Saskatchewan working on various projects, and that's when he met Mom in the small town of Macklin, where she was working as a nurse. Dad's sense of adventure wasn't over just yet. I have an old black and white photo of Dad roaring down a dusty country road going hell-bent for leather on a motorcycle. He owned a few bikes in that period and they were always Harley Davidsons and Indians. Nothing but the best for Andy.

I also have another picture from that era: their wedding photo. They made a very handsome couple. They settled in Regina where Donald was born in 1940 and Mary-Lynne in 1942. The wanderlust got hold of Dad again. 1943 saw them move to Trail, BC, where one of Mom's younger sisters, Janet, was living. One day while working with the maintenance department, Dad and his boss were given the task of removing some wooden posts. The foreman wasn't too impressed when he discovered, much to his horror, that they used dynamite to get the job done, so he sacked them both. I guess the only noteworthy thing about Trail was that the family lived there long enough for number two son, me, John Andrew Forbes, to be born before moving on.

NORTH VANCOUVER

Shortly after the dynamite incident, the family packed up again and headed for the West Coast, landing in North Vancouver, where the final addition to the growing family, Barbara, was born in 1945. Dad found work in the construction industry. There was a post-war building boom happening then, so money was good, which allowed us to buy an older house on West Kings Road, across the street from the North Star school. I have a few memories of the time we lived there. The earliest was when I was probably between three and four years old, and decided to overhaul and tune-up the family's mantle radio. Maybe I was a tad too young to be tinkering around inside an electrical device, especially when it was still plugged in. You can imagine what happened next when I put that screwdriver in the back of the radio. Sparks flew, I flew, and the circuit's fuse blew. I spent half the day hiding under my bed, scared witless, dreading what my father would do when he came home from work. Mom finally coaxed me out, promising that she wouldn't rat on me. It was our little secret, and my first, but not last, attempt at electronics.

One morning my friend John Langley, a British kid who lived up the street, and my sister Barbara, watched as the school teachers were busy hiding Easter eggs amongst the bushes around the school yard. When the teachers finished we snuck over and really cleaned up. We had our very own private Easter egg hunt, and gut aches to prove it.

There was a Scandinavian family with two boys in their mid-twenties who lived on our block. One hot summer day they were driving over to the "Milk Pond" for a dip and Mary-Lynne and I got permission to go with them. We called it the "Milk Pond," but thinking back the proper name had to be Mill Pond, because most likely a sawmill was located there years before homes were built in the area. The two brothers would lather up with a bar of soap and then jump into the deep end off a plank that served as a diving board. I wanted to follow suit but Mary-Lynne kept warning me not to because the water was way over my head.

"Just play in the shallow end at the beach," she said.

What does she know? I thought. She's just a dumb girl, so I leaped off the board just like the guys were doing, and sure enough, it was way over my head. Imagine that. And I couldn't swim a lick. My sister screamed bloody murder so the boys hauled me out. That wouldn't be the last time that I nearly drowned.

Another memory also involved water. When I was four or five my buddy, who lived in the neighbourhood, was going with his father, a commercial fisherman, to the docks where his gill netter was berthed. It was spring and he had to get the boat ship-shape for the upcoming fishing season. I was invited to go along. The docks were right in front of an Indian reservation on Burrard Inlet. While his father worked on the boat, Buddy—damned if I can remember his real name—had a nice double-holstered set of cap guns that he got for Christmas. We were having a grand old time with these guns until half a dozen native kids showed up and took away Buddy's pride and joy and chucked them into Burrard Inlet. I suppose it could have been much worse—we could have ended in the drink but thankfully that didn't happen. Buddy went crying to his dad but he didn't get much sympathy there.

He just said, "Look boys, I got a lot more work to do here. The tide's going out now so in an hour or two you can fish them out yourselves."

That was one incident where the cowboys didn't win the battle.

NO ROADS IN

By the early '50s house construction was sporadic at best in the Vancouver area, so Dad signed on with Crown Zellerbach, a pulp and paper mill located in Ocean Falls, 350 miles north of Vancouver on the mainland. He flew back and forth to Ocean Falls a number of times before we moved up there by passenger boat. There were no roads in. The mill and its workforce was expanding, but the town was up against the mountain with no more room to build additional housing, so the company pushed a road out to Martin Valley, one and a half miles away, with building lots made available to the employees. It was a company town. Crown Zellerbach offered cheap rent to entice the workers to stay put. In Martin Valley, they sold the lots for the princely sum of fifty cents each. Dad was feeling pretty flush that day—must have been pay day—so he plunked down one dollar and bought a double lot. Our neighbour Tom Mudie tried for years to buy

Family photo '52 Xmas Martin Inn
L-R - Mary-Lynne, me, Dad, Mom, Don, Barbara

that extra lot, but there was no way Dad was giving up that real estate. All the fifty-cent property owners in the Valley formed a co-op. They bought an old truck from the company plus two cement mixers and they were in business. They helped each other put in the foundations, erect walls, and nail the roof trusses in place. All the heavy work. Dad, being a carpenter, must have been one of the more popular guys in the co-op because most of the other folks didn't have a clue about house construction. They were papermakers, office staff, sawmill workers, to name a few. Within a few years Martin Valley took shape. Dad had been building our house off and on for about a year but it was still far from finished when we arrived. It had the bare essentials: exterior walls, a roof, and a working furnace. I can remember looking through knots in the sub floor of the upstairs to the unfinished basement bedroom, dirt floor and all, where a weasel with a white fur coat was living in what was soon to be the boys' bedroom once the concrete floor was poured.

Ocean Falls was a wonderful place to grow up in during the '50s and '60s, especially if you liked the great outdoors. We were hemmed in by high mountains on all sides, plenty of lakes and rivers and of course the Pacific Ocean was front and centre. But boy, could it ever rain! At an annual rainfall of 175 inches, three times Vancouver's total, we could count on fairly steady if not non-stop precipitation between October and mid-May. It could get depressing at times. There was no TV, and radio reception was limited to CBC during the day although in the evening it was possible to pull in many other stations from far away. House parties and movies were about the only outlets for the adults, but my father wasn't a very sociable person, so Mom eventually became depressed after a few years of living in the rain forest. More than once she had to fly to Vancouver to seek treatment.

OCEAN FALLS AND AREA

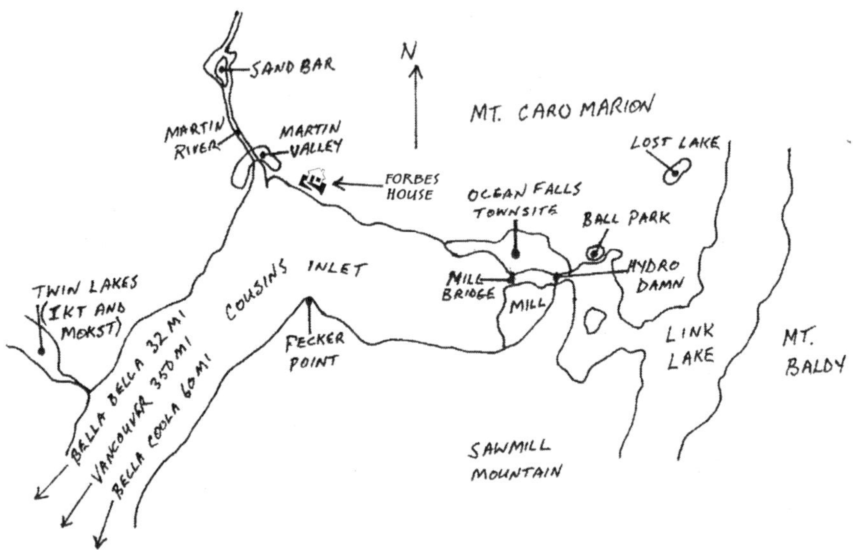

WEST COAST

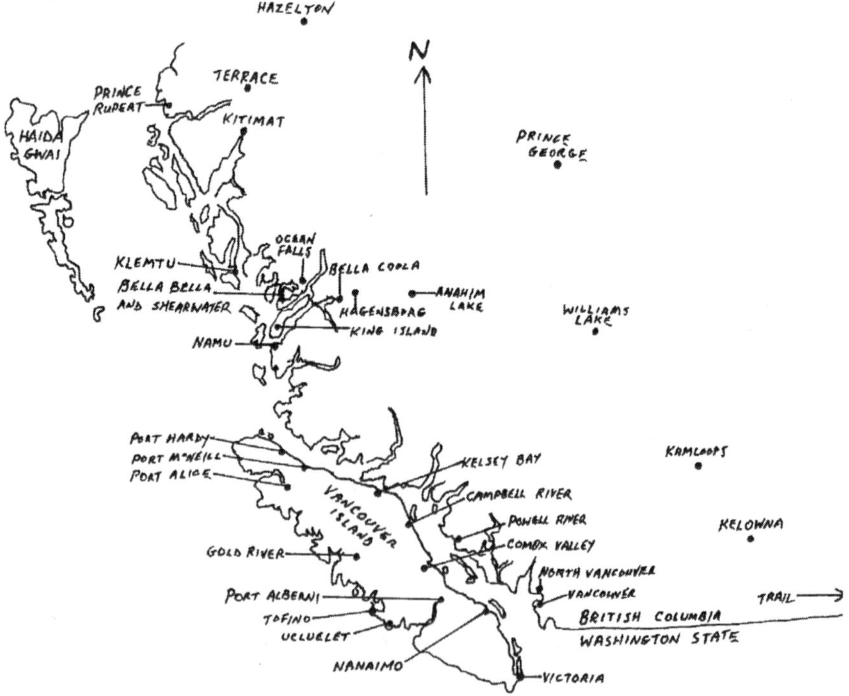

BUSH APES

The summers in Ocean Falls were great. With all the newly constructed houses filling up with families, it wasn't long before there were at least half a dozen boys my age living at what the townies called "The Farm." They also referred to us Valley kids as "Bush Apes." All summer long it was hiking, fishing, camping, getting into trouble and trying not to drown. The Martin River was one of our favourite haunts. A mile upstream from the river's mouth was the sand bar where we camped out many a night—under the stars—not many tents around in those early days. Once my next-door neighbour Jimmy McRae came with us. On a dare from Mike Whalen, I urinated into his gumboots. I thought it was hilarious until he found out who did the evil deed and chucked my boots into the river. Nothing like a moonlit swim at four a.m. to clear the mind. That was Jimmy's first and last trip with us. Maybe he didn't like our practical jokes, but the real problem was his father, who was a slave driver. George McRae ran the Standard Oil fuel station in the Valley and his son was cheap, make that free, labour. Many times Jimmy had to go directly from school to the fuel station where he worked until supper time wheeling 45 gallon oil barrels from the dock to the storage shed. Before the Great Depression in the '30s the Whalen family was quite wealthy, being heavily involved in logging and the pulp and paper industry. The town of Port Alice on northwest Vancouver Island was named after Mike's grandmother. Mike's father

Len was the creator of the Rangitangs, humorous paintings that portrayed West Coast loggers living in float camps. The cartoons appeared in many newspapers in BC for a number of years. Crown Zellerbach hired Len to work in the safety department at the mill creating safety related posters.

One year Jack Cronin and I noticed several dead fish and eels at the mouth of the river, so good upright citizens that we were, we gathered up a bucket full and brought them to the government fisheries officer in the Valley.

Me and John Riley at the Sand Bar on the Martin River

He thanked us and said,"I see we have eels in the river."

It turns out he had dumped serious chemicals from the bridge into the river to see what was living in it. Some kind of fisheries study I guess. I've heard of fishing with hand grenades and dynamite before, but not deadly poisons.

Another interesting activity happened in the fall when the salmon were spawning. After school, a bunch of us kids would go up the Martin River to a deep pool just across from what we called "The Frog Pond," a place ideal for jigging salmon. One kid would climb up a tree to be a look-out for the game warden. Another would go just downstream from the pool to spook the fish with a big rock, and the rest of us would give a mighty heave on the heavy line with all the treble hooks and lead weights as the school of salmon swam upstream over our lines. Not very sporting but moderately successful. Twice I witnessed kids with treble hooks through their fingers as they threw their lines out, and this was when all fishing hooks had barbs. Once, I landed a ten-pound Coho when Mr. Martin, a new high school teacher, and his wife came onto the scene. They had just immigrated from England. Both got quite excited about the fish, so I offered them my catch. Mr. And Mrs. Martin graciously accepted, but really, I should have released the fish. After a few weeks in fresh water a spawning salmon starts to turn bad and this one was just starting to discolour. It was likely okay, but who knows? I do know for a fact that the Martins survived because he taught for a few more years in the Falls.

Martin Valley consisted of perhaps three or four streets initially, but eventually a bridge was built over the river and houses started to pop up on the south end. Ocean Falls didn't have any room to expand and additional housing was required for employees and their families. Woody Green, a carpenter millwright like my father, came from Lethbridge, Alberta with his family and moved into a new house across the bridge, maybe 300 yards up the hill from the river. Woody's youngest son Lyle was my age and he was quite the lad. Fortunately, he survived his wild youth and later on he became quite successful in electronics. Lyle was definitely not dumb, just somewhat irresponsible. When Lyle was thirteen his mother bought him a decent pair of brown oxfords. The rest of the gang wore cheap sneakers or gumboots. Lyle hated his oxfords with a passion and let his mother know every chance he got, which was quite often. Lyle said that they looked like nurses' shoes, and to prove his point he slapped a coat of white paint on them. His poor mother.

It was around that time that we built a club house by the Martin River. We had Lyle, Archie Young, Jack Cronin, Blair Mackinnon and myself. Many a night the five of us would be sneaking around the Valley procuring materials such as two-by-fours and plywood for our co-op project. Beg, borrow or steal, but mainly steal! This was quite the club house. Three windows—no glass yet, just the openings—a door and five canvas bunks. Lyle even scrounged some house wiring that we ran from his house through the bushes to the club house so we had 110 volts. When the roof was underway we realized that with the monsoons starting up in four months, just plywood for the roof wasn't ideal. I was given the task of recruiting Gordon Mudie since we knew that his father had a big roll of tar paper. So I talked up the virtues of our club house and he bought in right away. Gordon hauled that roll over the bridge and we got to work right away. There were three of us nailing down the plywood sub roof, and just before we were ready to roll out the tar paper, the hammer slipped out of my hand, slid down the roof and bonked old Gord on the noggin. I imagine that it must have hurt like hell, but what really pissed him off was the fact that his new club mates were busting a gut, laughing non-stop. I almost fell off the roof at one point. Unfortunately, Gord picked up his tar paper, slung it over his shoulder and trudged on home. No amount of pleading would change his mind. To this day I can still remember in the summer heat looking across the river and watching our waterproof roofing slowly moving along Garden Drive to its home half a mile away. And that roll was damn heavy. Oh well, easy come, easy go and besides we had room for only five bunks. We had to put our heads together to come up with a solution for the rain problem. We decided to re-arrange the plywood sheets so they overlapped top to bottom, in effect using the sheets like giant shingles.

MARSHMALLOWS AND SHOTGUNS

Another one of our favourite haunts was Twin Lakes, two miles south of Martin Valley down Cousins Inlet. The original lake, Mokst Lake, was about four miles from the salt chuck, and between those two points was a beautiful valley full of prime timber. Back in the '30s a log and earth dam was constructed and the valley was logged off. A wooden flume was built to carry the logs from the artificial lake down to the ocean that was about half a mile away. This man-made lake was great for swimming and trout fishing. The problem was getting there as the trail was poorly maintained, or should I say *not* maintained until the late '50s when a road was finally pushed through. Another option before the road was built was to take our chances walking on the log booms on the ocean. We would fall in a few times but it was a lot easier than the so-called trail. Once we finally got to the lake we had to find a boat to borrow so we could fish for the day, and it wasn't like these boats were tied up waiting for us. Usually people hid the boats around a corner and up into dense brush, and in one case, someone had hoisted a rowboat up a tree with block and tackle. Gus Herman, an old Norwegian millwright who worked with Dad, built a really sturdy rowboat that saw a lot of use over the years. If a set of oars and oar locks came with the boat, we won the jackpot. The far end of the lake had the best spots for rainbow trout, and it seemed that every time we were heading back at the end of the day's fishing, the lake wasn't so smooth anymore, and of course the wind was directly in our faces. We never had outboard motors or life preservers but somehow we survived. What our parents didn't know.

Five thirty a.m. in March of '59, Jack Cronin, Gord Mudie, who had gotten over the hammer incident, and I sneaked into town to liberate a row boat that we thought would look good at Twin Lakes. This kid in Ocean Falls said he found it adrift in Cousins Inlet, so he claimed it as his own citing "salvation" laws on the high seas. What he meant was Salvage Laws of the sea. We always understood that the high seas meant anything out beyond seven miles of land. To our way of thinking this boat was fair game. From the docks in Ocean Falls we had almost four miles of salt chuck before we hit land at the mouth of the Twin Lakes river. At least the water was calm. Normally that early in the day there's no wind to speak of.

When we came ashore at the river's mouth we had our work cut out for us. It was all up hill with very rough terrain. That was one difficult job but we were determined, and it's a wonder that the bottom of the boat didn't fall out because of all the rocks that we dragged it over. Finally, after many hours of tough sledding, we got to the lake only to find that it was frozen solid. What a surprise. Normally you would be lucky to see two weeks in the winter when you could actually skate on the rivers and lakes. Not too many kids from Ocean Falls made it to the NHL. Fortunately, the ice wasn't too thick, so we spent the rest of the day breaking it up to get around the first corner in order to hide the boat. If you're reading this, Chester, my belated apologies for absconding with your boat. But we did have the best interests of your boat in mind because a wooden boat would last much longer in fresh water than the salty brine of the ocean.

When my brother Don graduated from high school in 1958, Dad was very proud of his firstborn, so he ordered a Timex watch from the Woodward's catalogue for Don's grad present. Dad had a grade eight education, and there was his son off to university in the fall, taking mechanical engineering. Dad should have stayed in school instead of taking off for parts unknown when he was a teenager. He was as smart as his brothers and they were all highly successful. Don was working in the mill that summer in the paper-testing lab—quality control for the newsprint that had just rolled off the paper machines. One weekend he was fishing at Twin Lakes with Sandy Collins when damned if he didn't drop his brand-new Timex in the water. Dad was none too pleased. He was born Scottish and lived through the Great Depression, so he didn't take things like this lightly. The next weekend Dad and I hiked out to the lake—not on the log booms as he was a serious non-swimmer—for the watch recovery operation. We were armed with a big magnet attached to a length of fishing line. We found a boat in short order, and I rowed it down to the far end of the lake where we fished for at least three hours for that stupid watch to no avail. As I mentioned previously, we were *sans* outboard motor and life jackets. Later in the afternoon the lake got quite choppy and the head winds stronger—guess who was manning the oars? It was a difficult day for the kid, and a long time to spend in a small boat with someone who wasn't overly talkative.

Four years later, when I "graduated," Dad asked me what I would like for a gift so I ordered a nice suitcase out of the catalogue, something that would float. Dad wondered why I didn't have a gown and mortar board, and I had to fess up that I hadn't actually graduated because I was short a few courses: Chemistry 91, which I eventually finished by correspondence while in the RCAF in Germany, and French which I hadn't really excelled at. Since both courses were requirements for university entrance, following in my brother Don's footsteps at UBC didn't look too promising. Yours truly ended up paying for his own "grad" present.

Two incidents at Twin Lakes could have turned out badly for me, but because I'm here writing this, I clearly survived. Once, Jack Cronin, Lyle Green and I were out in Gus Herman's boat, probably about five hundred to six hundred feet from shore, when a local yahoo started taking pot shots at us with his shotgun. It was our good fortune that we were in a well-constructed row boat and not a cheap plywood one. We ducked below the gunnels for a few minutes until he got bored, and started blasting away at birds and beer bottles instead. I don't know if any of the pellets actually hit the boat but nevertheless, we cowered down in case he got lucky, or unlucky. This character was a year older than we were at the time. He dropped out of school a few years later and ran with the wrong crowd, which resulted in a few scrapes with the law, but he eventually straightened out. When I met him years later he was a fairly successful businessman.

The second incident happened in the fall of the same year. It was a typical cold and damp day for that time of year. Jack and I scouted around the shore line and came across a kayak that was just begging to be taken for a spin on the lake. Being invincible teenagers with not an ounce of common sense, and of course not wearing life preservers, and novice kayakers to boot, we soon capsized some distance from shore. We were wearing heavy winter jackets that quickly water-logged and gumboots that sank to the bottom in seconds. The number one rule in this situation is to stay with the boat if it's still floating, which it was. Not us. We started swimming for shore but all we could manage was a pathetic dog paddle with those heavy clothes on. It took at least a half hour and was truly a miracle that we didn't drown in those freezing waters. I was laughing too much to be scared. Jack, not so much. When we finally reached safety, I looked back at the kayak, and there was a trail of white dots extending from it right to the shoreline. Jack had a large open bag of marshmallows inside his jacket and at regular intervals a little marshmallow would pop up to mark our route. That was the funny part. Walking barefoot and soaking wet for two miles to our homes wasn't so funny. Since the trail was in terrible condition with sharp rocks, mud and fallen trees, we agreed that the log boom was the best choice to get us back to the Valley. The worst part was hiking from the lake down to the salt chuck over the rocks. Luckily, half-way home, we were able to flag down an outboard that came along. These guys were sailors from a freighter that was in Ocean Falls taking on a load of newsprint. They had rented a boat and fishing gear for the day and just happened to land a couple of wet, shivering kids. When I finally got home I had to sneak in the back door or risk the wrath of Dad and a probable grounding.

In September of grade eleven, a classmate, Harry Diggens, was selling his sixteen-foot canvas covered canoe. It was in decent condition so I jumped at the chance. After school, I paddled it the one and a half miles from Ocean Falls to Martin Valley in record time. Our house was right on the water so I just pulled the canoe onto our property and ran up all excited to tell my Dad. He normally didn't get off work until five, but his union, Local 312, was on strike, so he was home. I found him in the basement and blurted out, “Hey Dad, guess what? I just bought a great canoe for fifteen bucks, paddle and all.”

“You what? Take that damn thing back where you got it from. There’s no way any kid of mine will be out canoeing around while I’m in charge. Too damn dangerous,” Dad said. I presented my arguments but he wouldn’t budge. My sister Mary-Lynne could win a few minor skirmishes with Dad but I never had much luck. It started to get heated and I got lippy, so he cuffed me on the ear. I ran up the stairs, Dad in hot pursuit. I’d never seen him move so fast and at the time he was fifty-five years old, give or take. As I opened the kitchen door to make good my escape, he helped me along by planting his size tens on my backside. Perfectly bad timing. At the very instant I was being propelled through the air, Mr. and Mrs. Martin, our school teachers, were walking by. That was embarrassing.

The shocked looks on their faces soon turned to smirks and I imagined Mrs. Martin turning to her husband saying, “Isn’t that the tosser who gave us that rotten fish last year?” As for my prize canoe, it found a home in exile at Twin Lakes, joining the ranks of the other various boats doing community service.

BOATS

Although Dad wasn't too keen on his youngest son owning a death-trap canoe, he eventually had a couple of inboards himself. When I was eleven, he bought the Carmona, a thirty-six-foot boat with six sleeping berths, a galley, and even a head. It was a wonderful boat. The first time out fishing he landed a thirty-pound salmon and a ninety-pound halibut and said to himself, "Wow, this is fantastic." Talk about beginner's luck. But that was it, nothing but cod and red snappers. No more salmon or halibut after his first fishing trip. At least we got to explore the various channels and inlets and the numerous beaches for miles around. One year, my brother Don, along with quite a few boys from Ocean Falls, spent the summer working for the fish cannery in the Indian village of Namu, fifty miles due south. We went down one weekend in the Carmona to visit my brother. Don told me about a humorous incident he had while working at the cannery. A few of the guys collected some fish guts and skin and very carefully packed it into a can, making sure it was the proper weight, then sent it through the process where the fish was cooked and the can sealed and labelled. Can you imagine the look on the lucky housewife's face when she opened up that can of salmon?

The following year the Carmona developed engine problems that proved the old axiom that "a boat is a big hole in the water that you keep pouring money into." So Dad unloaded it and bought a twenty-four-foot inboard that didn't have any of the comforts of boat number one; however, it was much faster. That meant we could cruise out to the prime trolling area, get skunked, and come home in a much shorter time. It was a win-win situation for the salmon.

One summer evening, it was getting dark and we didn't want to tie up at our proper berth which was a half mile walk from our house, so we docked at the Standard Oil station. The dock was comprised of a high wharf for tanker ships and down the gangway to two floating docks attached end-to-end for small craft for refuelling purposes. After tying up, Dad didn't notice the two-foot gap between the two docks and fell into the water. It was pitch black by then. Here was a non-swimmer with a now broken shoulder blade, and his scrawny son trying his best to pull him to safety. That was fun. He was laid up for a good two months after that.

The following year Dad took Bill the Boarder fishing. We now had a rental suite in the basement and Bill was our first tenant. He was most likely kicked out of the hotel in town and Dad took pity on him. Bill really liked his booze, so he provided the beer and Dad the gas. Big mistake. After getting skunked again, they pulled up their lines and headed for home in the late afternoon, but decided to bypass Martin Valley and instead headed into Ocean Falls and the pub. Not a wise choice. Since there was some water in the bilge, Dad opened the valve for the self-bailer which works fine when the boat is moving, but not so fine at rest. It's a good idea to shut off the valve when the boat is tied up, which they neglected to do. While Dad and Bill were knocking back the draft beer in the Martin Inn pub, the boat was slowing taking on water.

At the time, I was playing for the Local 312 softball team. Brother Don was on the team and they were chronically short of players, so I was signed on. I was the seventeen-year-old kid on the team, and the rest of the guys were older mill workers. I was all glove, no bat, but still a warm body. The game that evening was over by eight p.m., so I was hanging around the Martin Inn while Don and two other players, Ray Smith and Bob Wayne went into the pub for refreshments. They hardly had a chance to sit down and order a beer, when some guy rushed in and said that Andy Forbes' boat was sinking fast. The boys sprung into action, first buying two cases of beer, then dragging Dad out of the pub, leaving Bill, and picking me up as we made our way to the dock where, sure enough, the water level was part way up the engine. We turned off the self-bailer valve and then Ray brought his fourteen-foot outboard around and we started the long tow to Martin Valley. By then of course it was darker than all get out and no running lights on either boat. Dad was oblivious to the fact that his underage son was there guzzling beer. I was sitting on the gunnel and at one point we caught a wave the wrong way and I fell backwards, my hair just brushing the water when Bob hauled me back in and opened another beer for me. It was close to midnight when we finally arrived in the Valley. The high tide had peaked, so the plan was to beach the boat and open the self-bailer again to drain the water. Just as we got close, the "non-swimmer" jumped overboard up to his chest, and dragged his boat up onto the beach. Dad never mentioned that night. He was either too embarrassed or it was a complete blank. Surprisingly enough, except for a few minor electrical issues the engine didn't suffer any permanent damage after the self-bailer drained the boat.

After the Martin Valley Co-op members had built their own houses, they organized again to put up a volunteer fire hall. Since Dad was a carpenter he was made foreman for the build and then they appointed him fire chief for the first two years. One Friday night while in my bedroom I could hear Bill the Boarder, who, as I've said, liked to tie one on occasionally, stumble in. He was thrashing about, making a lot of noise but eventually he must have passed out because it was dead quiet. Not for long. There was a loud bang from *Chez* Bill, then silence again. What was that guy doing?? Then I caught a whiff of smoke so I knocked on his door. Nothing. Knocked again. Still nothing. Now I could see smoke so I burst into Sleeping Beauty's suite. Bill had the munchies when he got home so he decided to heat up a can of beans. He placed the beans into a frying pan and turned his hot plate full up. He missed one important step, the part where you open the can and dump out the beans into the pan. Thus the explosion. The beans knocked out three or four acoustic ceiling tiles and then shorted out the electrical wires and started a fire on the floor joists. Since both parents were in Vancouver, I yelled up to my sister Barbara to phone the fire department. I quickly filled up a large pot with water that I flung up into the ceiling. After three or four pots the fire was out, but nothing woke up Bill, even when the volunteer firemen charged onto the scene.

What I found humorous was when they found out how I extinguished the fire, one of the volunteers said to me, "You would think that the son of the former fire chief would know better than to put out an electrical fire with water."

Yes, I knew that water and electricity didn't mix, and I also knew that if I didn't act quickly, we would be out of house and home and maybe short a few lives, too.

In the summer of '61 I bought an eight-foot plywood runabout, powered by a ten-horse outboard. This boat would really skedaddle providing I didn't have any passengers along for the ride. In late September, Roy Chernishenko, nicknamed Shanko, said that he and his friend Jap, a young paper-maker who was boarding at Roy's house, were catching a ride Friday after school with a fish boat down to Bella Bella, a native village about thirty-five miles south, but they didn't have a way of getting home on the Sunday, and since I had a boat, maybe I could pick them up. I never did know Jap's real name. When he first came to Ocean Falls he nick-named Tom Powell, Spook, so Tom retaliated by hanging the handle Jap on him because he was brought up in Japan where his parents were Baptist missionaries.

I rounded up a case of beer and headed out on Saturday morning, invincible once again without a life preserver or even a map, just a five-gallon gas tank and a prayer. I was told to just go through Gunboat Passage, veer left 45 degrees after the second wooden triangle fishing boundary on your right and head for the distant lighthouse. You can't miss it. They were right. Who needs a map? A light drizzle came down the entire trip, so when I finally tied up in Bella Bella, my fingers were so cold that I had to use pliers to unzip my fly to relieve myself. I soon tracked down Roy and Jap, and before long my lone case of beer was history.

At one point during the night, a guy who lived across the bay at Shearwater approached me and offered me ten dollars if I would take him home. He was a bootlegger over to do some business in Bella Bella when his motor broke down. Because it was overcast, I didn't have any stars or even a moon to show me the way, just blind faith. When I got back safely to the dock, I said to myself, “Now that was stupid.” I found Ray and Jap and they had some disturbing news. The weather forecast was calling for a gale on Sunday. Not good. Ray tracked down his original ride and bribed him with a few dollars into giving us a lift back to the Falls with my outboard in tow. We were leaving at seven a.m.

We stretched out on the main drag, which consisted of large planks with a four-by-four wooden curb for a pillow. It was impossible to sleep. Not only was it a cool evening, but the local folk continually walked up and down the board walk. When I recall Bella Bella, I think of it as “the village that never sleeps.” Eventually our ride came along so we followed him down to the boat at the government wharf. Things were looking up until his brother, three sheets to the wind, showed up, intending to ride with us. He started out by being aggressive towards us and then at one point stood on the guard rail and threatened to jump into the salt chuck. After Roy pulled him off the rail, we decided that we didn’t really want to be stuck out on a fish boat in high winds with these characters, so we reluctantly went back to plan A, my outboard.

The marine gas station and store had its own separate dock which was approximately a quarter mile away, so we made our way over to top up the fuel tank. The owner assumed that we were just going to Shearwater. “No,” I replied, “Ocean Falls.”

“Are you serious? Good luck,” he said, shaking his head. “The winds will be picking up later on today.” Then he glanced over to the government wharf area and wondered why four fishing boats were slowly going back and forth and two scuba divers were on the shore. “Looking for crabs?” Roy said. But it was worse. Five women came storming down to the dock, pointing at us, blaming us for the brother’s drowning. Apparently just after the fish boat cast off from the wharf the brother went completely nuts and jumped overboard. He went down once, came up, and then down again for good. And these women were blaming us. One had out a note pad and was busy writing down our descriptions. Brown hair, brown eyes, maybe five feet, ten inches, blue jacket, kinda scrawny. She had me down to the T except she forgot the good-looking bit.

Now there was no doubt that we had to make tracks, gale warning or not. The village didn’t have a police force, so we figured that there was a good chance of being lynched. Off we went with our five gallons of gas in a boat built for one, not breaking too many world speed records. When we got up to Gunboat Passage we breathed a sigh of relief. It appeared that no boats were in hot pursuit and the ocean became calmer since the pass is quite sheltered. Halfway through Gunboat we realized that we couldn't use this short cut because the tide was too low. The pass was now impassable. They should have called it Canoe Pass. We had to back-track and go around the island, wasting valuable time and burning precious fuel. Within an hour of the Gunboat Passage fiasco our fuel tank was down to a quarter and the sea was getting rougher.

It was about then that Jap said, "If anybody knows how to pray, now would be a good time."

Our guardian angels were looking out for us that day. The weather didn't get much worse, not what was forecast, and damned if we weren't the only fools out there. Halfway across the channel was a sports fisherman from Martin Valley trolling in his sixteen-foot outboard. To our good fortune he had gas to spare so he topped up my fuel tank. He couldn't make change for the ten-dollar bill that we handed over, but we weren't about to quibble. Money well spent.

We finally limped into port sometime after three p.m., but now the worrying game began. Would we be arrested, jailed, charged with murder? On Monday morning, I was a tad anxious as I bused into town for school. By Friday I was breathing a little easier—nothing had happened yet. However, when school finished for the week, and I along with a few friends were about to walk into the pool hall at the Martin Inn, the marine division RCMP sergeant intercepted me and wanted to have a word. Off I went down to the police patrol boat under escort. The cop explained that he just wanted a general idea of what transpired the previous weekend in Bella Bella and nothing I said would be brought up in court, so I sang like a canary, boy did I ever.

I was given a date for a court appearance, with a parent, in two weeks' time. Now I really had a problem because the old man was going to throttle me much worse than the law could ever dish out. I had to come up with a cock-and-bull story, mainly bull, that my dad would buy.

The story went somewhere along the lines of "Remember in the spring when our high school basketball team went over to Bella Coola for an exhibition game?" So far, true. I continued, "In downtown Bella Coola, one side of the main drag where all the businesses are located is the 'white' side, and the other side is the boundary for the Indian reservation." Again, true. "Me and two other guys didn't know about this boundary, and the RCMP gave us a summons for trespassing." This was the false part.

Dad thought about it and said, "It doesn't seem to be too serious, just a stupid mistake, so your mother can go to court with you." He probably didn't feel like walking back into town in the rain for a seven o'clock court appearance after working all day in the mill. I dodged a bullet there. Mom was a real softie. The rest was anti-climactic. Roy and I were each fined twenty dollars for trespassing plus four dollars court costs. Jap was tried in adult court and was convicted of numerous offences, so his total fines amounted to a little over a hundred plus court costs. The sergeant pulled a fast one on me though. After telling me previously that what I had said wouldn't be admissible in court, when he took the witness stand he told the magistrate that John Forbes admitted underage drinking in Bella Bella. However, since there was no evidence, I walked on that one.

BASKETBALL TRIPS AND THE BIG HALL

Our basketball trips were fairly tame because Coach Wayne Erickson kept a watchful eye on the team. What sticks out in my mind when we played in Bella Bella, is that when you were going for a lay-up at the north end of the court, you could do yourself serious harm if somebody happened at that very moment to open the door to the hall. The outside door opened inward quite close to the backboard. On the Bella Coola trip nothing much remarkable occurred, except on the return ride home we had a few good laughs. The girls' high school team, the Charleson Charmers, were also along for the trip. Our team was called the Charleson Chieftains. We travelled there and back on this beautiful sixty-foot purse seiner that had no problem accommodating both teams. Pauline Baker had to use the biffy that was on the starboard deck. There were numerous vent holes higher up in the door that were the perfect size to accept firecrackers. If you think firecrackers are loud in a confined space, you should have heard Miss Baker. Everyone on the boat did, including Bob Scott, the coach of the Charmers who was also the school principal. No one owned up to the evil deed and it was one trip that Pauline will never forget.

When I was sixteen, I was playing in the junior league with the junior Royals when Coach Erickson promoted me to the Chieftains after permanently suspending two of his starting five, Rich Baker and Charlie Williamson, for smoking. The coach called it "puffing." The following year our team had great expectations for the Northwest BC high school playdowns, held in Prince Rupert. The coach had scouted the opposition and felt that we had a fighting chance. That winter the Chieftains were busy fund-raising with bottle drives, bake sales, you name it. If nothing else, we would be the best-dressed team, with our snazzy warm-up sweats and new team jackets. The 1958 Chieftains, with my brother in the starting five, turned a few heads when they unexpectedly placed ninth out of 90 teams in the provincial playdowns in Vancouver, setting the bar for us.

Our team was booked into an older hotel located in downtown Prince Rupert and a block up from the notorious Apache Pass where, a few years previously during the fishing season, the mayor of Rupert had to read the riot act. Sandy Gilchrist and I were rooming together on the fifth floor. Around four a.m. I went sleep-walking, wearing nothing but a pair of shorts. When I woke up on the third floor, I walked over to room 316 and tried the door. Locked of course, so I knocked then pounded to no avail and eventually realized I was out by two floors. So, I went up to room 516. Same thing. Locked out and no amount of pounding on the door would roust the bastard. Sandy was a pretty good basketball player, a world class swimmer, but what he really excelled at was sleeping. Out of desperation, I took the elevator down to the lobby to explain my predicament to the desk clerk. The night man was enormous, weighing in at a good 350 pounds. He didn't blink an eyelash when he saw this nearly naked teenager standing at the front desk in the wee hours of the morning. Perhaps because I couldn't prove who I said I was—I wasn't carrying any ID—he wouldn't give me a spare room key and send me on my way. Instead, he insisted on escorting me back to room 516. He shook Sandy awake to confirm that I did in fact belong in that room. Hey, I might have been a cat burglar travelling light.

As far as basketball went, we didn't have a great tournament, losing every game. Our coach figured the little village of Hazelton would be a cake walk. However, their team had other ideas. The host team, the Prince Rupert Rainmakers, were in a class of their own. Two factors that weighed heavily in their favour were their outside shooting and height, or should I say, our lack of height. We were definitely vertically challenged for this contest. Back home we competed in the men's league, playing in the Big

Hall that had a low ceiling, too low for long shots. Any arc on the shot and the ball would bounce off the ceiling beams. We were a tad intimidated even before the opening jump-off as we watched the Rainmaker's centre, Johnny Olsen, doing some serious slam-dunking during warm-ups. Our tallest player, Gordie Donald, was a measly six feet three inches, and if he somehow got lucky and did bring down an offensive rebound, he would quickly dribble outside the key and pass off to a guard instead of trying for a basket inside. The outcome of that game was never in doubt.

The next year, Grade 12, after being disciplined by Wayne Erickson in the P. E. class for inappropriate behaviour such as rough housing in the locker room and snapping towels which caused us to be late for the next class, I quit the team. I joined a men's team, competing against my old teammates. The only problem I encountered was refereeing games that involved the high school team. I was always "under the gun," so to speak, to be impartial and call a fair game. Once, I ejected Sandy Gilchrist for taking a swing at an opposition player. Fortunately, he hadn't connected with his punch and Wayne Erickson didn't protest too vigorously because he knew the rules.

I was probably a fairly average player with a decent jump shot. One night I was really hot, couldn't miss a shot. My big night made the sports page of the weekly paper, the *Ocean Falls Advertiser*. The headline read, "Forbes scores 45 points." Yes, the baskets were really dropping although, if you went beyond the headline it explained there were two games involved that night. After we finished the early game only one team showed up for the late competition, so they begged us for a game. What I remember most about the second game was the pain in both my legs cramping with charley horses. Two or three times my teammates dragged me out onto the outside fire escape and rubbed my legs down with snow until the cramps subsided, then threw me back into the fray.

SPORTS

Sports was a big part of our life in Ocean Falls. Crown Zellerbach had built an indoor pool attached to the basement of the Big Hall, and for years that undersized pool kept sending top ranked swimmers such as Allan, Ron and Sandy Gilchrist, Lenora Fisher, Jack Kelso and Ralph Hutton to the Olympics, the British Empire Games and the Pan-American Games, all with excellent results. Every school kid in the Falls was sent to the pool and taught to swim by the team coach, George Gates. For us mere mortals who didn't relish the thought of training early in the morning before school and then again after school to become stars in the aquatic world, we had little league baseball in the summer and junior basketball in the wet season. It seemed that every kid in Ocean Falls played baseball until he graduated to the softball league.

Don and me in '62

For junior basketball, the men's league provided coaches for the teams. Joe Check was the coach for my team, the Royals. We practiced every Saturday morning in the Big Hall, and there were many days when we were without a coach because Joe had a casual, laid-back demeanour or else he just wasn't motivated. Joe was a pipefitter and worked straight days, eight to five. He just liked to sleep in, I guess. At least Joe showed up for our games. Years later I met him at a reunion and his excuse for skipping practice was that he couldn't show us anything—we knew it all.

The mill was a regular United Nations, a melting pot of many nationalities such as Scottish, English, Italian and German. Each had its own soccer team entered in the local league. Frank Spina played for Team Italy, the Juventus, and since they were chronically short of footballers due to shift work, Frank convinced me, John Riley and John Sarnacki to bolster their ranks. Why not? A little bit of inexperience wouldn't hold us back. Kick the ball and run. Easy. We got involved but right away it was "off side" this, "off side" that. Since there was hardly any ice in the winter time for organized hockey, and no TV on which to watch soccer or hockey games, we didn't have a clue what this "off side" business was, so we cornered Sarnacki's father for a quick lesson. We didn't learn much because he spoke English with a Polish accent, so we moved on to Riley's father who had a pretty good Scottish accent going. Mr. Riley got out pencil and paper and straightened us out in short order. I scored three goals in my soccer career. One legitimate and the other two from scrums on corner kicks. One bounced off my hand undetected and one off my wrong foot. They all counted.

It seems most kids in Ocean Falls had a nickname. We started calling Frank Spina, Franco, then Frankenstein, and finally just Stein, which stuck for a number of years. Once during a party at Gilchrist's house the guys insisted that Stein "stomp the grapes" to showcase his Italian heritage. Grapes were in short supply, so the boys threw a handful of crab apples into the bathtub. Without shoes, Stein had a tough go of it. Painful arches, too. I was not exempt from the nickname game. Grandpa Forbes called me Jock when I was born and that stuck. It was okay BG (before girls), however, later on when I started dating I knew that things would have to change. To this day I still remember the embarrassment I felt one day as I strolled down Front Street with a girl, and Shanko, a block away, hollered out, "Hey Strap, where ya goin'?" In '63 when I signed up with the air force I reverted to my christened name, John.

The Big Hall was really the heart and soul of Ocean Falls. The main floor consisted of the basketball court that doubled as a dance floor, complete with a stage at one end and a balcony at the other. Down below was the swimming pool (the home of champions), a five-pin bowling alley, and a shooting club. I and all my buddies played in the junior bowling league, but it was never my favourite sport—far from it. The manager, Gordie McLean, didn't put up with any crap from the kids and spent a lot of energy yelling at us. Occasionally we would set pins for pocket change and that was definitely not my favourite job either. Gordie also hollered a lot at his young pin-setters.

The Big Hall was also where the boy scouts met once a week. After the evening scout meeting, Jack Cronin and I would often catch a movie at the Crown Theatre a block away. The trick was to sneak in after the show had started and very quietly find a seat in the rear, trying to avoid the ever-vigilant high school ushers, Paul Wagner and Darryl Hobson. At most movies, we never found out "who done it" because the ushers were pretty keen, giving us the bum's rush. When we were younger, twenty cents got us in to watch the Saturday matinee, which might be the Lone Ranger, Hopalong Cassidy, Roy Rogers or Gene Autry—good old western shoot'em ups. One Saturday I was sitting about twenty rows from the front and Howie Smith was perhaps six seats to my right. Three rows ahead of him was this nerdy kid whose name escapes me. The movie wasn't too exciting and I got bored so I started bouncing peanuts off this kid's head. The poor guy was going nuts: I had the range and could hardly miss. He started yelling at Howie and of course Howie told him to bugger off. When the peanuts kept scoring direct hits on the old noggin, the nerdy one complained to the manager who in turn kicked Howie out of the theatre. By then I was so doubled over with laughter that my gut was hurting. Entertainment happened where you could find it.

One summer, our boy scout troop took the passenger boat over to Bella Coola for a two-week camping trip. It didn't start off too well because as we were walking down the gangway after docking, a gust of wind caught my Stetson hat and sent it flying into the salt chuck. Thankfully a crew member somehow climbed down and fished it out for me. Our camp was eight to ten miles up the valley from Bella Coola, a few miles short of Hagensborg. Our site was a perfect setting for a camp, close to the river and quite flat, unlike our hometown that was hemmed in on all sides by the mountains. Two instances stand out in my memory. One of the scouts, Buddy Hebert, went missing one evening, so for about eight hours, we searched high and low with flashlights until he finally showed up on his own accord. He said what helped him survive was his boy scout training. Apparently, Buddy used his trusty jackknife to cut a button off his scout uniform and popped it into his mouth to create saliva. Now I never did fully understand this saliva business. Maybe that's why I never made Queen's Scout. Surely he could have helped himself to some of that fresh water flowing through the Valley. We must have waded through two or three creeks that night looking for the guy.

The second incident happened after a week of eating our own food, things like gourmet instant puddings and the old standby, flapjacks. Yours truly wasn't feeling too chipper—low energy and bad stomach ache. The scout master, Ernie Herd, decided that I should pay a visit to the Bella Coola hospital. I was okay with that until I found out that the mode of transport would be on foot. The sun was really beating down on us that day as we set out on our eight-mile trek into town. Thankfully I still had my Smokey the Bear hat to ward off the rays. At least six different vehicles stopped to offer us a ride, but good old Ernie was determined to soldier on despite the heat. The only handout we accepted on our forced march was the occasional drink of water from the houses along the road. At the hospital, the doctor quickly diagnosed me as being "backed-up," so an enema was ordered which seemed to do the trick. I was told to drink plenty of water every day, eat lots of fresh fruit and veggies and ease up on the puddings. I followed up on the water part, but not so much on the fruit and veggies which were not too plentiful out in the wilderness. Two weeks passed by too quickly. We really took a liking to the Bella Coola Valley and the added bonus of great weather.

Alexander Mackenzie, the first explorer north of Mexico to cross North America by land, made his historic journey to the Pacific Ocean in 1793, canoeing down the Bella Coola river. A hundred years later in 1894, a group of Norwegian Lutherans secured land grants and settled in the Hagensborg area. They had small farms and eventually over the years their descendants took up the more lucrative jobs in forestry and fishing, like their neighbours the Nuxalk First Nations people. An interesting event happened in 1953. The BC government refused to extend Highway 20 from Anahim Lake to the valley, so the good folks of the Bella Coola Valley banded together with two hundred and fifty dollars, dynamite, equipment and two years of blood, sweat and tears along with determination, and pushed a road through. It was slightly wider than a goat trail, but more winding. This would be a vital link to the outside world. The highway led into Williams Lake and then south via highway 97 to Vancouver and civilization. Thus the "Freedom Highway" was born. It has been described as an "interesting drive", a euphemism for just plain scary with many switchbacks and sheer drop offs. It's the steepest highway in Canada with grades as much as eighteen degrees.

THE MARTIN INN

If the Big Hall was the heart and soul of Ocean Falls, the Martin Inn was the hub. Various businesses operated within its walls: a beauty salon, barbershop, large restaurant, even larger cafeteria and the most important businesses in a small town—the pool hall and the pub. This was no country inn. The hotel opened in 1947 and when the annex was added it had upwards of 500 rooms, making it the fourth largest hotel in BC. Crown Zellerbach employees only paid a dollar a day to stay there. Anything to keep the workers happy and more importantly, to keep them in Ocean Falls.

The cashier in the restaurant, Monique, a single woman in her mid-40s who it was rumoured had a checkered past, was also the one to scoop out the ice cream if you ordered a cone. Quite often we would walk down at lunch time to ogle Monique as she filled our orders. Another waitress, a much younger and quite attractive gal, had a real full set of lips. This was before women started using silicone for the fuller-lip look. Lyle Green remarked that you'd have to tie a board across your butt if you were lucky enough to kiss her. She was a very nice person and a good sport. Half the single men who lived in the hotel were in love with her, and the other half had serious problems with their vision.

We had a regular gang of kids who would hang out in the hotel, normally in the evening when the manager Louis Churchfield wasn't around. Usually we didn't have too many problems getting by the night desk clerk. The trick was to walk by the front desk on the pretext of going to the washroom, then climb up one flight of stairs to get access to the elevators. Lyle Green used to stop the elevator between floors and then climb on top. Not recommended for the faint of heart, especially when the car is moving. What was advantageous was that if anyone wanted to report us for creating havoc, they couldn't call up the main desk because there were no phones in the individual rooms. By the time a resident made his way down to the lobby with a complaint for the night clerk, we would be long gone. The clerk worked alone and couldn't leave his post for any length of time anyway. We drove those poor desk clerks absolutely nuts for a good two or three years.

In the winter, our number one favourite pastime was making snowballs when we had sufficient snow. Four or five of us would gain access to the roof of the hotel and then stockpile half a dozen snowballs each and wait for some poor sucker to come strolling down Front Street. He wouldn't be strolling for long once we opened fire. Jack Cronin was especially effective because he had one hell of an arm, and he nailed more than his share of victims. What was even more entertaining was unleashing our entire arsenal at the fire hall down below. You could see the volunteer firemen inside the hall playing cards, drinking coffee, shooting the breeze, or whatever else firemen do when they're not putting out fires. All of a sudden the front of the building would be bombarded by a few dozen projectiles. They came charging over to the hotel hell-bent for leather to lay a beating on us little buggers, but we were never caught. In the summer, we would fling tiny pebbles that were conveniently part of a flat tarred roof. A few handfuls were just as effective as snowballs in getting some movement out of the firefighters. We might have riled up the boys but at least we didn't break any windows—through no fault of our own.

Dave Brassard joined our gang in grade ten and fit right in. His father was a sergeant with the RCMP who was transferred over from Ucluelet on Vancouver Island to take command of the local detachment. Dave didn't get any breaks from the sarge. Once, Ray Peterson and Dave were collared by his dad for firing a 22 rifle up the Martin River. Dave's main interests were fishing, playing pool and shooting guns, in that order, but definitely not school. So, as mentioned, he fit right in. Shortly after high school he made his way back to Ucluelet where he got on as crew on a fishing troller, his dream job. Eventually he worked his way up to skipper a fish boat and even sank one to make things interesting. Tragically, later he developed Korsakoff's Syndrome, a degenerative neurological disease, likely caused by consuming large amounts of alcohol for a long period. When I looked him up in Port Alberni in 1998 he was living in a rundown travel trailer in a rundown trailer park. He still looked basically the same as forty years previously, skinny and in need of a meal, but by then he walked crab-like, in great pain. Dave still drank and still fished on the river in his little row boat. Sad to say, he didn't make it past his late 50s.

Years later at an Ocean Falls reunion I was talking to Howie Smith about the good old days and he told me his Martin Inn stories. Howie was living in the hotel, so I'm assuming that his parents had retired and moved away since he was not living at home. He opened the window of his hotel room and set a few slices of bread on the sill, which attracted a flock of seagulls. He captured two birds, put them into the elevator, then sent them down to the main floor, right across from the desk. Can you imagine the scene as these seagulls ran all over the lobby, pooping and squawking as the night clerk tried to round them up and shoo them out the main entrance? Another time he put a sizable amount of human excrement into a large paper bag, placed it in the elevator and lit it on fire, then pressed the "M" button. When the doors opened, the poor night clerk rushed over to stamp out the fire with his shoes. Suffice it to say the air turned blue and it wasn't just from the smoke.

The year before I made the near fatal trip to Bella Bella, I was getting a lot of use out of my recently purchased eight-foot runabout. Dave Brassard and I went camping for two overnights down Cousins Inlet in a secluded cove that was picture-postcard perfect. Not only was it sheltered from the winds but was just crawling with crabs in 20 feet of water. We found remnants of a gill net on the shore. We cut a branch off a cedar tree to bend into a circle and made ourselves a makeshift crab net. For bait, we tied on Dave's ham sandwich and lowered the net down to the bottom with fishing line. Within a few hours we had a dozen decent-sized crabs but unfortunately no pots big enough to boil them in.

No problem, we thought. We'll just take them home and have ourselves a crab feast later. Can you imagine our disappointment when we arrived home two days later, only to be told by my mother that they had to go in the garbage because crabs need to be boiled alive in order to be safe to eat? We wouldn't make that mistake again.

About three-quarters of a mile across Cousins Inlet on the corner is a navigation beacon. On the marine charts it is called Coolidge Point but was universally referred to as Pecker Point where a house of ill repute was in operation throughout the '30s. The house had seven rooms, plenty of liquor for sale, no-limit poker games and a few ladies, if you were so inclined. The madam, Blanche, who weighed in at 300 lbs, saw double duty as a bouncer. The owner of the establishment, Captain Judd Parker, ran a shuttle, the Myrtle R, to and from the Falls. The clientele were fishermen, sailors from the freighters taking on a shipment of newsprint, and of course the odd mill worker. Captain Parker and Blanche were shut down by the Department of National Defence in 1940. In the '50s Dolly Henshaw inherited the property and lived there for awhile with her husband Paddy. He owned a tug boat and worked for Crown Zellerbach. In 1960 Jack Cronin and I went over in my boat, and by then the building was seriously dilapidated. Poking around in the wreck, we found a few empty liquor bottles and a mouldy recipe book for liquor orders. In '65 the Martin Valley Volunteer Fire Department burned it to the ground for fire practice.

SAWMILL AND BALDY MOUNTAIN

When we were in grade nine, five or six of us would hike up to Sawmill Mountain and stay at the ski lodge for a few days. We would leave on Friday right after school and come back on Sunday afternoon. Hardly anybody went there, so the trail was quite overgrown and fairly steep. Soon the unrelenting rain turned into snow and by four-thirty or five p.m. it was dark, which didn't help matters. It was a difficult hike. The higher we got the deeper the snow, especially when we left the trees behind and started across the meadows. By the time we reached our destination our clothes were soaked through because the snow was chest high by then, very wet and heavy. Once we reached the meadows everybody had to take a turn breaking a trail, so when we finally reached the chalet we were quite exhausted and cold. Then came the fun of trying to get a fire going with the wet kindling and firewood that was stacked outside in the elements. Gasoline from the rope tow engine usually did the trick after a few attempts, so we could at least dry out some of our sopping wet clothes.

I believe the chalet was built in the late '40s by the ski club volunteers. It was a decent-sized log cabin complete with a wood stove, fireplace and glass pane windows. It's amazing that everything except the logs were packed up that same trail on the backs of the ski club members. To this day I don't know and can't imagine how the rope tow engine magically appeared on the top of Sawmill Mountain. Thinking back, I still find it a mystery why we even bothered hiking for five hours in terrible conditions when we never did ski. There were a few pairs of wooden skis lying around the chalet but no ski boots in sight, and as far as we knew the rope tow engine wasn't even serviceable. Besides, deep, wet and unpacked snow weren't ideal conditions for novices. Snowshoeing would have been more appropriate.

We would spend most of our waking hours feeding the fire and chasing off the mice. The chalet was infested with the rodents that had been waiting all year for someone stupid enough to show up with fresh food. It didn't matter where you set down your food, as soon as you turned your back the little buggers would start nibbling away. At least the unopened cans were safe. Whenever we went camping, summer or winter, we would buy canned beans, our favourite brand being Bingo Beans. It wasn't the taste that dictated the selection but rather the cheap price.

The cabin's loft had a good number of bunks and after kicking out the mice we laid out our sleeping bags on mouldy straw mattresses to settle in for the night. Can you imagine six teenage boys in a confined space after they've been eating beans all day? Think *Blazing Saddles*. Of course, we could hear the mice scurrying about all over. Not a great night. The hike back down on Sunday was much easier with our lighter backpacks though naturally before we got to the trees we were soaked through again. I imagine the mice had a nice feast after we left.

The previous summer Bruce Gilchrist and Johnny Beggs were up there fooling around with a 22 rifle. The unofficial story was that Bruce was making Johnny dance by shooting down by his feet when he miscalculated and put a bullet in his leg. This didn't look good for either party involved. Bruce stopped the bleeding and then proceeded to pack poor Johnny down the mountain, no easy task when you consider that he was a least 170 pounds of dead weight. My brother Don had a similar experience about a year and a half before. He, along with three other high school kids, packed Patsy Thorstenson down Sawmill Mountain after she broke her leg skiing. Patsy should have gone with the snowshoes.

Bruce carried Johnny along the trail that ended at the mill. By then it was about three a.m., so they made it undetected to the bridge and somehow got past the mill's timekeeper/safety man and into town. They passed the hotel and fire hall all the way up the hill beyond the dam to the ball field by Link Lake. Bruce was either really strong or really scared but in all likelihood a lot of both as he pulled off this remarkable feat. The final stage of this operation was for Johnny to lie down on the ball diamond and yell for help while Bruce disappeared. When Johnny was rescued he had concocted a cock-and-bull story about being shot by someone hiding in the bushes. Bruce was home free in more ways than one. A few years later, the true details of the "ambush" were common knowledge to most of the town but not to the cops. In the summer of '62, the ski lodge burned to the ground under mysterious circumstances. Nobody was ever charged. However, we had a pretty good idea who the culprits were.

During the summer holidays in '61 we were working in the mill in various departments. I did numerous jobs such as welder's helper and carpenter's helper, as well as clearing brush with a machete. I also put in some shifts in the finishing-room, on the beaters, and on the sawmill booms. If working in the groundwood mill was like working in hell, working in the beaters was a close second, maybe just purgatory. Normally the foreign workers from war-torn countries in Europe who didn't have a grasp of the English language, and in most cases, were single, started out in the groundwood mill. If they stuck it out some of them graduated to the beaters. If a newsprint roll, after coming off the paper machines, didn't pass the quality inspection, it was sent down to the beaters to be stripped down sheet by sheet with a utility knife, and then fed into a huge tank where it was beaten with the aid of a chemical slurry back into pulp. The environment in the beaters was hot and toxic and poorly lit. It was a regular dungeon, so I was fortunate to do only a few shifts there.

Roy Chernishenko wanted to hike up Mount Baldy the first chance that our days off coincided. We recruited Mel Gribble, and when this UBC student from Vancouver who was working in the mill that summer got wind of the trip, we signed him on as our official bootlegger. If you ever see a photo of Ocean Falls taken from the air, on the bottom of the picture you'll see the ocean with the log booms, then the mill and town site with the hydro dam just above, holding back Link Lake that stretches for miles north and south. Above the lake is Mount Baldy, the imposing and beautiful backdrop to the town. Instead of being steep or jagged like most West Coast mountains, this one is quite rounded and the tree line ends 2/3 of the way up, hence the name Baldy.

Roy borrowed a friend's outboard which brought us to the trailhead approximately six miles north on Link Lake. We made pretty good progress in the morning, but by the time the sun came over the rise we were labouring with backpacks loaded down with food, sleeping bags and of course, beer. This was before that marvellous invention of canned beer. The bottles were much heavier, so we took a vote and decided to lighten the load. By the time we hiked out of the trees our packs were definitely lighter. Mel was unusually quiet so we suspected that he was hoarding his. That entire trip our UBC boy kept looking over his shoulder checking for bears, even at the top of Baldy. He hardly slept that night, feeding the camp fire and shining his flashlight every which way. We made camp fairly close to the summit, beside a pool that was about four feet deep. In the morning, we noticed that a previous hiker had thrown a can of fruit cocktail into the pond, so I stripped down and waded in to the icy waters to retrieve it. When I say icy, I'm not kidding. The pool was fed by melting snow. Just as I was about to reach down for my dessert, I heard the guys laughing it up, so I glanced over my shoulder to see Roy filming all the action with his 8mm camera. At least he had the decency to stop the camera rolling on my way back out. For years afterwards he showed that footage at parties at my expense. After I thawed out, I traded my hard-earned fruit cocktail for Mel's last beer and didn't share it with Roy.

ROCKS, RATS AND WOODCHIPS

Lyle Green

The roads in Ocean Falls for the most part were built of four-inch thick planks. That included all the streets along the ocean and also up the hillsides because wood was plentiful, and blasting out the mountainside with dynamite would be too costly and time consuming. Since the wooden roadways were elevated, the steam pipes from the mill that heated the houses could be run underneath, out of sight and harm's way. Maintenance couldn't be easier. Along Marine Drive at the edge of town where Martin Valley road began, was a single-family house on the left, then four bunkhouses and lastly another single-family home. The bunkhouses were built in the '20s for the Chinese, Japanese and Hindu single workers, but by the '50s only the Chinese were still around. Up until 1941 the Japanese, with numerous families, had a strong presence in the Falls. They even had a Buddhist Temple and a school house. Percy Monroe and his family lived in the first house. Al Monroe, the youngest son, was at least two or three years older than the rest of us and was slightly challenged, never going beyond grade eight. His talents lay elsewhere. With his long and nimble fingers, Al's expertise was in building model airplanes and boats. He was showing us his collection one day, numerous models, beautifully hand painted. One wall in his room was completely covered with cut outs from the Eaton's catalogue women's underwear pages.

Anyway, one night a pack of us, all around fifteen years old, were walking the plank road that rose about eight feet above Monroe's house when Lyle Green decided to liven things up. Without any warning, he picked up a fifteen-pound rock and let it fall down the eight-foot drop to Monroe's front door, which made one hell of a racket and almost went right through the landing. Al's older brother Ernie, who was a mill electrician, came running out the door with a big screwdriver in one hand and blood in this eye. We were fortunate that it was fairly dark because old Ernie was some pissed. Some of the guys headed for the hills, but most of us ducked under either the wooden road or the bunkhouses which were sitting on pilings. We cowered under there for at least thirty minutes until Ernie calmed down and went home.

Eventually, after high school, Al found work cooking in logging camps, but sadly he died of heart disease in his mid 50s. As for Ernie, I met him and his wife at a reunion on Vancouver Island years later and somehow failed to mention the boulder incident. He was the nicest person, but I didn't want to find out if he carried a grudge.

Our grade six teacher was fresh out of teacher's college. Don Little was definitely not little, at least six feet three inches tall with a brush cut and a great attitude. Everybody liked him, especially the girls, because he was also good looking and young. In addition, he was a first-rate basketball player who in '58 coached the high school team in the BC playdowns. For our class, he started a project that involved white rats and nutrition. We would feed two rats healthy food and the other two junk food and do weight comparisons to show the students the effects of proper nutrition. He knew that my dad was a carpenter so he asked me to build the cages for the project at home. When Dad found out what all the noise in the basement was about, he was none too pleased. He called me a fool and a sucker, thinking that I was being taken advantage of because I was supplying all the materials. Did I mention Dad was Scottish? What Dad really meant was that *he* was supplying all the materials. The cages were built in spite of Dad's objections. Three or four of the girls were entrusted with a key to the school because naturally these rodents had to eat every day. The names that come to mind are Alannah Kelso, Ruth Boillet and Linda Hogg. One weekend one of the girls opened the cage, maybe to clean it, and one of the rats did a runner, thus the data for the project were somewhat skewed. That's the only time we ever saw Mr. Little upset.

Looking back, I now realize that building those cages was my first experience working with wood, and later on woodworking turned out to be a great hobby along with restoring antique furniture. Mr. Little's teaching career wasn't very long. After three years he left Ocean Falls to join the air force, taking officer training and eventually becoming a navigator on the CF-100 Canuck, a jet interceptor/fighter affectionately known as the "Clunk" or the "Gravel Truck." Two years after joining up, Don came back to Ocean Falls on leave and gave a spiel to the high school students extolling the virtues of the RCAF. So, there you go. He got me started on woodworking and also planted a seed in my mind about a career in the military.

The last house along Marine Drive after the bunkhouses was occupied by Wong Chee and his family. Every Halloween he would order in fireworks to sell to the local kids so that we could create mayhem legally. Wong Chee was the boss on the wooden flume that floated the wood blocks from the sawmill to the groundwood and chipper mill. Dave Brassard and I worked on the flume for two weeks one summer and we found it a soft touch, especially on a warm day, because all we had to do was break up the blocks when they jammed up the odd time. Working on the chip barges was a different matter altogether. The company purchased two really old metal-hulled sailing ships that were converted into barges for transporting wood chips from various sawmills up and down the BC coast to Ocean Falls to be "cooked" into pulp. These sailing vessels were stripped of everything such as the cabin, masts and deck, so what remained was basically just a hull with a lot of capacity for the chips. The only additions were good sized logs fastened to the gunnels on both sides and a level floor at the bottom of the hull. The barge would be towed into port and tied up to the Island Titan, a pile-driving rig that could be converted with a huge bucket on a boom for unloading the chips. Once the bucket scooped out most of the load, the operator, John Cherris, couldn't see over the gunnels so that's where we came in. Dave took the first four hours, straddling the log gunnel, giving hand signals to the operator who was virtually operating the bucket blind at this point. And because there was now a D-4 caterpillar in the hold to push out the chips from the sides and both ends, it was also a good idea if the bucket didn't flatten the cat skinner.

My job down below was to rake the wood chips off the ribs and to keep well clear of the cat. It was a soft touch but not so for the signal man, as he was up there in all weather conditions without a chance of relaxing. At midnight we would crawl over on a plank to the Island Titan to eat lunch and more importantly warm up, and then it would be my turn. I don't know what he was thinking, but before Dave left the ship he took off his life jacket. He slipped on the plank and fell at least 20' into the water, just missing by inches the log against the pilings. His aim was perfect, hitting the open water, because if he had fallen on any part of that log, it wouldn't have been a happy ending. We lowered an extension ladder and somehow got him out. Not surprisingly he wasn't his normal cheerful self. John Cherris was none too pleased either when he saw that Dave wasn't wearing his life jacket. After lunch they found some dry clothes for Dave, and then banished him for the remainder of the shift to the ship's hold. At five a.m. when we walked through the mill to punch out at the time clock, the sawmill superintendent, Al Jeffrey, intercepted us to give us hell. Knowing that he shouldn't have been at his office till eight a.m. and he was there three hours early, we knew someone had alerted him and we were in trouble. He was yelling about safety records, life jackets, dumb kids. The air was getting bluer and bluer as he wound up. I wanted to point out that I didn't violate the life jacket regulation, but I was afraid to interrupt him. In 1961 our mill had won the trophy for the safest mill in BC, and a couple of high school kids weren't about to jeopardize that record.

CHARLESON HIGH

Our homeroom teacher in grade eight was Helen Moore. She was in her forties, quite short, and a bit on the stout side. That year the grade eight class was putting on the play *I Remember Mama*, and she had one heck of a time recruiting boys for the male parts. One of the principal male parts went to Hanalore Meinke who did a pretty good job although her voice was a few octaves too high.

The best thing to happen that year was that Principal John Moe, who had been teaching at Charleson since the late '40s, was retiring. Not too many students were sorry to see him go. He was a very strict, cold person who believed in corporal punishment with a capital C. The vice-principal, Bob Scott, would take over the helm the following year. I believe that he was generally well liked by the kids and faculty alike. Scott was fair and had a heart, unlike his predecessor. Mrs. Scott taught us Social Studies and she made it fun to be in her class. She was probably my favourite teacher, if I had to choose.

I liked John Robinson, our homeroom teacher in grade seven. Jack Cronin and I got our fair share of whacks across the palms for goofing off in class, but we deserved them and Robbie was just doing his job.

Most of us boys carried jack knives in our pockets. Once I made the mistake of bringing this cheap little Japanese *hari-kari* knife to school. It had a thin three-inch blade with a wooden handle and a wooden sheath. As I was showing it off in the classroom between classes, one of my classmates snatched the knife away and jabbed Blair McKinnon in the thigh. I don't know what possessed him. The blade must have cut an artery because blood gushed out fast and furious from his wound. As they hauled Blair off to the hospital for repairs, they hauled me down to the principal's office for the inquisition. I took the brunt of the blame as I had provided the weapon even though I didn't actually do the evil deed. Mr. Moe really enjoyed giving me the strap on the backside that day. He was big and strong and just waled away. I got the point after one wallop but he insisted on giving me five more. I didn't chip in for Moe's retirement gift that year.

Some of the guys used to really torment Mrs. Moore. Lyle Green was quite the shit disturber in her classes. Once he put a handful of earth worms in her desk drawer, which almost sent her around the bend. During summer holidays she and her husband Frank, another school teacher, went over to France and they brought back a few posters from Paris and proudly displayed them on the back wall. When she stepped out of the class for a few minutes Dave Brassard torched the Eiffel Tower one. She didn't notice it when she first came back in, but she could smell something and knew it wasn't quite right. She kept sniffing and we all held our breath until she finally glanced at the back wall, let out a mighty scream and then stormed out of the room. Now that was cruel.

In September when our class was entering senior high, we had to put up with the annual initiation ritual that consisted of the grade eleven boys tormenting us all week—fun activities like knocking the school books out of our hands or turning over our desks. We survived the week alright until Friday when between classes we were climbing the stairs en route to the science lab. I could sense that we'd have to run the gauntlet. The senior boys were waiting for us at the top, and out of nowhere Darryl Hodson sucker-punched me in the chops. It was my good fortune that a few of my buddies caught me because he really clocked me and I was a bit groggy. Thankfully initiations are being phased out now. Those weren't the good old days.

That year, grade ten, was almost my last year for formal education because I was nearly expelled through no fault of my own, of course.

Someone in the class had drawn a picture of a big dog, complete with male genitalia, and the dog's face looked much like the teacher standing at the front of the class, Mr. Martin. The artist even gave the dog a moustache and a trilby hat. Just like Martin. After he completed his handiwork, he handed it back and the work of art made the rounds in the classroom. Some of the guys added to it. Instead of a feather in the hat band, a small Union Jack flag was inserted and naturally, a few choice comments added as well. By the time the paper reached me the dog was wearing two pairs of argyle socks with three different colours inked in. Mr. Martin must have figured by then that something was up because he could hear the snickers as he wrote on the board. He turned just in time to see me putting the paper on my desk after it was handed off to me. Busted. He was normally a very calm, level-headed teacher, but when he saw that canine sporting the British flag he went totally ballistic, hauling me down to the principal's office where I remained for the rest of the day, even through lunch hour. No Monique today. Principal Bob Scott tried to coax a confession out of me but I maintained my innocence right to the end. I was thanking my lucky stars that Moe had retired the previous year. The boys upstairs weren't about to acknowledge their part in this mess, since they had their sacrificial lamb down below being forced into submission and possibly expulsion. Finally, out of desperation, every boy's pen in Martin's class was labelled and then brought to the office where it was compared to the art work. By three p.m., I was released with a warning, and after all that detective work, nobody was charged. The graffiti artists were lucky those were the pre-DNA testing days.

I had the misfortune of having Frank Canty for a homeroom teacher in grade nine and again in grade twelve. Of all my teachers, he was definitely my number one least favourite. Old Frankie was a lifelong bachelor, quite bald, with a demeanour better suited to a sergeant major in an army boot camp. He wouldn't tolerate anything but the business at hand: learning. Everything else was *verboten*. The only time I saw him crack a smile was when he was flipping up John Sarnacki's shirt collar. Not to hold it against him but Mr. Canty had a funny way of pronouncing "ar." He would say Larry but it would rhyme with starry as in "Starry starry night."

When Jack Cronin mimicked him, he would say, "Har-r-r-y, Lar-r-r-y, and Bar-r-r-y went over the falls in a bar-r-rel." Jack was careful not to mimic our favourite teacher-target during school however. Canty taught math, sciences, and health and personal development. During HPD classes he liked to read chapters from Emily Post. Some of those tips actually came in handy in later years: remove hats indoors, open doors and pull out chairs for dates. Ruth Boillet wasn't in Frank Canty's fan club. She was one of the more popular girls in the class and quite attractive. During one HPD lesson we were learning about the dangers of alcohol and the effects it had on the brain and internal organs when Ruth let out this barely audible snicker. Very few heard it, but Mr. Personality did. He erupted, putting Mr. Martin of the canine-cartoon fame to shame. We had never seen anything like it. It was downright scary.

He screamed, "Ruth Boillet, five years from now you could be a hopeless alcoholic living under a bridge or even worse, lying dead in a ditch." After a few more words of encouragement, he stormed out of the room. You could have heard a pin drop. After high school, I thought I'd seen the last of him, but four years later our paths would cross again in Germany, thousands of miles away.

In order to be admitted to university we needed to graduate with a foreign language so in grade eleven I took French. However, I didn't get much further than the *un, deux, trois* stage. No mistake about it, I was a lousy student in French that year and my attitude was not much better. Our French teacher, Mrs. Christopherson, had quite the Australian accent, so naturally I blamed that on my difficulties with *le français* lingo although it didn't seem to hinder the rest of the class. Halfway through the year I was given the old heave-ho from French 10, so university was no longer an option. My final year in French, in grade twelve, wasn't much better. I failed the final exam but at least Mrs. Christopherson didn't expel me. Small victories.

The principal, Bob Scott, was also my English 40 teacher in grade twelve. To formally graduate I needed two years of French, which I was failing badly, and Chemistry 91 didn't look too promising either. As it turned out, I passed my lab portion of chemistry but flunked the final exam. I finally got my Chem 91 by correspondence four years later. Mr.

Scott was trying to encourage me, telling me I had the potential to succeed since my IQ was equal to that of my brother who was soon to graduate from UBC as a mechanical engineer. A requirement in English class was to hand in an essay every Friday for the entire school year. In early May, Mr. Scott informed me that he would have no choice but to fail me in English 40, regardless of my final mark in the exam, unless I handed in the twenty-two essays that were overdue. Now that caught my attention. Twenty-two essays in three weeks. I definitely wanted a passing grade, and I also didn't want to disappoint my teacher because I had a lot of respect for him. The pressure was on, so I buckled down and actually did grind out the essays on time, although it wasn't easy. By number twenty-two I was desperate for a topic and in my brother's book collection chanced upon a really thin pocket book about microbes, of all things. Every year Don would bring home from university his required reading books. Interesting stories like *Catcher in the Rye* and *Catch 22*. How appropriate. What's the catch? Catch 22 essays. Anyway, the microbe book was dryer than dry but at least it was small, maybe one hundred and twenty pages at most. I ploughed through it in record time and the resulting essay was one of my better efforts.

When our class graduated in '62, I wasn't allowed to take part in the ceremonies because I didn't have the required credits. Disappointing for me, and when my father found out later he wasn't too happy either. However, I did attend the post-grad bash at Rick White's house up on 10th Street, but I wished that I hadn't. I was standing on the deck outside, leaning against the railing, minding my own business, when an undergrad gave me a little push and I went flying off the deck, along with ten feet of railing, landing flat on my back. The next morning my lower back was all black and blue, and ever since then I've spent a small fortune on chiropractors. The undergrad wasn't trying to be malicious, maybe just exuberant and tipsy. His name was David Dink Dowling, and believe it or not, both his father and his older brother whom I had never met, were also known as Dink Dowling. They were a family of Dinks.

Rick White had the brightest future in our class. In school, he always had top marks and he was cool before cool was cool. But that brilliant future was not to be. Booze was his downfall. After one year of university he dropped out and started working in an oil refinery in Burnaby. He did okay there, making decent wages, retiring early, but Rick was one bitter person, hating almost everything. I made the mistake once of giving him my Edmonton phone number and every so often he would phone, always late at night and of course looped, and start his ongoing rant against the world. My wife wasn't impressed. That was before we had call display. A number of times I tried to get him interested in Ocean Falls reunions that were happening every four years, but he always came up with some flimsy excuse why he couldn't make it "this time." In his younger days, he had a full head of jet-black hair, but in his 50s, Rick had serious hair loss. Whenever we got together he would ask about our former classmates and did they have a full head of hair or were they balding. My take on the situation was that he was too vain to show up at a reunion looking like Frank Canty with a seriously receding hair line. Rick didn't get much past his early 60s when he passed away.

PLAY IT AGAIN, BILL

Lyle Green bought an electric guitar and taught himself how to play with the help of a Chet Atkins song book. Three other guys joined with Lyle to form "The Wild Ones," but really it was the piano player Bill Frew who was the real deal. The other three basically supported Bill and his keyboard. Bill would hear a tune once or twice and it was memorized and played anywhere on demand. He wasn't short-suited in musical talent. Many times after school, Bill would make his way to the music department of the Hudson's Bay Company where he would lift the latest 45 record fresh out on the hit parade. The store clerk knew what he was up to, but she never did nail him. In his bedroom were two stacks of 45 records, both about three feet high. A few times he even pilfered LP records. That was no easy task when you consider how much bigger they were compared to the smaller 45s. Archie Young nicknamed him "Fingers Frew," and he wasn't referring to his piano-playing skills. Bill actually got his start playing the accordion. Back in about '57, Opal Wareham, a divorcée, came to the Falls and married a machinist by the name of Art Koppang. Her son Bob ended up in our class, and after completing grade eleven, with Principal Bob Scott's blessing, he dropped out of school to join his uncle in Taller O'Shea's country band touring western Canada. Opal was from a well-known musical family in BC that toured all over the province with country and western bands. She was also a music teacher, and soon it seemed that every second kid in Ocean Falls had pestered their parents for an accordion and signed up with her to take lessons. Just before the big accordion infestation happened, Dad bought an old beat-up piano for a reasonable price and said to Mary-Lynne, "You know, I don't care if you ever get to be a classical pianist, but it would be nice if you could walk into a party and sit down and play the piano all night long."

My sister took weekly lessons from Mrs. Ungerer, but it wasn't an instant success like Dad envisioned. After eight weeks Mrs. Ungerer terminated Mary-Lynne because she wouldn't practise. Clearly, she had better things to do, so I was next in the firing line. The piano that he paid good money for wasn't about to sit idle. I really and truly hated it, so after six months of pure torture I jumped ship and signed on with Opal Koppang, hoping that her rock and roll style would be more enjoyable than classical music. It was, but just barely. One night Opal's students put on a big concert in the Crown Theatre, showcasing all our many talents. Accordion and piano. There I was, up on the big stage in front of a sold-out house, banging away on the keys, when I lost my train of thought, and of course my place on the music sheet. Talk about panic, and no place to hide. After what seemed like minutes but most likely was closer to five seconds, I somehow found my place and finished the tune, not to a standing ovation, I might add. That was the pinnacle of my musical career. I will never forget the piece that I was playing. It was "Don't be Cruel" by Elvis Presley. How appropriate. I begged off piano lessons. And that wasn't just a figure of speech. I literally begged. Poor little sister Barbara then stepped into the breach and she carried on with the Forbes tradition. Amongst the three of us we didn't have a single musical bone in our bodies. Not so Fingers Frew. Even after two heart attacks in his mid 50s and hearing loss from operating a diesel tugboat for many years at Port Alberni, he's still very active on his beloved piano and electric organ. He's in a six-piece band that plays rock-a-billy music by Buddy Holly and Jerry Lee Lewis, among others, mentors teenage musical groups, and even finds the time to entertain seniors at nursing homes. You can't keep a good man down.

CARS, BIKES AND FORKLIFTS

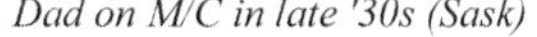

Dad on M/C in late '30s (Sask)

Me in '61 on Matchless 500

In August of '61 two of my classmates, Lorne Gilchrist and Harry Diggens, bought used motorcycles in Vancouver and had quite the adventure touring all over B. C. After they came back in September for grade twelve, they were the envy of all the teenage boys in town. When I mentioned in passing to my Dad about my friends' trip, I couldn't believe my ears when he said that in a few weeks he had to fly to Vancouver, and he would pick up a used bike for me. I would pay for it of course, but still, here was a man pushing me towards a motorcycle, yet a canoe was a "death trap". Don't they call bikers "organ donors?" Apparently, he had owned numerous Harley-Davidson and Indian bikes on the prairies, in another life, and survived. A few weeks later a '56 Matchless 500cc bike was off-loaded at the Johnston Terminals wharf. One of the Johnston workers, Pete Humphries, fired it up on the third kick, and with me hanging on behind him, we roared out to my house in Martin Valley. "Wow, this is great," I said. "My own bike." The euphoria didn't last too long. I don't think I put more than twenty miles on that damn machine. After the first day, it was hard to start. The clutch was shot, the gear box was buggered and the magneto was suspect. Other than those minor problems, it was just fine. But it did look good. Thank you very much Fred Deely Motorcycles Limited. The first day I got it running I was going from Jack Cronin's house to mine a little too fast, lost control on a corner and almost ended up in the cemetery, literally. My dream soon died but not me. A university student working in the mill that summer who had a few clues about bikes stripped it down in our basement, and put it back together with some new parts, but we weren't much further ahead. He was honest with me and said there were too many problems and it would be throwing good money after bad. The only positive part of this whole sad saga was that for awhile my nickname was Matchless Forbes instead of Jockstrap.

Because I had worked in the mill for two months the previous summer and was now working every weekend, my bank account was looking very healthy. After all, there wasn't much to spend your money on in Ocean Falls, so I decided to fly to Vancouver for the Easter break. I was itching to experience civilization and Prince Rupert didn't count. I landed in Vancouver with my eyes wide open, taking in everything for the first time. I was overwhelmed by the tall buildings, the tens of thousands of cars, most of which weren't in the beater class, and of course the girls. In Ocean Falls you could go all day and be lucky to see a handful of babes, but the big city was just crawling with them. Babe Central. I could get used to this. At the downtown intersections not controlled with traffic lights I would just stand for minutes on end like a real hick, wondering how it would be possible to cross without becoming another traffic fatality. Finally, I asked a stranger what the trick was. He rolled his eyes, and then explained that by law cars had to stop for pedestrians in crosswalks. If not for him I would still be standing there. I stayed in the Belmont Hotel on Granville Street, just at the foot of the Granville St. bridge in downtown Vancouver. For two dollars extra a day, I had the bellhop wheel in a portable black and white TV. After he plugged it in and adjusted the rabbit ears I settled down to watch my first program on the small screen. I didn't last half an hour because I thought it was pretty stupid to fly 350 miles to watch a grainy black and white picture when the big bad world was right outside my door.

The next morning was a repeat of my Prince Rupert hotel experience, only worse. My room, which didn't have a bathroom, was halfway down a wing around the corner from a bank of elevators. Wearing only my shorts, I stepped directly across the hallway to the bathroom, and because my window and the bathroom windows were open, there was enough of a breeze to slam my door shut, locking me out. Now what? I could hear little kids playing in the hallway down by the elevators, so I couldn't very well venture down there in my nearly naked state. Eventually the kids went back to their room, and just as I was going to make my move I heard other people talking while they waited for an elevator. When they left I sprinted to the elevators, pushed the button, and then quickly ran back to my observation post around the corner. Finally, after what seemed to be an eternity but was probably just a minute, I heard the elevator door open and out stepped the bellhop, complete with his organ grinder monkey hat. He looked around and then noticed me down at the corner frantically waving at him. After a good laugh, he went down for a key, and best of all he didn't insist that I accompany him to the front desk. Note to self: buy pyjamas.

Charlie Williamson, who was a year older than me, showed up at the Belmont on my second day in the big city, looking for a favour. He was a burly guy, quite popular, who over the years remained a good friend. Charlie had been in a fender bender while driving a rental car the day before. Because Charlie was using a friend's driver's license, he had paid cash for the damage on condition that the other driver didn't report the accident. The problem was, he was short of funds, and needed a carpet to sleep on for a few days until he flew home. Athletic Charlie would jump up and pull down the exterior fire escape stairs, and climb up to the third floor and through my unlocked window, always at night, so he wasn't detected and booted out. I felt that I owed him for a previous incident at the high school. We were climbing up the stairs by the school and not thinking. I gave him a little shove where there wasn't a railing. Down he went, about six feet, but immediately bounded up. He probably had a good thirty pounds on me and had a reputation for being pretty handy with his fists. I saw my life flash before my eyes. This is game over I thought to myself, but fortunately Charlie wasn't hurt, just dirty, so we had a good laugh. My lucky day, Chuck chuckles.

Another guy got in touch with me during that Easter break. Vern was originally from Weyburn, Saskatchewan, and he worked in the mill just long enough to earn enough money to buy an older car. He was in a rooming house up on Kingsway Ave, drawing unemployment insurance, and surviving on a steady diet of fried egg sandwiches that he did up on a hot plate. Vern really wanted to go to the Seattle World's Fair, so we agreed that if I bought the gas we would drive down in his '55 Pontiac. I also bought him the odd hamburger because he had an obvious cash flow problem, and it worked out just fine. We saw a lot that day, walked miles, even went up the Space Needle. Thinking back, the highlight for me that week wasn't really the trip to Seattle, but rather the realization that there was something much greater than my hometown and that something was civilization.

Between the ages of sixteen to eighteen, we regarded the mill property as our own personal playground. Security was lax after hours so there was no problem sneaking into the mill. A covered conveyor belt, about a half mile long, took the hog fuel—bark—from the sawmill to the power plant where it was burned to generate steam. A bunch of us kids would ride that belt, but it proved to be almost fatal for Jack Cronin. Jack was a bit of a daredevil. If there was a cliff to jump off into the lake he would always dive in head first, trusting that he wouldn't kill himself on a submerged rock, whereas I would take the more conservative, some would say chicken approach, and jump in feet first. On the conveyor belt one night he miscalculated on his dismount, and was about one second from falling into the hopper along with the hog fuel. He couldn't jump on the catwalk because it ended a few feet back, so instead he had to jump up to grab onto a rafter, and then make his way back hand over hand to safety. All in a day's work for Jack. His father ran the dairy department for the Hudson's Bay store and had quite a reputation for drinking, and it wasn't milk. Jack started drinking beer in his high school years, and to him it was all about speed. Two gulps would do it, then he would be reaching for another bottle. Like his father before him, it was only a matter of time before Jack became an alcoholic. Sometime in his forties, he came to the realization that he wasn't long for this world if he didn't change his ways, so much to everyone's surprise, Jack quit cold turkey. We were all glad for him because he was such a great guy, well liked, a good friend for life. Jack lived in Kamloops for many years, where two of his younger sisters lived. Unfortunately, he died of pancreatic cancer in his late sixties, living much longer than we initially thought he would.

Roy Chernishenko introduced me to jitney racing. A jitney is similar to a large fork lift, but instead of the forks, there is a grappling device that is used for loading rolls of newsprint onto the barges. The warehouse that stored the rolls was all of two city blocks long, plenty of room to hold our drag races. One night we took off down the track and I just couldn't catch Roy's jitney. As we came to the finish line, I was engulfed in smoke because I hadn't released my parking brake, and then from another direction came a jitney driver with a fire extinguisher. He smelled the smoke from quite a distance away, and lucky for us decided to investigate before pulling the fire alarm. Also lucky was that I knew him from the basketball league so he didn't turn us in, just gave us hell, pointing out that the warehouse was built entirely out of wood, and it contained millions and millions of dollars worth of newsprint. That was the end of the jitney races.

One Friday night I took a small forklift from the lumber yard for a joyride. Before leaving the yard, I put an empty pallet unto the forks to make it look authentic in case I encountered anyone. As I was driving past the sawmill, Leo Turcotte, a sawmill relief foreman, jumped out of nowhere and put his hand up for me to stop. This didn't look good—my driving career nipped in the bud. It turned out that Leo was on his lunch break and he just loved to shoot the breeze. He didn't clue in that I was joyriding, maybe because of that pallet on the forks, but after twenty minutes I told him that I had to get going. I had a pick-up to do. The entire time that I sat there listening to Leo, the transmission was in gear, with my foot pushing down on the clutch because I wasn't sure that I could find the proper gear again, and I didn't want to stall the engine and blow my cover. By the time I slowly drove away my leg was throbbing. My ears were too because Leo sure could talk.

BOOTLEGGERS AND BEER

From the age of sixteen until I left Ocean Falls three years later, I and my friends used two different bootleggers although, to be truthful, they weren't true bootleggers because they never marked up the booze. If a case of beer was selling for two dollars and forty cents in the government liquor store, that's what we paid. Norm Christie was a man in his mid 40s who was lying low from the Vancouver City police as he earned an honest living in the Falls. Norm was a scary looking character with a receding hairline hiding under a pork pie hat, who in his previous life was a thug on the downtown east side, namely amongst the skid row pubs on Hastings Street. He only lasted a few months in the Martin Inn before being evicted, probably for beating up some poor sucker, so he ended up living in a boat at the docks. Perhaps because he had a captive audience that would listen to all his outlandish stories, he wouldn't charge us extra for the alcohol. At the time, the liquor of choice was lemon gin. It was a lot easier to conceal under our jackets than a dozen beers, but to me it tasted like perfume. In less that two years our bootlegger left for the big city where he was either in his old stomping grounds or in jail. Both scenarios fit Norm Christie to a T.

One night I was walking on the Martin Valley road with a case of bootlegged beer when I saw the police jeep coming towards me, so I quickly stashed the beer in the ditch and carried on. Everyone recognized the jeep at night because of the high headlights that were close together.

When the cop passed me, I recovered the beer but the wily old cop, Sergeant Brassard, had made a U-turn, turned off his headlights, and came back and nailed me. He didn't charge me, just relieved me of the beer. Bill Frew was telling me that the Sarg liked to throw parties at his house and occasionally he would have Bill come over to pound out tunes on the piano. I was glad to help.

Our best bootlegger was brought in to work as a meat cutter at the Hudson's Bay store. Harvey Werner wasn't much older than we were, but he was of legal age and he also didn't charge extra. Harv was more of a friend than a bootlegger. He was slim with red curly hair and a shy demeanour. His main passion was playing poker. If we wanted to have a few beers, he would leave a case in his hotel room and then lend us his room key while he sat in on an all-night poker game elsewhere in the hotel. One Saturday night in the summer of '62, Roy Chernishenko, Cec Walker, myself and this older guy whose name I can't recall were up in Harvey's room having a bit of a party when there was a loud knock on the door. A voice yelled out, "Open up, police." Both Roy and I were minors, and Cec, whom we called Johnny, a mill worker, was also underage. In a flash, the older guy jumped into the clothes closet with his beer and cigarette and both Johnny and Roy threw their beers out the window. The door wasn't locked so Constable Ken Parkes burst in and caught me red-handed, drinking a beer. So off I go to the police station, charged with underage drinking. Constable Parkes relieved me of my shoe laces and belt and locked me up in a cell.

Harvey Werner on Granville St. in Vancouver

This reminds me of folk singer Arlo Guthrie's huge hit in 1967, "Alice's Restaurant". When Officer Obie arrested Arlo for littering and put him in a cell, taking his belt, Arlo said, "Obie, did you think I was going to hang myself for littering?" Within minutes Johnny Walker showed up at the station and started hassling the poor constable.

Johnny was going on, saying, "Look at the big cop, arresting Jock for no reason, look at all the buttons on his tunic," and then poking his finger on each button down Parkes' chest, saying, "Look at the buttons, one, two, three, four, five, six buttons. Wow, big cop."

It was a wonder that he wasn't jailed right alongside me. I must say, that cop sure had a lot of patience, but after half an hour of Johnny's abuse, it wore a little thin so he gave me back my laces and belt and set me free. Harvey the bootlegger wasn't so lucky. A few months later when he was putting on his expensive suit, he noticed the sleeve had a nice round burn hole in it caused by a cigarette.

In the spring of '63 I met Harvey in Vancouver and ended up staying at his parents' house in Richmond. On the Saturday night, we went out to the Smilin Buddha Cabaret on East Hastings with his older brother and his brother's wife. At the time, the place didn't have a liquor license so you had to smuggle in your own booze and then buy the mix for five dollars a bottle. The trick was to have your female companion carry a large handbag to hide the liquor when the cops raided, which they did twice that night. When the cabaret's lights flickered, that was the early warning signal that in twenty seconds, ten cops with powerful flashlights would be searching the joint. All the liquor quickly went into the handbags. I don't remember who was playing that night in the Smilin Buddha, but I do know that they hosted acts like Jimi Hendrix, Jefferson Airplane and The Payolas.

Like I said, Harvey lived for poker. I remember him telling me once that he was "pretty lucky" in an all-night poker game, so he flew to Vancouver for a weeks' holiday and bought a new Chevrolet. When he came back he promptly lost a ton of money and had to sell his new car in a hurry or risk getting beaten up for not paying off the debt that he'd accumulated in one night of gambling. In the mid '80s, my wife and I were at an Ocean Falls reunion in Nanaimo when out of the blue Harvey showed up. I hadn't seen him in over twenty years, and because he didn't know that many people in the hall, he sat with us and he basically bought every drink for the entire table all night long. He wanted to dance with my wife Evelyne, but she wasn't too keen on waltzing with a complete and slightly tipsy stranger, so she mentioned that she liked the polka, which was a little white lie. A few times Harvey went up to the DJ requesting a polka to no avail until finally he waved fifty dollars in his face. The DJ agreed; then Harv pulled out another fifty and said, "Make that two."

When we left for our hotel he asked if we would mind giving him a ride, so we dropped him off in a seedy-looking back alley in the downtown area where an all-night poker game was happening. He must have done okay because the next day he showed up in a taxi at the reunion picnic with a large Styrofoam cooler overflowing with hard liquor, wine, beer and mix, plus plastic cups, and everyone was welcome to partake. Harvey Werner, last of the big-time spenders. He was telling me that after he left the Falls he ended up at the Calgary Stampede where you could find some high-stakes poker games. As the story goes, he lost his shirt and couldn't even afford a bus ticket back to Vancouver, so he stayed in Calgary, driving a cab. Eventually he won enough to buy one taxi, then won seven, then he lost them all in poker, then won them all back again. The story goes on about taxis, caterpillars, construction, Vegas trips. It was mind-boggling. I couldn't separate fact from fiction. For Harvey, it was easy come, easy go, repeat if necessary.

It was in the summer of '62 that the Ocean Falls Johnston Terminals Beer Heist took place. Sometime after midnight the door on the Johnston Terminals warehouse down by the dock was forced, and numerous cases of beer were taken. Somehow Roy figured that Johnny Beggs and a few of his cohorts were involved. They had "borrowed" kids' wagons that were lying about and wheeled the beer up Front Street and then up the Dam Hill Road to the ballpark at Link Lake, where they then cached their booty in the dense bushes surrounding the park. Only in Ocean Falls would you find a crime of this nature that didn't have a get-way vehicle,

Johnny Beggs

mainly because there were only about thirty-five cars in town, and thieves weren't sophisticated enough to know how to hot-wire a car. Roy, Jack Cronin, Bill Frew and I decided to wander up to the ballpark and have a look-see. Much to our disappointment we came up empty-handed although, in the bush, we found a pair of sunglasses that looked a lot like those Johnny always wore. The ownership of these sunglasses was never in question because he was probably the only guy in the Falls to wear shades, and our town wasn't a hotbed for the latest fashions. Circumstantial evidence pointed to John Francis Beggs.

WATER-LOGGED

After graduation, most of us worked in the mill for the summer. I applied for the sawmill boom, and it didn't hurt my cause that the superintendent, Al Jeffrey, was the manager of our softball team, Local 312. I promised him that I would wear a life jacket at all times while working on the water. The sawmill operated seven days a week with two shifts, eight a.m. to five p.m. and eight p.m. to five a.m. We had a lunch break at either noon or midnight and the three hours between shifts was when all the sawmill equipment would be oiled and greased. Jack Steepe, the oiler on our shift, was a skinny little bald-headed character of sixty-four, who in his former life was a pharmacist in Vancouver. He looked like a refugee from skid row which he most likely was, and his clothes were as greasy as the rags that he carried in his back pocket. He lost everything because of alcohol although his brain still worked just fine. Jack used to entertain us with stories of the big city, and especially of horse racing of which he was particularly fond. He lived on an old leaky former fishing boat tied up at the wharf because his stay in the Martin Inn was short-lived due to some alcohol-related incident. When he turned sixty-five the following spring, the sawmill division put on a retirement party for old Jack in the banquet room at the Martin Inn. Al Jeffrey sent two of us down to the wharf to collect him before he had too much to drink. While we were there to steer him to the party, he mumbled something about the bilge, so I hand pumped out some water until he was satisfied. At his party he told a few tall tales, had more than a few whiskeys, even thanked the superintendent for giving him a second chance, and then started to nod off. We dragged him back to his yacht for his final night in the Falls. The next day he stumbled over to the sea plane terminal and flew to Vancouver, never to return. Within twenty-four hours Jack's boat had sunk to the bottom of the harbour. Only an oil slick marked its berth.

I worked with two others on the booms, Dave Tatrie, the leadhand, and his buddy Grant Reed, both from the prairies, but by September they had enough of the isolation and headed for the big lights down south. My foreman, Bill Braschuk, liked my work so he promoted me to leadhand which resulted in a nice pay raise and first choice of days off. I chose to work from Sunday to Thursday with every Friday and Saturday off. Perfect. And of course, Sunday was time and a half. When Archie Young and Sid Fredrickson started on my crew in September, they weren't too pleased with the shift arrangements, but I had seniority, all two months of it. Sid was about our age and was from Hagensborg in the Bella Coola Valley. He pushed logs with us for only about three months, just long enough to earn a great nickname. One beautiful fall day, before the monsoons started, he was feeding logs onto the jack ladder when a low-flying seagull scored a direct hit on the side of his head. He was known as "Shithead Sid" after that. Sid should have been wearing a hard hat but probably didn't want to end up with hat hair.

I was fortunate to have Bill Braschuk as a boss. Everyone seemed to respect him because he never flew off the handle when things went sideways. My classmate Rick White's father, also Bill, was a very stern unfriendly foreman, but the one to avoid at all costs was Nick Slater. He acted like he had a lot of shares in Crown Zellerbach and those shares wouldn't be dropping in value on his watch. During the winter months, the winds would push all the logs way back in the pocket, which would result in gaps on the jack ladder to feed the sawmill. Gaps meant fewer logs on the sawmill assembly line, which translated into the possibility of idle workers in the sawmill. Not good for the bottom line. If Slater was on duty he would throw a fit and come running down to the log booms to fill in the gaps. He was like a man possessed, springing into action, pike pole in hand, and, of course, no caulk boots or life jacket.

If the sawmill was cutting pulp for newsprint, we had to have roughly a 60:40 ratio of spruce and hemlock. Fir and hemlock look similar, but you couldn't introduce the fir log into the mix because it would ruin the pulp. Fir was only for kraft paper like brown paper bags and such.

When I first started, Nick explained how to tell the difference. "Its all in the bark," he said. "Poke your pike pole into the bark and if it's red under the surface, it's a hemlock log. If there's still any doubt break off a piece of bark and chew it, it should taste like turpentine." Isn't that what the ancient Greeks drank when they wanted to commit suicide, juice from hemlock bark?

Slater's regular boom leadhand was this stocky little older worker of either Polish or Ukrainian heritage who answered to the name of Kulat Bill. Kulat is a Russian word that means "wealthy peasant," but old Bill was more of a serf to the boss. He was deathly afraid of Slater. He was without a doubt one of the hardest-working and most loyal employees for Crown Zellerbach. Bill acted like he would be fired any minute and be shipped back to Siberia. He was in his mid 50s, so I'm sure he had some bad memories of the communists in eastern Europe.

I was forever grateful to have Bill Braschuk for my regular foreman. The only positive thing about Nick Slater was that his daughter, Claudia, was a real sweetheart, a real looker, but unfortunately, she was taken. My good friend Roy was dating her, even though Daddy didn't approve because Roy was now working in the steam plant instead of attending university. The relief foreman, Leo Turcotte, was okay to work for. He never did recognize me as that forklift operator from the previous summer. We nicknamed him "Leo da Lion" but we should have called him "The Chatterbox." Because it was so noisy inside the sawmill with all the various saws screaming constantly, Leo had no one to talk to, so a few times a shift, da Lion would nip down to the booms to bullshit with us. How so un-Slater like.

We would occasionally handle cottonwood logs which are used to produce tissue paper. The larger logs were so heavy and water-logged that about ninety percent of the log was below the surface, so if you made the mistake of standing on one, it would sink. The smaller cottonwood logs would arrive in the form of a mini Davis raft which was a huge bundle of logs strapped together with three steel cables. It was pretty dicey liberating the raft of logs and staying dry. The trick was to cut two of the cables with a double-bitted axe, and then whack the last cable about three quarters of the way through. With a final swing of the axe, we would leap to safety as the logs exploded. Jumping with an axe in hand was the scary part.

After graduation, two of my classmates, John Riley and Bill Frew, flew over to Britain for an extended holiday instead of working in the mill. John came to us from Aberdeen Scotland in time for grade four. He was just a wee lad with a big booming voice. Despite being at least a head shorter than the rest of us, he turned into a fairly good basketball player. Early on, Archie nicknamed him "Peanut" so John countered by calling Archie "Lofty." John and Bill travelled all over England and Scotland, and it wasn't long before they were seriously short of funds and had to write home for money to fly back. Much to everyone's surprise, when John stepped off the seaplane in Ocean Falls he had a wife in tow. Pat felt right at home with all the Scottish accents in town and the dreary overcast skies. John joined Archie and myself on the sawmill booms since Sid had moved on by then. It was just like a class reunion. John didn't last too long because he had an accident on the boom dozer, a little tug with a hole in the centre that housed the outboard engine that we used when the winter winds were blowing the wrong way. He wasn't really banged up much, but the safety department felt that John was too short to operate the dozer, so they recommended a transfer. It was the best thing that could have happened to John because the following week he started in the steam plant where it was always warm and dry and best of all, no Nick Slater. John was always good in math so he had no problem passing his 4th Class Steam Engineering ticket and eventually became a 1st Class which opened a lot of doors for him.

Archie and I were working the night shift once when the paper machines had a scheduled shut-down, so the sawmill was at a standstill. Unfortunately, our boss that night was Nick Slater. Company man that he was, we were told to cut up the garbage logs into sixteen-inch logs for fireplaces in the townsite. "We can't have any idle time boys." There was an old electric saw similar to a mitre saw to work with, only much bigger and quite noisy. After three hours of slave labour, we had to come up with a plan because, after all, this wasn't what we signed up for. We jammed the blade in a gnarly old log until the fuse blew on the motor. We then suggested to Nick that he had better phone for the duty electrician. Two hours later Dave Owens showed up, meter in hand, to trouble-shoot the saw. After forty-five minutes, he declared the machine serviceable, much to our disappointment, but at least we had a good break from the thankless job. Nick was hinting that we had sabotaged the saw on purpose but we pleaded ignorance and claimed innocence. He couldn't bear to see workers sitting around being non-productive, and even worse, drawing wages. Nick was the ideal foreman unless you had the misfortune to be on his shift.

The jack ladder that hauled the logs into the sawmill was quite steep, gaining thirty to forty feet in altitude. Much of our spruce was towed down from Masset in the Queen Charlotte Islands, now called Haida Gwaii, and it was prime timber. I thought it was a crime that wood so straight and knot free like Stika spruce would be ground up into pulp. Once on a day shift we loaded up the jack ladder with these beautiful spruce logs that were five to six feet in diameter, and made the near-fatal mistake of not leaving any space between the butts. With all that weight the chain broke, but as luck would have it the safety brake prevented literally tons of logs from sliding back into the water, right where we were standing. It would take the millwrights and welders a good six hours to repair the chain, so we had a mini shutdown on the booms, but I felt so guilty about over-loading the jack ladder that I booked off and went home.

For six months of the year it was quite enjoyable working on the booms. If we fell off a log, it was no big deal because we kept spare clothes and boots in the boom shack. The rest of the year was a different matter altogether. We constantly had to wear rain gear and, if it was snowing or really blowing hard, it just added to the challenge. Balancing on a log that was covered with snow wasn't much fun, and it took a lot of skill and luck not to end up in the chuck. In the boom shack, we had an oil stove going day and night with wet clothes strung out above it. One morning in early March when we came to work, we were greeted with a disheartening sight. Our beloved boom shack, our warm refuge from the winter elements, had burned to the ground. Check that, it had burned to the waterline. The company was generous with our losses. I ended up with two brand new pairs of caulk boots and some warm clothing and of course a first-rate rain suit. By the end of the month the carpenter millwrights put together a new boom shack; however, it didn't come with an oil heater.

THE RCAF YEARS

1963 - 1987

THE GREAT ESCAPE

It was probably around that time, maybe after falling in the water for the second time that week, that I had serious doubts about my future as a boom man. As I grew older, jumping around on the booms like a fool like old Kulak wasn't very appealing, especially if half the year was miserable. The money was decent but the future was dismal, so I thought about what my former sixth grade teacher, Don Little, said about the air force. Electronics was the magic word, the end all and be all. And more importantly at that time, a ticket out of Ocean Falls. What was their logo then? "Join the air force and see the world." I wrote the RCAF recruitment centre in Vancouver, and they replied right away that I should come down for an interview. In April I showed up at the recruitment centre on Seymour St. in Vancouver for my interview and aptitude tests. The sergeant said I would be informed by mail within a few months if I was accepted. Sure enough, I received a letter mid-June stating that I was a suitable candidate for the RCAF, and to report to Vancouver for my physical in early July. I was ecstatic because I would be escaping the one-horse town that didn't have a single traffic light to its name, had terrible radio reception, and of course had no TV. I was going to see the world or at least a bit of civilization beyond Ocean Falls. Three weeks after receiving my acceptance letter I flew to Vancouver and breezed through the medical.

The clerk at the recruitment centre was arranging a return ticket by boat to Ocean Falls and back, and instructed me to be at the CPR train station on West Hastings on the 23rd of July, 1963. I told them that I would be on the train but they could forget about the sea cruise because I'd given my notice at the mill and that part of my life was now history. Much to my surprise, they gave me a living allowance for two weeks, so I found an older house on Nelson St. in Vancouver's west end that offered room and board by the week. This was before the area was invaded by high-rises. Many of the houses were three and four stories. The best part was that downtown, as well as Stanley Park and the numerous beaches, were all within easy walking distance.

In those two weeks, I don't recall that it rained even once, so I hiked all over the west end. One day I phoned Bozena Watroba, a grade-ten student at Charleston High whom I had dated a few times back home. She was living with her aunt and uncle in one of the Vancouver suburbs and attending summer school to pick up a course that she had failed. Bozena was bored silly because she was under strict orders not to socialize with anyone. Translation—no boys. Just to stick to her school books and stay in the house. After three bus transfers I made it out to her street and waited for her to slip out the back door. We talked for about twenty minutes, and then a quick kiss and I was out of her life, not seeing her again until a reunion thirty-five years later in Campbell River.

My wife and I were sitting with Roy Chernishenko and his wife Marlene and Roy said, "You know, Jock, Bo is here and she is sitting about six tables over there."

So I wandered over but didn't recognize her. Finally, Roy brought me over to this stranger whom I still didn't recognize until she spoke a few words. We had a few laughs and then, pointing out our three or four years difference in age, I jokingly said that I had really been robbing the cradle.

Bozena countered with, "It was more like I was jail bait."

The train ride to Montreal was a blast. The last two passenger cars were reserved for the air force recruits, and every stop the train made a few more boys climbed aboard to join the party. The club car wasn't very strict about checking our ID cards so the beer was a-flowing. For a parting gift, my brother Don had given me his ID card which simplified matters.

One of the recruits who boarded in Banff mentioned that a government liquor store was close to the train station in Calgary, so some of us pooled our resources and walked up and bought six cases of beer with my fake ID card. After we left the store we noticed that two men in suits were following us about five hundred feet back. We were speculating that they could be detectives. The train whistle sounded when we had a block and a half to go, so we picked up the pace and damned if the two men did also. Then it was an all-out sprint which saved our bacon because the train was now moving out of the station. We just got on, but not our friends. They were a-huffing and a-puffing, all red-faced, as we turned around and waved at them from the safety of our coach.

Our train rolled into Montreal in the evening and we quickly transferred to military buses that would take us to our new home for the next nine weeks, thirty miles south at the Manning Depot, RCAF Station St. Jean. An older friend back home gave me the lowdown on what to expect if I wanted to survive boot camp. He said it was the job of the disciplinarians, or discipts as we called them, to treat us like dirt, try to break us, but no matter what, you couldn't take it personal, just keep reminding yourself that this wasn't the real world. The discipt for course 6331 was Cpl. Pritchard and he assigned his flunky, Leading Aircraftsman Hillier, shortened to LAC, to march all the new recruits to the H huts. It wasn't "left-right, left-right" but rather "f-ite, f-ite," and "halt" was more like "alt." That was fun because my whole life I sauntered along with big steps and now I had to shorten my stride to not run over the guy ahead of me in line. Add a large, heavy suitcase into the mix, plus the fact that I had two left feet, it made for an interesting introduction to military life. Between the f-ite f-ites, LAC Hillier was screaming like a banshee at the lot of us. Grin and bear it, John. To think that I gave up a job paying eighty per cent more than this one. Grin and bear it.

The barracks were two-storey H huts, WWII vintage, that housed all one hundred and thirty-one recruits of 6331, with twenty to a room. Our furnishings were pretty basic: one chair, a bunk bed, and a locker per person. Maybe that's what basic training meant. By the time we settled in and made our beds—no chambermaid there—we were pretty bushed because it was after midnight, so we were looking forward to a nice long sleep. But it wasn’t to be, thanks to Cpl. Pritchard and his cohorts who rudely woke us up at six a.m. It was a mad dash to get to the showers, shave, and throw on our clothes so we could be marched in three ranks to the mess hall for a quick breakfast. Then our day really began.

BASIC TRAINING

I was forever grateful that my name was Forbes and not Zimmerman because every parade—haircut parade, clothing parade, needle parade—was performed in alphabetical order. Quite a few of the guys had fairly short haircuts before they boarded the recruitment train, but they wasted their money because in two minutes, the barbers almost scalped us. Some of the boys were nearly in tears. I didn't see anyone tipping the barbers. The clothing line-ups lasted hours as we were issued summer dress, winter dress, shoes, overshoes, underwear, shaving kit, sewing kit, and a large barrack box to haul it away in. That's when Aircraftsman 2nd Class, AC2 Zimmerman learned a lot about patience. Needle parade was short but not sweet since the all-in-one inoculation meant a very painful arm for a few days. By the end of the day the standing joke was that you didn't have to go on piss parade in alphabetical order, you just had to take a number.

My Roommates in Basic Training
L-R - Surfer Joe, Horst, Rick, Courtenay, Jim, Wally

There were a handful of recruits on our course who had been in either the air cadets or the reserve, which came in handy because they knew all about spit-shining shoes. Everyone was issued a shoe brush but we never did figure out why. We spent hours and hours in the laundry room under the tutelage of the "veterans" to learn the fine art of spit-shining a shoe. And when I say hours and hours, it's no exaggeration. The shoe brush couldn't even be used on our floors because they were also highly polished. Once our living quarters and uniforms were sorted out, we settled into a routine of drill and general service knowledge lessons in classrooms. We learned about air force history, such as the Victoria Cross winners Billy Bishop and Andrew Mynarsky, and a smattering of military law terms. AWOL (away without official leave) is an American acronym whereas the proper Canadian acronym is AWA – away without authority. First aid training included how to deliver babies, but thank God, I never had to put that knowledge to the test.

One of the first things that I bought at the base exchange was a steam iron which got a lot of use pressing my fatigue pants daily. We were allowed to substitute a polyester shirt from the base exchange for our standard-issue cotton shirts, which simplified matters because we would shower while wearing the shirt and then hang it to dry. For military drill, Cpl. Pritchard and LAC Hillier would put us through our paces at least two hours a day, and it could get quite humorous with all the screw-ups. We didn't dare laugh or crack a smile or we'd suffer the consequences. The discipts would get quite vocal with us and all we could do was stare straight ahead and say, "Yes, Cpl., no Cpl." In rifle drill we had to be extra careful not to slam the rifle stock on our beautiful spit-shone shoes.

For some reason that year St. Jean was a dry station. In early years it wasn't but just our luck that in '63 there wasn't a beer to be had for the recruits, so the only entertainment was a theatre and a dry canteen that had a jukebox and a snack bar. What didn't help matters was the distinct lack of women. Pre-1963 and post-1963 there were a few courses of WDs going through basic training but sadly not during our year. WDs was short for Women's Division and their nickname was "Wub Dubs." I don't want to know what they called us. The number one song on the hit parade in June of '63 in Canada was a Japanese song by Kyu Sakamoto called Sukiyaki, and I swear that it was played at least three times an hour on the jukebox, but it definitely wasn't on my quarter. It was *numero uno* across the country in June and all summer and into the fall in the dry canteen. Months after I left Manning Depot that tune was still rattling around in my head.

For pay parade, yes, another parade, we would march up to the table, come to attention, salute the finance officer, state our rank and surname and the last three digits of our regimental number, pocket our measly amount, and then take one step back, salute again, then make an about turn and march off. A friend of mine recently told me that his brother was a finance officer in Bagotville, QC, in the '60s, doling out money on pay day, when this young AC1 came up to receive his money. Apparently, there had been an error the previous week when he was overpaid by quite a bit. The young lad did everything correctly until he was handed all of a dollar and sixty-five cents. He just pocketed his "pay" and marched off without saluting. The Sergeant at Arms called out, "Airman, get back here. You didn't salute the flight lieutenant," to which the AC1 replied, "What do you expect for a buck sixty-five?" By then the officer was almost rolling on the floor with laughter, so he told the Sergeant to let him go.

Halfway through our basic training, a sports competition was organized among the various courses at St. Jean. Technically it was an inter-course rivalry, no pun intended. I signed up for basketball and on Friday our team made it to the finals against course 6329 whose star player, it was alleged, had played recently with the University of Saskatchewan Huskies. He was around six feet three inches versus my five feet ten height, and although my roommate Herb Hebert was only five feet eight, he was quick. The U of S guy was very arrogant and cocky, and when he looked us over he just laughed because he figured the outcome was a foregone conclusion. I'll never forget the look on his face when the final whistle blew and 6331 beat 6329 by three points. Herb and I came up with a foolproof defence. He was a one-man team who didn't believe in passing the ball so we just double-teamed him to death, forcing numerous turnovers. When we shook hands at the end of the game he wouldn't make eye contact with us. That was a very satisfying victory and it was just for bragging rights.

In the mess hall the tables had room for eight people, and if we sat with a stranger eventually we'd ask him what his course number was. If he said 6333 or 6335, we would say to him in a condescending manner, "Get some time in, coolie," because, after all, we had two to four weeks seniority on the kid.

During off duty hours such as evenings or weekends we had to wear a uniform and there was no walking allowed—it was marching or nothing. None of this sauntering along like I was used to, even if I was alone. I remember many times when staff personnel yelled at me, "Airman, swing those arms," and heaven forbid that you were caught with your hands in your pockets. It was almost a capital offence. They would holler "Airman, take off those American gloves."

After five long weeks at St. Jean our course was granted the weekend off, so naturally we all took the bus into Montreal. Everyone except the odd recruit who was CB, Confined to Base, for some infraction like talking back to staff. As we passed through the guard house the Air Force Police (AFP) would be handing out condoms. A few smart asses would say, "Only one?" and the cop would reply, "Now that's original." In Montreal two guys would be sent into a rundown hotel to rent a room and then at least a dozen of their buddies would sneak in to sleep on the carpet. It was basically wall-to-wall bodies with not a lot of room to manoeuvre. Courtenay Clark, who slept in the bunk above me in the barracks was in our room, and he picked out a spot just inside the door, pulled out a hunting knife with a six-inch blade and stuck it into the floor, then curled around his knife and settled in for the night. If the door was opened by any uninvited folks it would bump his head and he would spring into action. No one would be robbing us on Courtenay's watch. Another unusual thing about him was that he had at least three-hundred keys in his locker in the barracks, and I often wondered what the hell he did with them. Very strange indeed. Courtenay's hometown was Burnaby, BC, and years later I bumped into him at an Ocean Falls reunion on Vancouver Island. He wound up with Air Force Police as a trade, and after graduating from Camp Borden, he had the misfortune to be posted back there but didn't last the year. He took his release and headed back to BC and eventually to Ocean Falls where he worked for two years. I asked him about all those keys, wondering if he was into B & E's. He said, "No, not really, I just like keys."

Actually, spending the weekend in Montreal was a bit of a letdown after anticipating the great time that we would be having. We just wandered around the downtown area and had the odd beer in a few sleazy bars and generally behaved ourselves except for one skinny kid from northern Ontario, who was beaten up and relieved of his wallet after having too much to drink and striking out on his own.

After week seven, our course had another weekend pass, and many of us, myself included, didn't bother with the big city this time, mainly because St Jean-sur-Richelieu was much closer, cheaper and safer if we wanted to unwind with a beer. The kid from Northern Ontario was CB for the duration of basic training because he lost his ID card in Montreal and by week eight, he was shipped home anyway. Course 6331 started with one hundred and thirty-one recruits but only one hundred and fourteen made it to graduation. Some couldn't cope with military routine; others were just physically unfit, and the rest were probably just immature and missed their mommies. This wasn't a Boy Scout troop.

When I signed on the dotted line in Vancouver it was with the understanding that I would be in an electronics trade; however, before we left basic training, the air force had different ideas. The Cold War was at its height in 1963, and the United States was supplying all our CF-104 Starfighter squadrons in Europe with nuclear weapons, so the RCAF required an abnormally large number of AFP's for extra security at the overseas bases. Over fifty percent of our course was selected AFP and just my luck I was one of them. If I'd known beforehand I would have stayed at home, happily or unhappily pushing logs up the jack ladder.

I was determined to make a better account of myself in the air force, especially after the disastrous year that I had in grade twelve, just scraping through. Back then, when Dad realized that I wouldn't be following my brother Don to university, he was quite disappointed in me. He stated that since I was now working in the mill, I should be paying him room and board. I agreed but we couldn't settle on the amount, so in a huff he said, "Fine, don't pay me anything." For thirteen months I took him at his word and didn't.

About the time that I learned that electronics was now out of the picture, I also had second thoughts about the room and board issue so I sent him a cheque for thirteen-months back rent, settling on an amount somewhere in the middle of the two original figures. I also mentioned my disappointment on being selected AFP. Within a week he fired back a letter, thanking me for the cheque and then stating in no uncertain terms that he didn't raise a son to be a "flatfoot." To my recollection that letter was the only letter that he ever wrote me. It was short and to the point and later would turn out to be significant in my life.

In basic training, there were seven different subjects that we were marked on. My best marks were in composite (general service knowledge), survival, and physical training. With my two left feet, my military drill mark was slightly below the class average. In my overall mark I placed eleventh out of one hundred and fourteen recruits, so the AFP selection really rankled me. We spent nine weeks at St. Jean, and I can honestly say that I didn't mind my stay there. The weather was great and I met a good number of decent guys and a few oddballs. All in all, it was a rewarding experience.

CAMP BOREDOM AND CLINTON

We boarded the train in Montreal and headed west to Ontario, most of us travelling to Camp Borden and the remainder, the lucky ones, to the School of Electronics in Clinton. Camp Borden is situated approximately forty-five miles north of Toronto and ten miles south of Barrie, and consists of an army training base on the north side and the air force trade schools on the south side. The AFP barrack block was a fairly new three-storey building separate from the other barracks, which housed the other trades. Every morning when the AFP students marched in formation between the other trades' barracks, many of the guys would open their windows and scream out "Meatheads chew, meatheads chew." It was so loud you could hear it blocks away. That's when I knew for sure I didn't want to become a "flatfoot," so I arranged an interview with the unit education officer in headquarters. I told him how disappointed I was with the selection process and that I was seriously thinking of applying for my release. Even though we had signed a five-year contract, it wasn't written in stone. If we opted out early, the penalty was only five dollars for every month short of five years. The flight lieutenant was very understanding and much to my surprise he had me write aptitude tests again. When the results were tabulated he told me the good news. I was allowed to re-muster. A staff member would drive me down to Clinton as soon as I cleared the base. Just in the nick of time because my AFP course was starting the following week. "Meatheads chew." I wrote my parents right away with the glad tidings and then celebrated with my buddies in the wet canteen.

A little east of Lake Huron and about fifty miles north of London, Ontario, Clinton had a population of 3500 people. Since I still had a long wait before my basic electronics course started, I had to report to pre-course pool every morning. The military wasn't about to waste all that free manpower, so every day the idle airmen who were marking time were farmed out to different sections on the base. When I was told that my course wouldn't be starting until late November, I thought that a holiday would be more enjoyable than mess hall duties, so I applied for two weeks annual leave. I decided to hitchhike in uniform to the West Coast because it was much easier to catch rides that way, and at that time the military still allowed it.

Once I got onto the Trans Canada Highway I had some first-rate rides that ate up the miles. At Sault Ste. Marie, an off-duty Ontario provincial policeman drove me all the way to Thunder Bay, a good eight hours. He told me that if I had been in civilian clothes he never would have stopped. After walking for an hour through Thunder Bay, a trucker hauling a trailer-load full of new cars gave me a lift to Calgary. Just before the Manitoba border he had me hide in the car that was over his cab because, as he explained it, he didn't want to shift all the cars back and forth to satisfy the axle limit regulations at the next weigh station in Manitoba. I guess my 160 pounds plus luggage must have done the trick because he had no problem at the scales. By Winnipeg, the driver was getting pretty tired. He asked me if I wouldn't mind driving. I told him that I drove boats and forklifts but that my transport truck experience was fairly limited.

He thought this over for a minute and then said, "No problem. This highway is as straight as an arrow and I could 'learn' you in five minutes." And that's exactly what he did. In less than five minutes he "learned" me how to operate a rig hauling an expensive payload. The transmission had ten gears and for the majority of the trip I used the ninth gear, only dropping down to eighth or seventh on the occasional incline. He watched me for a few minutes and then said, "It looks like you've got the hang of it. Wake me up on the east side of Regina." Then he promptly fell asleep in the bunk behind the seat. Talk about faith. When it dawned on me that

I was on my own, guiding tons of steel and rubber down the highway at 60mph, my heart started pounding. But before long, I settled down because I realized that I did have the hang of it after all. It was just after midnight and the traffic was light, mainly transports and the odd car. I even learned to flash the headlights to signal to the truck overtaking me that it was safe for him to pull back into the right-hand lane. Basically, I just had to make sure that I kept between the lines and didn't fall asleep, and I had no problems on either accord.

Approaching Regina after six hours, I woke up the driver and he acted like it was an everyday occurrence, having some young stranger with zero experience driving his expensive equipment in the middle of the night while he got his beauty rest. At Calgary, he headed north to Edmonton to deliver his cargo, and I carried on westward with my hitchhiking adventure. It took me three rides to get from Calgary to Banff where I caught another great ride. A couple from Medicine Hat had to get to a funeral in Vancouver, so they were driving non-stop to the coast. The best part was they didn't seem to mind if I nodded off in the back seat. The Rogers Pass in the Rockies had an early dump of snow, but they were sensible drivers with decent tires which made all the difference.

When I flew into Ocean Falls the monsoon season was in full swing, which triggered memories of why I left in the first place. At least Dad was much friendlier this time around. We buried the hatchet. He finally accepted that I wouldn't be following Don into university but that I would be making my own path. My stay in the Falls was pretty low-key. I hung around the pool hall during the day and basically just killed time because many of my friends were shift workers in the mill. Maybe I was bored, having outgrown my hometown once I'd seen the real world. I treated myself to a flight with Air Canada to Toronto for the return trip back east because the prairies were now in a big deep freeze. To stay in shape, I thumbed it from Toronto to Clinton.

After my two weeks leave, pre-course pool assigned me to the unit mail room to sort letters, which beat the hell out of swabbing the decks in the mess hall. The postal corps sergeant and I got along well, so he arranged to have me there until my basic electronics started. He was close to retirement age and didn't want to break anyone else in. I remember

'57 Dodge Custom Royal

happily sorting mail on November 22 when we heard on the radio that JFK was assassinated in Dallas. I thought for sure that WWIII was about to begin, but thankfully that blew over. In retrospect, I think the Sarge had an ulterior motive in keeping me because he heard me mention that I had quit a decent paying job before enlisting. At that time, 1963, a large majority of the recruits joined up because they didn't have a job. This led the good Sarge to believe that AC2 Forbes likely had a healthy bank account, and the Sarge had a car that he wanted to unload.

Within a few weeks I was the proud owner of a 1957 black and yellow Dodge Custom Royal. The body was in decent shape, it was huge, and the yellow paint job went well with the lemon theme. After a few months, I noticed that the amount of blue smoke coming out of the tail pipe cut down in direct proportion to the amount of STP lubricant added to the engine oil. A few of my friends helped with some driving lessons on and off the base. I was probably one of the few persons at RCAF Station Clinton who didn't have a driver's license—operating boats didn't cut it. After a few weeks' practice and a quick study of the driver's manual, I took the Ontario Driver's exam in downtown Clinton. Much to everyone's surprise, including mine, I passed on the first attempt. All of us were surprised because the examiner was quite strict and failed a good number of the out-of-province drivers. I suspect the experienced drivers failed because of their acquired bad habits, whereas I didn't have any.

When we finally began the basic electronics course, I was very relieved but soon found that it wouldn't be a walk in the park and that wet canteen activities would have to be curtailed if I wanted to succeed. The higher your final score, the better your choice of trade and posting. My roommate, Charlie Horstman, was also on my electronics course. There was never a dull moment when he was in the room. A very likeable guy, he acted like there was a rock-and-roll tune playing somewhere, bobbing his head and snapping his fingers to a beat only he could hear. Charlie had it made. He could drink beer all night long, not crack a book and still pass with decent marks, unlike yours truly. After I spent a month on the course, the school shut down for Christmas break and I decided to stay put since I had just recently gone home. The trip home was just too far to go for a week. That was one long, boring week because very few stayed on base, certainly none of my friends. Two things I remember most about those holidays are driving around the Clinton area in my big beast of a car, trying to stay out of the ditches because we'd had a huge dump of snow, and walking into the mess hall where there were more staff than students.

In January, it was back to the grindstone. The vacuum tube was still king back in those days, and we just barely scratched the surface on solid-state and transistor theory. Our class was probably one of the last to study vacuum tube theory. In a few short years the transistor would take over. As an example, the ARC-34 UHF radio transmitter that was in both the Voodoo jet and the Hercules transport aircraft was very unreliable due to the technology—or lack of it, and it weighed about sixty pounds. The replacement radio, the solid-state ARC-164 seldom broke down and weighed about six pounds.

TRAVELS WITH CHARLIE

The school shut down again at Easter for a week, so we were once again granted a week's leave. Not too keen on staying in Clinton all alone again, Charlie and I decided to visit his hometown of Bridgewater, Nova Scotia, south of Halifax. *We* didn't decide. Charlie insisted that I should enjoy the culture of Canada's East Coast, so I reluctantly agreed although the weather didn't look too promising and our mode of transportation would be via the thumb. I didn't really trust my Dodge to get us to the Maritimes and back. Short trips were okay as long as I had a good supply of engine oil and STP on hand.

Hitchhiking in uniform was our choice, mainly because we weren't about to waste our monthly wages of eighty-four dollars on transportation. The trip went smoothly until we hit eastern Ontario when a few flakes started to fall. By the time we rolled into Montreal it was coming down pretty good but no problem for a couple of air force pigeons—that's what the other services called us. (We called the soldiers grunts or pongos. I won't mention how we referred to the sailors.) Between Montreal and Quebec City, with two different rides, we ended up in a ditch twice. The weather had turned into a full-blown blizzard with white-out conditions and plunging temperatures.

We really appreciated our greatcoats on that trip. How would I describe them? Long and coarse, like a horse blanket with buttons and a collar. After our second bout in the ditch (as Henri, one of our classmates, would say, "We took da ditch"), we stuck out our thumbs again at the bottom of a long hill, just past Quebec City on the south-east side of the St. Lawrence River. Our prospects didn't look too promising because the drivers were afraid that if they stopped for us they wouldn't get enough traction to get going again. That day would have been a perfect time to run a commercial for snow tires or chains.

Eventually we did manage to get a ride from a guy who was driving from Hamilton to Cape Breton. Back then he would have been called your typical "hood." You know the type: black leather jacket, black T-shirt, shit-kicking boots, greasy hair, and an attitude. He needed us as much as we needed him. We pushed him up that hill and many more on his worn-out summer tires all the way to Rivière-du-Loup, QC where the conditions deteriorated into serious snow—heavy and horizontal. It turned out that Cal was paid by a businessman to "pick some guy's nose", which we took to be hood parlance for beat him up. With the Hamilton cops wanting to have a word with him, he was going to Cape Breton come hell or high water to hide out with his relatives. When I think about that trip, a few things come to mind: snow, more snow, snow banks, snowplows, and very limited visibility. Oh, and how could I forget, pushing a '56 Mercury across most of New Brunswick. I should have stayed in Clinton but I would have been bored silly and missed out on all the fun. Just like Jack Kerouac's best seller *On the Road*, this was the deep-freeze version.

A few times we were stopped completely because the highway was closed for some serious snow removal. On one occasion, since sleeping was out of the question and I wasn't too fond of Charlie and Cal's second-hand smoke, after three hours of waiting behind a long line of vehicles, I decided to walk up to the head of the stalled convoy. I discovered that the road was now cleared and the driver of the lead vehicle, a transport truck, was sleeping soundly in his cab. Did I wake up the truck driver? Not on your life! I quickly made it back to the boys and we passed everyone, bald tires and all. We eventually arrived safely in Saint John, New Brunswick where Charlie and I caught the ferry boat over to Nova Scotia. I suppose because we saved his bacon, so to speak, Cal drove out of his way to drop us off at the ferry terminal before he headed northeast to Cape Breton.

The first law of hitchhiking is never fall asleep so you can keep the driver awake. We did our job but we were pretty bushed by the time we hit Bridgewater.

Charlie was raised by his aunt and uncle. They were very kind people. His aunt welcomed us with open arms, these two dishevelled and unshaven knights of the road. It was good to eat some home cooking instead of greasy hamburgers that seemed to be the norm for hitchhiking grub. His uncle, Harry Rafuse, owned a hardware store that Charlie took over years later. He eventually turned it into a taxi stand and bicycle shop since he couldn't compete with the larger hardware chains.

The people who founded Bridgewater were of Dutch and German descent, and their descendants had quite the accent. Talking about his aunt, Charlie would say, "An aunt (ant) is an insect that crawls on the ground, but an aunt (ont) is my mother's sister." Charlie's "ont" was a wonderful lady who just doted on us like a mother hen. He was fortunate to have these folks in his life. Borrowing Uncle Harry's car, we checked out some of Charlie's old haunts in the neighbouring towns such as Lunenburg, Liverpool, and Mahone Bay. We went to a few dances on Friday night, but it appeared that Chas lost his touch because the local girls weren't falling all over us. When it came time to leave Bridgewater, his "ont" insisted that we take public transportation because, although the storm had passed through, it was still "dreadfully" cold to be hitchhiking, and besides, we could get mugged by "ruffians".

We took a bus into Halifax and then grabbed the first train heading west. When we pulled into Montreal we had a five-hour layover until our next connection, so we stored our luggage in a locker at the train station and went for a few refreshments around the corner into a bar where our money quickly disappeared. Not only were we now virtually penniless, we came awfully close to being beaten up for speaking *anglais*. Our plan was to catch some shut-eye on a bench at the station until daylight and then start thumbing our way home. Unfortunately, bums are frowned upon in the Montreal train station, so we were promptly sent packing. At four a.m., bitterly cold out on the streets, we stumbled into a fancy looking hotel like we owned the place, took the elevator up to the fifth floor, went down one of the wings, and fell asleep on the nice plush carpet. That lasted ten minutes, then along came the hotel detective who gave us the boot, but not at the same time, so Charlie and I were separated on the mean streets of downtown Montreal. I was freezing by then, so I headed back to the train station where my luggage was, but I didn't dare lie down on the bench this time. An hour later, old Charlie showed up and said that he had gone into a 24-hour greasy spoon, where he ordered a cheeseburger and a coke. After the meal, he realized he couldn't afford to pay, so he fled the diner, only to be tracked down within two blocks by two guys in a car. He coughed up the entire contents of his pockets—one dollar and eighty-five cents—thereby evading a sound thrashing.

On to Plan B. We changed into our uniforms in the washroom and tried thumbing out of the city but without success. So a modified Plan B went into effect: we spent my last five dollars on a city bus that took us to the outskirts of Montreal to give hitchhiking another try. We got lucky, sort of. An army type, a grunt, stopped for us before we froze to death, and he said that his unit was in London, Ontario. Wonderful. Except that his car was a real beater, a '49 Kaiser without a working in-car heater. Thank God for greatcoats! I was in the back seat and it felt like I was sitting on a block of ice. Charlie was up front where it was marginally warmer because he was closer to the engine. At least we were out of the biting wind. We made it back to base and somehow woke up in time for class the next morning.

We should have stayed in Clinton that week, but somehow we survived. Don't believe what some wise man once said, "A bad memory is better than no memory at all." Later in the spring when the weather warmed up, four of us decided to head over to Grand Bend on Lake Huron, approximately thirty-five miles away: Charlie Horstman, Gaston D'Entremont, and a third person whose name escapes me. Hey, that was over fifty years ago. Gaston was an Acadian from a small fishing village called West Pubnico on the southern tip of Nova Scotia. After two or three years of seminary studies working towards Catholic brotherhood, Gaston decided to switch careers, trading in his black uniform for a blue one. He was a shy little guy who had led a very sheltered life up until he enlisted and started hanging out with the likes of Mr. Horstman. He was handy to have around because he was old enough to legally shop in government liquor stores. I was also somewhat popular since I had a set of wheels. Grand Bend had a huge beach with hard-packed sand that was ideal for cruising. We hadn't driven two hundred yards on the sand when we found ourselves surrounded by three police cruisers. Was it a slow day or was it the short hair that did it? Whatever it was, they confiscated our recently purchased beer and then presented Gaston with a citation for having open alcohol in an automobile. I suppose three of us could have been nailed for being minors in possession, but they gave us a break. Gaston didn't think it was much of a break, but of course we all chipped in for the fine. Anyway, it put a damper on what started out to be a fine weekend. Some would think that because Gaston was older than we were, he was leading us astray, but in this case, it was definitely the opposite.

BACK TO BOREDOM

By early summer we finished the basic electronics course and Charlie and I both got into Communications Technician Air (CTA) trade, which was exactly what we were hoping for. The "air" meant communications and navigation systems on aircraft, which translated into much better postings, normally by larger cities or in Europe, versus the Communications Technician Ground (CTG) trade, which in a lot of cases stuck you in the middle of nowhere on Pine Tree Line radar stations. The next phase for us was the aircraft equipment courses located at Camp Borden. Because I had my own transportation I drove up to Borden on Friday afternoon while the rest of my classmates arrived via an air force bus shuttle the next day. After reporting to base housing and stowing my luggage in my assigned room in the barracks, I headed over to the Airmen's Mess where I ran into a few of the guys that I knew from basic training in St. Jean and also from Clinton. BIG MISTAKE. I was sicker than a dog that night and the next morning was not any better. Must have picked up a bug in my travels – couldn't have been the beer. I was afflicted with the 3 D's – dehydrated, dizzy and dumb. By noon, with no improvement in sight, I drove over to the dreaded army side of Camp Borden to the base hospital where I was hoping to get some sympathy, and maybe a pain killer or two. No such luck. The nurse on duty admitted me for observation. I was formally diagnosed with a case of gastroenteritis which in layman's terms is stomach flu. By

Sunday I was feeling much better but that didn't help matters because only a doctor could release me from captivity. The nurse told me that the doctor didn't come in on weekends except for emergencies and this was definitely not the case. I thought otherwise because my Comm Tech course was due to start Monday morning, but no amount of pleading and whining would help her change her mind. So, the next morning Squadron Leader RWD Low finally showed up in my ward and discharged me at nine-thirty a.m., and then I roared back to the air force side, a cloud of blue smoke trailing behind the Custom Royal, ran into the barracks, threw on a uniform, and hustled over to the classroom six blocks away where I was told that I was too late. Missed the course by two hours. Apparently, there were seventeen Comm Tech Air students waiting to be loaded onto a course, but only room for sixteen for that particular class, so guess who was the odd man out.

And it gets worse. The next course wasn't scheduled for another two and a half months. You can imagine my mental state at that point. I was extremely choked up, I was despondent, I was—it was like my girlfriend left me and my dog died all on the same day. Now for the good news. The equipment course starting in September wasn't for general aircraft like the one I just missed, but for the CF-104 Starfighter jet only. It would be a smaller class, twelve students, shorter by three weeks, and best of all, ten of the twelve graduates would be going overseas for a three-year posting. It felt like I won the lottery. Overseas. The carrot at the end of the stick. All I had to do was put up with the drudgery of swabbing the decks in the mess hall for a few months. I could do that standing on my head.

So Charlie and I parted company, he with the lucky/unlucky sixteen, and me reporting for mop duties in the mess hall, marking time once again. It was about that time that the Dodge began to make funny noises, so I drove it to a garage in Alliston and received some bad news. The crankshaft and valves were shot, so I decided to cut my losses and sold it to the garage for twenty-five cents on the dollar. I wasn't about to spend a whole whack of money on an engine job. It wasn't the end of the world because, after all, I would be in Europe by the New Year. Just a little setback. In mid-June, Bob Beech, who I had originally met in Clinton, was organizing a trip to Vancouver, and he was looking for passengers to share the expenses and the driving. Bob's car wasn't the greatest for touring and with four guys and all their luggage it wasn't the fastest either. Straight through, no stopping except for gas and oil and junk food. By the time we hit Alberta we were pretty well exhausted, so we picked up a hitchhiker whom we pressed into driving for us. He was a rodeo cowboy following the circuit to High River, and somehow, we found room in the trunk for his saddle and small gym bag. Five guys crammed into a car in the summer on the prairies. To say the least, it was quite rank in there. The cowboy drove for three or four hours before he headed off south to Lethbridge, so at least we did catch a few winks while he was driving.

When we parted company in Vancouver, the four of us weren't really on speaking terms, so to speak. I never did tell Bob what Charlie and I did to him one night back in Clinton. His room was right next to ours, and he had an annoying habit of talking loudly, late at night when we were trying to get some sleep. We crept into his room and flipped his bed over while he was in mid-sentence. He didn't have a clue who did the nasty deed, so if you're reading this Bob, I could say sorry, but I won't.

I caught the plane up to Ocean Falls and after a few days was getting bored, so on a lark I phoned up my old superintendent in the sawmill, Al Jeffery, and said that I was available for work. Much to my surprise he offered me five night shifts at my old job on the sawmill booms. I still had my caulk boots and hard hat at home, so I was good to go. Since I was soon to be a world traveller, the extra money wouldn't hurt. One night around 11 p.m., my former high school classmate Archie Young and the local meat cutter/bootlegger Harvey Werner snuck in under cover of darkness to pay me a visit. They had been drinking, Harvey especially, so we fitted him up with equipment laying around the boom shack: life preserver, caulk boots, hard hat and pike pole. We had him pushing logs onto the jack ladder to feed the sawmill. It's a miracle old Harv didn't fall in the salt chuck and even more miraculous that the shift foreman didn't discover what was up, but basically as long as the sawmill had a steady stream of logs coming up the jack ladder, he had no reason to check out the boys on the booms.

At midnight, we shut down for lunch hour, so I helped Archie get Harvey back to his room in the Martin Inn. He was getting more unsteady by the minute in the walking and staying awake department. He had grown quite attached to the caulk boots and hard hat by then, so he wasn't about to surrender them without a fight. The look on the desk clerk's face was priceless as we dragged Harv in his steel-studded boots through the tiled lobby and into the elevator. Our novice boom man was passed out with a big smile on his face before we got him back to his room. After about a week in the hometown, I caught the Canadian Pacific boat northbound to Prince Rupert, then bused on over to Terrace to spend a few days with my older sister Mary-Lynne, her husband Tony and their young daughters.

The second day in Terrace I borrowed a fishing rod from Tony and walked over to the Skeena River to try my luck. No fish, but I did catch a kitten. I was casting under this really high train trestle bridge when I thought I heard a cat meowing. I looked and looked and finally saw a tiny kitten fairly high up on a beam. Very cautiously I climbed up and rescued the feline and straight away took it to the local animal shelter. I sweated bullets up there because I'm not too fond of heights.

Years later Mary-Lynne said, "Jeesh, Jock, I lived in Terrace for years and never got in the local paper in any way, shape or form, and on your second day in town you make the front page." Small towns don't have too many newsworthy happenings I guess. From Terrace, I took the train to Saskatoon where my cousin David Haberman picked me up, and we drove to the Humboldt/Peterson/Bruno area on Highway 5, east of Saskatoon where I met a bunch of relatives for the first time. Then back to Borden via the thumb—a better way to travel, I thought, than car-pooling with Bob Beech.

The summer of '64 was a hot one and the humidity in southern Ontario was something that I never did get used to. A few of my friends in the barracks had cars, so we got out and about fairly often. Any amount of time spent off the base was time well spent. Our favourite place on the weekends was Wasaga Beach on Georgian Bay, north of Barrie. One Friday, just after supper, four of us were heading for the beach when we noticed a red and black '56 Ford convertible in a driveway with a for sale sign and a phone number. At the beach, I found a phone booth, dialled the number and told the guy I would be there in twenty minutes to have a look. When we pulled into the driveway, the car was idling nicely and the exhaust wasn't blue, which was promising. We checked the oil level and there was no indication of STP on the dip stick, another plus. Next, we put up the top and it had a few small slits in the canvas but nothing too serious. The body seemed okay, which probably meant that the owner was pretty handy with Bondo body filler because Ontario road cancer was a given where large amounts of salt were used in the winter months. We agreed on a price that seemed reasonable, and I now had some wheels to see me through the summer. The next night a guy from my hometown, Terry Rowe, who was at Borden to take his Air Traffic Controller's course, went into Barrie with me to a dance hall. After two or three hours of dancing and hustling up the girls and striking out, we jumped in the car, but the damn thing didn't have any reverse so we had to push it out of the parking stall. No reverse until the transmission was warmed up and then it worked fine.

So that's why the guy had the car idling in his driveway. Sucked in again. I soon learned to back into a parking stall but eventually took it to my favourite garage in Alliston where they tightened up a few bands in the transmission and replaced the transmission fluid. When the mechanic took it out for a test drive the hood flew up at 60 mph and it self-destructed instantly. He didn't realize that I was using a piece of wire for a backup because the hood latch was questionable. The garage knocked five dollars off the final bill, so I bought another hood at an auto wrecker, which meant that I now had a red, black and white convertible with a latch that actually locked.

The transmission was much better, so I was in no danger of dying of boredom on the weekends when there was a long spell of marking time. Besides Wasaga Beach, I also drove down to Toronto and Ottawa a few times. When Charlie graduated, he was posted to Downsview in Toronto. It wouldn't have been my first choice, but he liked the big city and there he could continue his search for his birth mother. When we were stationed at Clinton I was aware of at least two weekends when he bused into Toronto to check out the bars on Yonge Street, looking for a mother he never knew. Maybe he had heard whispers or rumours of his mom leaving Bridgewater when Charlie was a toddler, and eventually ending up in Ontario where she had two girls, half sisters to Charlie. I don't believe that he ever tracked them down but he had fun trying.

Charlie was attached to 411 Squadron, a search and rescue unit that flew light transport Expeditors and single engine Otters. Not too exciting. Since 411 was a reserve squadron, most of the aircrew and technicians were weekend warriors. Probably due to lack of funds, but mainly due to boredom, Charlie picked up the odd shift at a moving company and one Friday night he signed me up. There were five of us and we emptied an office building completely in downtown Toronto in about three hours. I never forgot the boss. He was always at our heels, yelling and cussing up a storm.

"Hurry, hurry, let's go, pick it up."

I couldn't move fast enough for him. All that grief for a dollar forty an hour.

"But it's cash under the table," Charlie said.

It reminded me of the stories you'd hear of a couple who would return home to their house in the country after working in the city all day only to find the house completely emptied of furniture, appliances, even the curtains and curtain rods. That was us alright, even taking a half-empty box of Kleenex out the door. I could think of better and more enjoyable things to do on my weekends off. Another weekend when I visited Charlie we went to a Roy Orbison rock concert in a North Toronto high school gymnasium. The "Big O," dark shades and all, put on quite the performance, what we could hear of it anyway, because we were surrounded by three thousand screaming teenage girls.

In September, the CF-104 equipment course finally started, and the twelve of us students in some cases would be together for the next three and a half years. One of the characters was Roger Beebe from either Big River or Carrot River, Saskatchewan. I never could remember, but any way you slice it, he was from the sticks. Roger didn't have movie-star looks, but that wasn't a deterrent in his pursuit of women. Kim Burley was also from Saskatchewan and we hit it off right away. Another classmate was David Elton Clarke, born in England but raised in Acton in southern Ontario. His father was an engineer who helped develop the Avro Arrow, the jet aircraft that was capable of flying at fifty thousand feet at speeds close to Mach 2, the one that John Diefenbaker's government cancelled in 1959. Many of the engineers found employment with the NASA space program after all fourteen thousand employees were fired, but sadly, Dave's father wasn't one of them. He died of a heart attack at a young age.

The reason why our course was so short was that the CF-104 had only a few communications systems on board: basically a UHF transceiver, an emergency UHF transceiver and an intercom system if the aircraft was a dual for training purposes. The navigational systems were handled by the radar and the integral systems technicians. I was thankful that I wasn't an armament systems tech because they had the nuclear delivery component that was quite complicated and involved. In early October, we graduated and I tied for first place on the course with 86.6%, and the even better news was, I was posted to 3 Wing Germany for three years along with Dave Clarke and Ed Herechuk.

TEN FOOT TWO AND MUD

The next step would be the CF-104 aircraft course in #10 Field Technical Training Unit—10 FTTU—at RCAF Station Cold Lake, Alberta. 10 FTTU was affectionately known as 10 Foot 2. The day after our graduation I picked up my travel claim at headquarters and headed west once again, but this time I would be doing the driving. I decided to take the US route across the northern states, crossing at Sault Ste. Marie into Michigan. The car was running okay and I had a good trip, but the first night I pulled over twice because I thought I had a flat tire. It finally dawned on me that my tires had drifted onto the shoulder, giving me a rough ride. After the second incident, it was obvious that I needed to find a motel and get some sleep. At Minot, North Dakota, I headed northwest into Regina and stayed at my Uncle Ian's for the night. My uncle was quite distant and seemed to be a bit of a snob. Maybe it was because he was a university grad and all four of his kids had been or were presently going to university and here I was, practically a high school dropout. That was my take on it anyway. I had no complaints about my Aunt Marge though. She was a very nice, friendly woman. The next day I drove over to see Dad's youngest brother Archie, his wife Babs and their son Barry, three years my junior.

Babs had quite an interesting life. She was born in England in 1915. Her father died in the Great War, her mother four years later, and her maternal grandmother shortly after that. Life wasn't kind to Babs early on.

By the time she was ten she was shipped off to South Africa to live with her paternal grandfather, but that didn't pan out either because now Babs was placed into a South African orphanage. Nobody knew the reason she ended up in the orphanage. Was she a difficult child to manage? Was her grandfather simply too old to raise her? Or did he, perhaps, pass away? It was too painful for her to talk about that dark period of her life. When she turned eighteen, Babs went back to England to reconnect with her cousins in Elstow, but that didn't go well either. After a failed marriage, she met Uncle Archie who was stationed in England with the Canadian Army during WWII, and they married in 1946. I really liked Archie. Two of his brothers, Dad and Ian, could have learned some lessons from him. When I first met him, instead of a handshake, he gave me a big hug and seemed genuinely happy to meet me and showed an interest in my life. Like all the brothers, he was six feet tall and very striking with his full head of white hair. Apparently by the age of twenty-five all of the brothers' hair turned white. When he pulled up to the house I had to laugh as he climbed out of the smallest car I'd ever seen, an Italian micro car with only three wheels called the Isetta, commonly known as the "Bubble" car. Over the years we kept in touch even though they moved to Indio in California, and my cousin Barry ended up in Tempe, Arizona. Twice in the '90s, Archie flew up from Indio to Edmonton for a visit. Later on, when my wife and I holidayed in Sedona, Arizona, we would see Barry and his clan in Tempe, by Phoenix. And when I say clan, I'm not kidding. Barry and Linda have two children and fifteen grandchildren.

Next stop on my odyssey was my Aunt Martha's farm where I had dropped in briefly in the early summer. The farm was fairly close to the hamlet of Meacham, population ninety, with a gas station and a restaurant, about fifty miles east of Saskatoon. Shortly after driving through Watrous, I had a flat tire. After changing the tire, I threw the flat into the trunk, intending to get it repaired at a convenient time. At Meacham, I had a few miles to travel on a grid road to reach the farm, and as I was driving up a small hill I gave the car too much gas and slid into the ditch. It had rained the night before, making the grid roads very greasy. I walked to a nearby farmhouse, phoned my uncle Leo, and with my cousin Lorne he showed up in a pickup truck and pulled me out. Little did I know that when I took the ditch, my heavy tool box, just issued to me in Borden, hit the trunk latch and mangled the locking mechanism. I wasn't too lucky with car latches. Had I known at that time, we could have repaired it at the farm, but because my overnight bag was in the back seat, I had no reason to access the trunk with a key.

In spite of the lousy start to the visit I enjoyed meeting my relatives again. Aunt Martha was slightly older than Mom and was a no-nonsense type of person. Her husband Leo had a good sense of humour and I quite liked him. They had three kids. Lucille, the oldest was a school teacher in Bruno a few miles away. David, my age, was at the University of Saskatchewan studying accounting, and Lorne, about seventeen, would eventually take over the family farm. That night Lorne drove me over to introduce me to his girlfriend Donna who he would marry a few years later. They would eventually have three boys.

I had one more stop to make before Cold Lake. My Aunt Margaret lived on a farm a little south of Cudworth, about forty-five miles from Meacham. Uncle Leo told me not to go as far as Cudworth, just to drive straight north on Highway 2, and after passing RCAF Station Dana, a radar base on the left, to turn right on the grid road, go two miles, then turn south for one mile. And then he pronounced the four magic words, "You can't miss it."

Well, I could and I did. What I thought was the grid road petered out to a narrow path of mud, and of course when I tried to turn around I became hopelessly mired in the muck. I could see an old farmhouse about a half mile ahead, so I trudged over to it hoping somebody could tell me if Margaret and Emmerick Kohle were in the area. No such luck. An old Ukrainian couple greeted me at the door with a lot of smiles, but not much else because they didn't know two words of English. I carried on, heading south for one mile and then west for another mile, coming back out at Highway 2 and the turnoff to the Radar Station. I thought that if I walked to the station, surely they would come to the aid of one of their brothers in need.

Not likely. The Air Force Police in the guardhouse just laughed at me and suggested that I look for a tow truck or a friendly farmer with a tractor. "Meatheads chew." By then I was pretty pissed and getting tired from all that walking, half of it in mud, so I made my way up Highway 2 where I had originally turned off. Right across the highway was a farmhouse and the man didn't hesitate when I asked for a tow, even though he had just put his tractor away for the winter and again had to fill up the radiator with water. I tried to pay him for his troubles but he refused to accept anything other than my thanks.

It turned out that the farmer was also a substitute school teacher who had taught Vesta, my aunt's oldest daughter. He knew exactly where the Kohles lived so sent me on my way complete with a hand-drawn map. I didn't miss it this time. My aunt was one of Mom's younger sisters, a real sweetheart, and my favourite. Her husband Em was a real character and soon became my favourite uncle on my mother's side. Both of them were very involved with their five kids. Em grew up just around the corner from the original Kohle farm that his parents homesteaded years ago. The quarter section of land was divided equally between Em and his older brother Otto, so they each ended up with an eighth of a section, which is tiny for a grain operation. Otto had eleven kids to feed. Eventually Otto had to sell his farm and move into Saskatoon, where he found work in an Army and Navy department store. Margaret and Em didn't have much money, but what they did have was a lot of love. I had planned on staying for only one day but stretched it to two because they were such a joy to visit.

Since farmers in general are early risers, I got away by nine in the morning for my final day of driving, which would be about seven hours if all went well. When I pulled into Lloydminster at the Alberta border for a bite to eat I thought I'd better get my flat fixed before I went much farther. That's when I discovered the problem with the trunk latch. Then I was really thinking that hitchhiking had its merits. I wanted to take a short cut through the Frog Lake area where, in 1885, the Cree, under war chief Wandering Spirit, massacred two Catholic priests and seven other Europeans, part of the North-West Rebellion that was started by Louis Riel and his Metis followers. The road was gravel and by all accounts it was in good shape. No rain had fallen for a few days, and even better, the drive would be at least an hour shorter. What were the chances of getting another flat tire? Pretty slim, I thought, so I decided to roll the dice, turning north at Kitscoty to check out a bit of Canadian history instead of taking the longer route through Vermillion and Bonnyville on paved roads. I didn't see much of historical interest, and frankly the drive was quite boring, until I was about halfway up the gravel road. I pulled over to check my tires, and sure enough, my rear tire was a little low. What a surprise, I thought. What are the chances? Now I was getting stressed because sixty miles south of nowhere is not a good place to be stranded without a spare or a car jack in the late afternoon in the fall.

I was hoping the tire pressure would hold up until I reached Grande Centre but with my luck lately I had serious doubts. Thankfully, I came upon a little country store standing there all alone—a beautiful sight to behold. I bought a cheap socket set and a flashlight in case I had to loosen off the back seat to pull out the car jack. That's exactly what transpired because twenty miles south of Grande Centre the tire was too low to continue. After a few bruised knuckles and a lot of cursing, I managed to loosen the back seat enough to shine the flashlight into the trunk where I located the wheel wrench and the jack and pulled them out. By the time I had the flat tire off the car it looked like I'd been in a brawl in some back alley, and I was the loser. Then I stood alongside the car for at least half an hour waiting for a good Samaritan heading north. Finally, a pickup truck stopped for me and my flat and drove me to a service station in Grande Centre. I was really uneasy leaving the car and its contents, which was everything I owned, but I had no alternative. Within half an hour my tire was repaired and I hired a taxi to rescue my car. My faith in mankind was restored when I found my vehicle intact. By the time the wheel was re-installed and I got under way it was pitch black and the temperature had dropped quite a few degrees. I suppose you could say I was unlucky, however, putting a positive spin on it, that episode could have turned out a lot worse than it did. I was some relieved when I drove past the guardhouse and onto RCAF Station Cold Lake. I'd seen enough mud and ditches and flat tires to last me a life time.

Our CF-104 aircraft course started on the Monday and ran for a month. Nothing too remarkable in classes at "10 Foot 2." What we did learn was that all the communications and radar equipment was jammed into the e-bay right behind the cockpit. Replacing black boxes was easy enough, but heaven help you if you had any kind of wiring problems because you had to basically stand on your head in narrow openings for access. Another thing I learned was that Cold Lake would never be my first choice for postings. In '64 the surrounding area didn't have much to offer unless you were inclined towards hunting and fishing. Edmonton was one hundred and eighty miles southwest and over half that distance wasn't even paved yet.

After settling in at Cold Lake, I visited the local auto wreckers to pick up a new trunk latch and of course now I had a serviceable spare tire, which thankfully I never needed again. The second weekend out west I drove down to RCAF Station Namao, which is located five miles north of Edmonton. I stayed in Ray Morton's room in the barracks. I knew him from St. Jean and he was also my roommate in Borden while he took his Comm Tech Aircraft course. Mort used a straight razor and no matter how big a hangover he woke up with, as far as I know he never ever nicked himself shaving. He was a charter member of the Ponderosa Club—twelve airmen paying sixty dollars a month for a two-bedroom bungalow on an acreage close to St. Albert, about ten miles west of the base. They had themselves quite the frat house. They all lived in the barracks and used the Ponderosa for their off-duty entertainment. A good friend of mine, Dennis Coughlin, whom I met four years later, was the treasurer of this gang of twelve. He told me that if he ever wrote about the goings-on there he would be afraid of libel suits. Mort was driving a Pontiac but his life-long dream was to own a Norton motorcycle. His friends couldn't wait for that to happen so they could say, "There goes snortin' Morton on his Norton."

When Mort was posted to Germany in 1969 he realized his dream and purchased a Norton, but tragically he drove it off the road and died. Mort *est mort.* I don't think Ray's nickname had anything to do with his early demise: his love of beer was probably the major factor.

The twelve of us comm techs were in class for a month at "10 Foot 2," graduating on a Friday, so naturally we celebrated with a big party that night. It had rained that day and when the temperature dropped down that evening the base turned into one gigantic skating rink. After the grad party, a few of us were chasing each other around the base in our cars, doing donuts and four-wheel skids on the slick surface. It was fun until I smacked into a concrete bumper by the headquarters building. The way the front end was sitting didn't give me much confidence in the health of my car. Sure enough, the next day a mechanic in Grande Centre told me that the A frame was cracked and it was illegal to weld it. Another car bites the dust. I sold it to the garage for parts. Except for the two classmates who were staying in Cold Lake, Stu McDonald and Terry Walker, the rest of us had to return to Camp Borden. I had picked up my travel claim Friday from the orderly room and neglected to inform the authorities the next day that I no longer needed it because of the accident. My excuse was that the orderly room wasn't open on the weekends. The plan was to cool our heels in Borden for awhile, take two weeks embarkation leave to go home, then report to RCAF Station Trenton on the 28th of December to fly over to Europe. Military logic. Travel all the way east to Ontario and then go back to the West Coast for holidays. I thought Cold Lake to Vancouver made much more sense but the powers that be didn't see it that way.

Before heading out, Stu McDonald hauled all my belongings into Grande Centre so they could be shipped to Borden. Stu had a Ford Edsel that he'd driven out from Ontario. The car was only in production for three short years, and the word Edsel quickly became synonymous with failure. The push button automatic transmission selector that was housed in the hub of the steering wheel wasn't one of Ford's better innovations, as Stu was to discover on more than one occasion. When he dropped me off at the edge of town we shook hands and he wished me luck in catching a ride. Stu spent seventeen years in Cold Lake before he finally got a posting to Ontario. He must have loved his hunting and fishing by then.

My first ride out of Grande Centre was with a driver in a 3-ton truck going only as far as Bonnyville, thirty miles away. He made me very nervous because he was tailgating and so busy talking that he didn't notice the driver ahead of us signalling left and slowing down. He had to slam on the brakes, and as a result we ended up in the ditch, unhurt but totally stuck. I told the driver that I would thumb a ride into Bonnyville and have a tow truck sent out. The next car to pick me up was my best ride ever, taking me all the way to North Bay, Ontario. After a quick stop in Bonnyville, we headed south to Vermillion, then southeast to the Trans-Canada Highway. Once we hit Saskatchewan, it starting snowing heavily with a strong wind and didn't let up until we were well into Northern Ontario, but my new friends were determined to reach their destination in record time. Nothing would stop these guys. Eventually I sat in the front passenger seat keeping the driver awake while the off-duty driver slept on the back seat. They were both airframe techs in the air force and took their release after their five-year commitment was up. If they could have wrangled an overseas posting like mine, they would have re-signed in a heartbeat. I was dropped off at a truck stop in North Bay and they carried on to Ottawa and Trois-Rivières. A trucker gave me a lift to Barrie and then one more ride brought me to the barracks at Borden. I couldn't complain about travelling all that distance in two days in less than ideal driving conditions.

GREY CUP AND EMBARKATION

I caught up on much needed sleep. Since my travel allowance gave me more than two days to drive from Alberta to Ontario in my "dearly departed" car, I didn't bother reporting in until Friday. I was in no hurry because no doubt pre-course pool would be looking for warm bodies to farm out. Monday morning my comm tech classmates and myself were on roll call at eight a.m. Sgt. Switzer was the NCO in charge now, and he was a real soft touch, just putting in time until his impending retirement and not too concerned about military protocol. What also worked to our advantage was a large influx of "coolies" from basic training so we "veterans" hung around more times than not, playing cards instead of mopping out the mess hall and other mundane jobs.

I phoned Charlie on the weekend and he drove up from Downsview. By then he had purchased a car that he paid all of two hundred and fifty dollars for, a 1954 Ford, rusted out, and with a muffler that didn't have much noise suppression happening. Perfect for Charlie. He mentioned that Downsview was putting on an honour guard of thirty airmen for the Grey Cup game the following Sunday, November 28, and the corporal in charge was short of a few bodies because Downsview was such a small base. Charlie said he would talk to the corporal on Monday and put in a good word for me. He loaned me his car to drive back to Borden and when I phoned him on Monday afternoon, Charlie said I was in provided

I practised with the guard Tuesday to Friday. I really wanted to be at that Grey Cup game because this was the first year that the BC Lions had made the final, but I didn't really want to go on charge for being AWA. I thought about it long and hard for about five minutes and decided that I would take the chance because Sgt. Switzer ran such a loose ship. I asked some of my classmates to answer for me at morning roll call, and later if the good Sarge was looking for AC1 Forbes, just say that I was feeling sick and went back to the barracks.

Monday night I packed up my dress uniform complete with greatcoat and drove down to join Charlie on the honour guard. We practised for four days, and Charlie showed me a few of his haunts in the greater Toronto area.

We had seats at field level on the thirty-yard line for the game, and once again I was grateful for the greatcoat because it wasn't particularly warm that afternoon. Our moment of glory was at half-time when we marched up the centre of the field at Exhibition Stadium in the mud. I was just praying that the TV cameras didn't show close-ups of our faces and if they did that Sgt. Switzer wasn't a football fan. It was an entertaining game featuring future Hall-of-Fame quarterback Joe Kapp and wide receiver Willie Fleming of BC against future Hall-of-Fame quarterback Bernie Faloney and Angelo Mosca—all three hundred and ten pounds of him. BC won their first Grey Cup, beating the Hamilton Tigercats thirty-four to twenty-four. When the game ended we were bused back to the base where Charlie and I quickly changed into civilian clothes and then headed back downtown. The traffic on Yonge Street was bumper-to-bumper with many drunken yahoos hanging out the car windows whooping it up. Charlie just loved it, laying rubber up and down Toronto's main drag with a very remote chance of being pulled over by the police. All that fun and we weren't even drinking. After the celebration, we picked up my luggage and he drove me back to Borden. Monday morning, I answered my name for roll call and the powers that be didn't have an inkling I was AWA for the week.

After the Grey Cup game, we had two weeks of utter boredom in Camp Borden before we were allowed to go on our fourteen-day embarkation leave. I didn't like the idea of hitchhiking to the coast in December, but then again, I'd had such fantastic success in the past that

I thought, why not try it one more time. Maybe I was getting cocky but it seemed so easy wearing a uniform. It was like that big 1965 rock and roll hit by the Beatles, throw on a tunic and "I've got a ticket to ride." In most cases on that trek, the longest time I spent standing on the side of the highway was thirty minutes. In Regina, I phoned up Uncle Archie and he picked me up for a much-needed overnight stay. I had a good visit and really appreciated the decent food, warm bed, and of course the hot shower. The only other noteworthy part of the trip was in the Rogers Pass west of Golden when we had to wait a few hours for the snowplows to clear a minor avalanche.

When I reached the coast, I phoned my Aunt Fran in Burnaby and invited myself over for the night. The food and hot showers were once again appreciated but the main reason I was delaying the last leg of my trip was because Ocean Falls in December is non-stop rain. There is a good reason why the residents of Ocean Falls are referred to as "The Rain People."

Fran's husband Peter Seifert worked for years as an accountant for the Canadian Fish Company, and in the early years he would be posted in the summer fishing season to cannery towns up and down the coast to run the company store and also do the books for the cannery operation. One summer, my sister Mary-Lynne went to Tallheo by Bella Coola to help Fran with her small children. Another year when Peter was assigned to Butedale, my brother Donald spent the summer there working in the store. After their kids got older and Peter had more seniority, he was permanently attached to the company's head office in Vancouver, much to Fran's relief.

Xmas '64 Ocean Falls. Sister Barb Forbes and Jack Cronin

When I flew into my hometown I did the rounds and managed to stay out of trouble. I was invited to Archie Young's house for supper one night, and

I had an interesting conversation with his father, Archie senior. I didn't realize he was such a huge football fan, especially for the BC Lions. Archie Sr. must have listened to the Grey Cup game on CBC radio because the town didn't even have TV until years later. He was asking me about the tackles and scoring plays and I had to embellish the facts quite a bit or ruin the moment because, really, field-level seating is not the best location to watch a football game. He probably "saw" more of the game than I did.

At home, I got a bit of a chuckle when I was poking around in the basement, looking for my old 22 rifle. I found the barrel, and when I enquired about the wooden stock, I was informed that Dad had thrown it into the fireplace. I often wondered about that. Was he short of firewood that winter or was he just dead set against firearms? At that time we were getting along pretty well for a change, so I didn't pursue the subject. In a few days I would be long gone. My trusty old bootlegger, Harvey, gave me a mickey of rye whisky as a parting gift, even though as a general rule I didn't drink "hard stuff" unless it was mixed five to one with coke. I would have preferred beer, but it wasn't all that practical since I would be travelling by air. Roy Chernishenko and John Riley along with his wife Pat and their wee one Brian came down to the airplane dock to see me off.

I had booked a flight to Vancouver for Boxing Day. Of course, that was dependent on the weather, especially since BC Airlines used Cousins Inlet as the runway, and if the water was too choppy, I wasn't going anywhere soon. Thankfully it wasn't too windy so we did manage to get airborne on the first attempt. My flight was in a Grummen Mallard twelve-passenger, two- engine amphibian aircraft that had a fairly good safety record, but all bets were off if it hit a deadhead on takeoff or landing. On my previous flight in a Mallard, the ticket agent was pushing on the side window porthole by my seat to get the aircraft clear of the dock when the glass cracked. I notified the pilot who determined that it was safe to fly as long as we didn't climb over five hundred feet. The pilot asked me to hold my air force forage cap over the cracked porthole, as if that would do any good. The flight to Vancouver took much longer than normal because we had to follow the coastline instead of flying in a straight line over the coastal mountains. A good portion of that trip was much lower than five hundred feet because of the clouds, so I imagine we startled more than a few small boats along the way. Thankfully we didn't encounter any deadheads or broken portholes on Boxing Day.

Once again, I phoned Aunt Fran and she sent Peter to the airport to pick me up. The next morning, we woke up to a big surprise. The lower mainland was covered in a blanket of snow. Vancouver seldom has a white Christmas and that year they missed it by two days. I was fortunate that Peter left Burnaby in plenty of time because the roads were in terrible shape, and I just made my flight to Toronto with minutes to spare. From the Toronto airport, I had approximately one hundred miles east on the 401 freeway to RCAF Station Trenton. It took one ride to reach the turnoff from the 401 into Trenton and two short rides and I was home free. I gave the trucker who picked me up by the airport my unopened mickey of whisky with a "Thanks for the ride and Merry Christmas." He was dumbfounded that a hitchhiker would be giving away free alcohol.

Once on the base I checked into transit quarters and then headed over to the Airmen's Mess where I ran into Dave Clarke and three other guys from my course. Exhausted and jet lagged, and facing a minimum twelve-hour flight over the Atlantic the next day, I had only a few beers with the boys. I had to give Dave some serious shaking to roust him the next morning because he was what you would call a sound sleeper. Maybe Dave wasn't too excited about the next three years, but I certainly was. I tossed and turned all night, thinking about what was in store for me and what a golden opportunity was handed to me to see Europe at the government's expense. Timing is everything. When I caught the "flu" six months previously, it changed my life drastically. I felt like I was the chosen one. Life is good. After showers and breakfast in the mess, we reported to the terminal for our flight on the Yukon, a four-engine turbo prop that had a capacity of one hundred and thirty-five passengers. We were informed that we would be boarding in three hours, but it was closer to four. Typical military operation, hurry up and wait. Our plane landed in Marville in northeastern France around seven a.m. local time. It was the home of #1 Fighter Wing that flew CF-104 jet interceptor/bombers in support of NATO.

WELCOME TO EUROPE

After a short stay on *terra firma* and a hot meal that wasn't a box lunch, we were on the move again on a military bus headed east. Beebe, Hayes and Watson were staying in France and the remaining seven of us would be posted to 3 and 4 Wing in West Germany. Our first stop was at Metz, France, which was the headquarters for RCAF 1 Air Division. Normally, the second stop would be 2 Fighter Wing at Grostenquin, also in northeastern France, but it was now closed. Charles de Gaulle and the French government were playing hardball with NATO, demanding that the foreign forces stationed on French soil come under French command or leave. Canada opted for the latter, sending 2 Wing's Fighter Squadrons across the border to Germany. 1 Wing Marville held on until 1967 and then moved lock, stock, and barrel, to Lahr, Germany, about forty-five miles south down the autobahn from 4 Wing, Baden-Soellingen. Our bus finally pulled into 3 Fighter Wing in the late afternoon, and I was assigned a room in barrack block 14, just down from the mess hall. My roommate was Bob Emmerson, an integral systems tech who hailed from Maple Ridge, BC. The next morning Dave Clarke, Ed Herechuk and myself reported for duty at the Telecom Air section located in the secure area of the base where the aircraft operations were happening. Flight Sergeant Chiasson, who was referred to as Flt. Sgt. Chainsaw, welcomed us aboard and then handed us off to Sgt. McLean. The good old Sarge promptly dismissed us, saying that because it was so close to New Year's Eve, we could come back in four days.

Right then and there Sgt. McLean got my vote for *numero uno* NCO. He was a crusty old guy, very likeable, who always treated us fairly as long as we played within the rules. He had half a dozen kids and a big older model Mercedes to haul them around in. When the floorboards of his car started to rust out, he just mixed up some concrete and literally paved the floor. The Sarge wasn't too concerned about minor issues like weight and fuel efficiency because gas on the base was fifteen cents a litre.

Someone had told Ed Herechuk that Luxemburg was one of the liveliest hot spots in Europe, so we decided to spend New Year's there. Mike Pierce, a refinishing tech who flew over with us on the Yukon, joined Ed, Dave and myself for our first European excursion. Mike was a big, easy-going Saskatchewan stubble-jumper who would never say no to a beer. I should really say "could never" not "would never." Armed with a map we took a cab to the *bahnhof* and bought train tickets and transfers. Three hours later we were in Luxembourg's underground train station. The boys were anxious to find a cold beer, but I was even more anxious to find a bathroom before we ventured out. I spotted a lit "toilet" sign and proceeded into a huge washroom, passing a cleaning lady sitting by the entrance, and sat down in a stall. I had barely locked the door when there was a furious pounding on it, and some woman screaming, *"Monsieur, monsieur"* followed by many French words that didn't make any sense to my *anglais* ears. She was yelling so loud and fast that I doubt that even had I passed my high school French, I could have comprehended what the hell was going on. I thought the *gare* was on fire and I had to evacuate, no pun intended, so I unlatched the door. That wasn't such a great idea because the cleaning lady came charging in and almost landed on top of me. I quickly pushed her out, re-locked the door, finished my business and then tried to leave without getting beat up. She was still pretty vocal and was pointing to a dish on her desk and a sign stating how many francs I was required to pay her for using the public washroom. Welcome to Europe, John.

We checked into a cheap hotel and had a few rounds in the bar. Dave insisted that we try out Charlie's Bar because he had read about it in *Playboy* magazine. It had the reputation for being one of the top bars in Europe, so we made our way to it to line up outside the door. When the doorman finally let us in, it was obvious that it was out of our league class-wise and price-wise.

Our cheap hotel had good beer at cheap prices. We couldn't eat enough of the *thuringers,* a spicy version of the German *bratwurst,* a sausage in a bun sold by street vendors all over the downtown district. The North American hot dog couldn't compare to the *bratwurst* and *thuringers* of Europe. Our hot dogs were a distant second to the European version, a poor relative from the trailer park on the other side of town. And we had no complaints about the beer, either. On New Year's Eve, the bar in our hotel got fairly lively with quite a few military types in there, standing room only. There was no shortage of air force and army bases within shouting distance of Luxembourg. The area was well represented by the American forces, and 1 Fighter Wing at Marville was approximately forty miles southwest. Bitburg AB, a large US air force base, was only thirty miles northeast of Luxembourg. On New Year's Day, the weather turned cold and wet, so after a few more *thuringers* we decided that we had experienced enough of Europe's hot spot and headed home to 3 Wing.

While I was in Germany, disaster struck my hometown. On January 13, 1965, Ocean Falls had an abnormal amount of snow in the surrounding mountains. That, coupled with the heavy rainfall, caused the power to go out. The townspeople then heard a tremendous roar, which could only mean one thing. A landslide went through the middle of town, wiping out two duplexes, a clothing store, the credit union office, and the *Ocean Falls* Advertiser—the local newspaper plant and office. It was a miracle that only seven people died that night.

Within six weeks Dave and I were selected for two different honour guards. The first one was a very somber event but the second one not so. The honour guard was bused to the Choloy Cemetery just past Nancy in France, where the Canadian post-war military and dependents graves were located, about a three-hour drive from 3 Wing. One of our pilots had thundered into the ground in January. The CF-104 Starfighter's role in NATO was to deliver a nuclear warhead to targets east of the iron curtain if war was declared with the Warsaw Pact Forces. It was originally designed to be a high-speed Mach 2, high altitude—fifty thousand feet—fighter/interceptor, but to keep under enemy radar, it was required to fly at low levels over hilly terrain, and if you factored in mechanical problems, inertial navigation problems, even bird strikes, the accident rate of the CF-104 was extremely high. If the single engine flamed out, the aircraft with its stubby wings would glide like a rock. When the pilot was doing his pre-flight check, inspecting landing gear, hydraulic lines, etc., the ground-crew man had to put his hand over the sharp leading edge of the wing to guard against the pilot cutting his head when he straightened up. Most of the NATO countries flew the F-104, and it wasn't long before it acquired the nickname "Widow Maker," although the pilots would never use that term for fear of jinxing themselves. They affectionately called the Starfighter the "Lawn Dart." In twenty-five years of CF-104 operations, over one hundred jets in the RCAF were written off with thirty-seven fatalities. Thank God for ejection seats. At the funeral in Choloy, there was the grief-stricken widow, all dressed in black, with her two young children.

The second honour guard was not only a happy occasion but an historic one for Canada. February 15,1965 was the date the new Canadian flag, the Maple Leaf, was run up our flagpole at the headquarters building for the first time. We finally put all the rifle drill in basic training to good use. Corporal Pritchard would have been proud. Lester B. Pearson, the Liberal Prime Minister, was the man responsible for getting the job done. Numerous designs were put forth, and, of course, it was debated for months and months in Parliament, with John Diefenbaker and his Conservatives fighting tooth and nail for the old standby, the Canadian Ensign. After we hoisted the new flag, for the next three years I would see more and more Maple Leaf flags attached to hitchhikers' backpacks, and chances were that if you stopped for them, they were US citizens. The Americans at that time weren't too popular in Europe, especially in France, because of de Gaulle and his beef with NATO.

It soon became obvious that if I wanted to make the most out of my European posting, I would need a good reliable vehicle, so in early February I purchased a '65 Volvo 544. No more beaters for me. Barry English, a young clerk admin LAC (leading aircraftsman) who worked in the headquarters building, was selling his new car because he needed the money to bring his fiancée over from Canada for the wedding. Even though I'd lost a few dollars on my two previous cars, I still had a relatively healthy bank account, so I was now the owner of a fire-engine red two-door vehicle with only sixteen hundred km on the odometer. If Henry Ford was still alive, he would have been happy too, because, as they say, imitation is the greatest form of flattery, and the 544 was a smaller version of the '46 Ford. Some of my friends thought that it looked more like a pregnant Volkswagen bug but regardless, the car was economical and reliable.

Dave Clarke and my Volvo

Just over the border was a small French city called Bitche, twelve miles south of Zweibrücken, and we all pronounced it incorrectly as "bitch" except for Barry English. He was a born-again Christian, and there was no way a cuss word would ever pass his lips.

Zweibrücken, which in German literally means two bridges or twin bridges, had a population of thirty-five thousand and an interesting history. So close to the French border, the Siegfried line went right through the surrounding countryside. The line consisted of eighteen thousand bunkers, tunnels and tank traps that were built in WWI and stretched for over four hundred miles. A few of us got past the barbed wire and climbed into one of the bunkers. It was enormous and built to last. After the First World War, French troops occupied Zwiebrüchen until 1930. WWII was much harder on the city. On March 14, 1945, RCAF bomber command destroyed much of Zwiebrüchen on an air raid to wipe out a ball bearing factory in the city. The US army marched into the city a week later. There were still scars on the buildings, evidence of the fighting.

Our favourite street was a two-block section of Ixheihmstrasse where most of the bars were located. The bar girls were forever pestering the guys to play foosball—table soccer—similar to the table hockey games that we played as kids back home. If we lost, we had to buy the girl an expensive cognac, but I soon learned that it wasn't "if" but "when" because these girls were experts at foosball and made their living at fleecing the customers. When Bill Kowalchuk showed up for a beer, the bar girls always seemed to be busy with other duties, because word soon got out that Bill was a foosball wizard. We also learned that the "cognac" that we paid for was in fact tea with a dash of cola mixed in.

I don't know if it was true, but we understood that in order to encourage new businesses, the German government didn't levy a business tax for the first year of operation, so all the Jewish bar owners formed a syndicate, and at year's end, they would sell their bar on paper to one of their buddies in the syndicate to avoid paying taxes. Payback time I guess.

Our favourite bar on the strip was the Papa Club. I remember on New Year's Eve the place was really hopping—standing room only. The owner was a veteran Israeli paratrooper who had lost an arm in one of Israel's wars. The law stated that on New Year's Eve the bars had to close by one a.m., so he locked the door to stop new customers from piling in, but it was a losing battle because every time he would let two out, three or more would barge their way in. Being a one-armed doorman is a tough gig.

While on the subject of war veterans and amputees, I have memories of a trip to Saarbrüchen, a half hour drive by autobahn, to watch Saarbrüchen FC, one of the top professional football teams in Germany. At the ticket counter in the stadium, I noticed one long line-up for ten Deutschmark (DM) admission and a much shorter one for only one DM. I chose the cheap one, but when I got to the ticket seller, he started yelling at me in German, and then pointing to the sign over the booth, then at my leg, and then at the other customers behind me. I noticed, much to my embarrassment, that all the folks in the one-DM queue were either hobbling along with crutches, missing arms or hands, or wearing eye patches. I'm glad I couldn't understand any language other than English that day although I did hear the odd *dummkopf* muttered, and I probably deserved it. When I finally bought my "all limbs attached" ticket, all the seats were sold out, so I stood halfway up the stadium against a railing. I had a perfect view, perfect until the match started, and then I soon found myself six rows back from the railing, because of all the shoving and elbowing going on. After ten minutes of standing on my tiptoes to see the action, I got disgusted and drove home. Unlike the English, the Germans aren't noted for their queuing skills. A good friend of mine stationed in 4 Wing did quite a bit of skiing in southern Germany and Austria, and he was telling me that he had many more scratches on the top of his skis than on the bottom, all from other skiers walking over his skis while he queued up in the lift lines.

Our barracks at 3 Wing were quite adequate and included the services of a *putzfrau*—a cleaning lady who looked after all the common areas like hallways and washrooms. We were responsible only for our own room, and it was inspected once a week by the Station Warrant Officer (SWO). The barrack warden was a German national who was in charge of all the station *putzfraus*, and each week he handed out the freshly laundered bed sheets. I suspect that *Herr* Winter had a pretty fat bank account because he was also the Zurich car insurance agent through whom every Canadian driver ended up buying insurance.

The first thing we all bought for our rooms was a beer fridge and a good hi-fi system, purchased from the base exchange where everything was duty-free. I was glad that I was a non-smoker and didn't really care for hard liquor because the temptation was there with Canadian cigarettes going for a dollar a carton and forty ounces of Canadian Club for two dollars. When Rory down the hall from me woke up in the morning, he would reach over to his fridge and down two beers before he even crawled out of bed. At the mess hall, he'd have a quick breakfast and then walk over to the hangar line. For lunch, he would walk right past the mess hall on his way to the Airmen's Mess where he would order two double ryes. Rory was so shaky at this point that he would need two hands to down his first drink, but normally by the second one he could do it solo. After work, it was back to the Airmen's Mess until closing time. Day after day. We could buy good German beer for ten cents a bottle or five cents a draft in the mess. It was fortunate that I had a good memory of how much I had suffered with a hangover because the beer certainly was tempting. I can still remember this older very likeable airman who, after two years, was flown back to Canada, strapped to a stretcher. Too much of a good thing is not a good thing.

FASCHING AND ROME

The week after the fighter pilot's funeral in France, Dave and I decided to drive over to 4 Fighter Wing at Baden-Soellingen, about eighty-five miles southeast, to visit with our former classmates. *Fasching* was just winding down because Ash Wednesday, the start of Lent, was close. The Germans take *Fasching* very seriously. It's comparable to *Mardi Gras* in New Orleans. Another name for it is *Fastnacht* which translates to "the night of being wild and foolish," a perfect description because of all the alcohol consumed. I drove Kim Burley, Ray Childs and Dave to a large hall in Rastatt where the wild and foolish was happening on Saturday night. We were probably the only people in the hall not wearing a costume or a mask, but that didn't stop us from joining in the festivities, especially Dave, as it turned out. When it was time to leave, Dave was nowhere to be found. We thought that he probably hooked up with some young *Fraulein,* so we drove back to the base *sans* Dave. At five a.m., he stumbled into the barracks looking like a truck ran over him. What had happened was, after drinking far too much and wanting to go on a joyride, he checked out all the cars parked on the street until he found one with the keys in the ignition, which didn't help matters. Unfortunately, most secondary roads in Germany are quite windy, and Dave missed a corner, ending upside down in a farmer's field. He lost his glasses, which wasn't good because Dave was blind as a bat without them. Other than a few cuts and bruises, he was okay. He had a hell of a time making his way back to the base because most people wouldn't pick up a hitchhiker late at night in the middle of nowhere, especially if he looked like a drunken bum.

The next morning Dave was feeling very remorseful about his wild and foolish *Fasching* experience. It got worse when he discovered a stranger's wallet in his jacket pocket, presumably the property of the guy whose car was now in the field. We looked through it and found money and pictures of the poor guy's wife and kids, so we concocted a plan that involved getting the wallet back to the rightful owner and keeping Dave out of jail or even getting deported. We drove over to Baden-Baden, a famous resort city of fifty thousand that had spas and casinos for wealthy folks. We sat in the patio section and ordered a beer and a bratwurst although I seem to recall that Dave passed on the beer. Since the patio was quite deserted, we had no problem placing the wallet in a potted plant without being detected. This incident was so out of character for Dave, normally an honest person. He sweated over it for a few months, concerned that some astute detective would find his glasses and trace them back to his hometown of Acton, Ontario.

The fiscal year in the military began on April 1, and I had to burn off my remaining annual leave by the end of March. Dave had used up his leave, so I decided to drive solo down to Italy to look up Pete Mammo who had recently moved back to Carrara in Tuscany. Pete spent a number of years serving with the *Carabinieri,* the national police force, before moving to Ocean Falls in the late '50s. Pete had the typical Italian hairdo, but his build was very atypical. He could have been mistaken for a fullback on a football team. His easygoing demeanour came in handy working on the booms because Kulak Bill was his leadhand and Nick Slater his shift foreman. In 1961, he married a local girl in Carrara and brought her back to Ocean Falls, but she lasted just long enough to get pregnant before flying back to Italy. If you've ever been to Tuscany, you'll understand why she wasn't very fond of our west coast weather, especially in the winter months. After a few more years of pushing logs, Pete built up his bank account sufficiently and followed his young wife back to Italy where he was hired on at the world-famous marble quarries of Carrara. They lived on the fourteenth floor of a high-rise and had a wonderful view of the mountains and the city. When I showed up at his door, I gave him a forty-ouncer of rye and two cartons of Player's Filter cigarettes, and Pete was so grateful that he almost got down and kissed my feet. He told me that he had to work for six hours to earn enough to buy one pack of Italian cigarettes and that they tasted terrible. He was happily married with a nice little family, complete with a mother-in-law dressed in the customary black of a widow, living in a spectacular area within a few miles of the Mediterranean, but I was under the impression that he missed working on the sawmill booms with Kulak Bill and the boys. Maybe it was just the pay cheques that he missed.

On my way to Carrara I stayed overnight in Genova, the birthplace of Christopher Columbus. I now understand why Chris wanted to discover greener pastures because what I saw of Genova wasn't very favourable. Two words that came to mind were dirty and polluted. Perhaps because the temperatures were warmer and more humid, but more likely because of the diesel exhaust from vehicles, I found that the major Italian cities had a lot of air pollution. I soon learned that "ring around the collar" was inevitable if I wore a white shirt.

Just south of Marina de Carrara, I stopped on the Italian Riviera to see the *Mare Mediterraneo*. There I met two young Canadians from Vancouver who were also driving a 544 Volvo. The previous day someone had broken into their car and stolen a camera bag containing not only an expensive camera, but also six months of undeveloped film of their once-in-a-lifetime European holiday. They talked me into using my Volvo as a bait car to catch the lowlifes who did this. I agreed as long as we didn't lock the doors and I substituted a few rocks for the camera in my camera bag. I didn't want a broken vent window like my new friends had, and I wasn't about to take the chance that the thieves could outrun us. We hid behind a sand dune all afternoon, drank cheap Italian red wine and got sunburned, but not a single person approached my car. If this was a Hollywood movie, we would have busted a crime ring, but it was reality, so we came up empty-handed and slightly tipsy. At six o'clock I followed them over to their hostel where I booked in for the night and payed next to nothing for supper. Two old Italian women were like mother hens as they shovelled huge quantities of bread and spaghetti at us and, of course, more cheap red wine that I didn't really need. The next morning, I headed south to Rome and the now camera-less Canucks drove towards the French Riviera.

When I was approaching Rome in the late afternoon, I noticed two or three long-legged attractive girls at every bus stop along the highway. This was at the height of the mini skirt craze, and they were looking pretty good, but they never seemed to get on the buses. It finally dawned on me that these "girls" were actually ladies of the night who had a jumpstart on the night. No pun intended here either.

I wanted to do all the touristy things in Rome, but I could see that driving was out of the question, so the following day I hooked up with a guide who came with his own vehicle. Hiring a guide was one of my better decisions. Although being a passenger was scary enough, at least it wouldn't be my car getting banged up. Navigating a traffic circle in Rome was a real ordeal for a rookie, especially when a vehicle entering a circle has the right of way, but Mario would make a Grand Prix driver proud. I finally asked him the secret of his success, and he told me the following three things: first, use the horn a lot; second, drive a larger car—his was one of the bigger Fiat models; third, and most important, watch to see if the vehicle bearing down on the right was braking. If the front end was dipping down, then that car was braking. If not, you had better start braking because it wouldn't be stopping.

The Coliseum traffic circle at rush hour is a sight to behold. Throw in some machismo, add a touch of testosterone, and you've got a recipe for mayhem. In one day, we saw everything that was on my list, and to make it more interesting, Mario threw in the odd gem that only a local would know. Even though some of his stories were a little far-fetched, I thought that my tour was good value. I saw the Catacombs, the Coliseum, St. Peter's Square, St. Peter's Basilica, a few historical landmarks that didn't really register with me, and the famous Trevi Fountain that was featured in the movie *Three Coins in a Fountain*. I threw in a coin, made a wish and lo and behold, my wish was granted five years later.

Cameras aren't allowed inside St. Peter's, so tourists have no option but to buy postcards and colour slides from the church if they want keepsakes of the spectacular interior. I was raised a Catholic and wasn't very impressed with the church squeezing every last penny out of the tourists, especially after viewing the untold riches in the Treasury Room of the Basilica.

For lunch, we ate on the run, but the deal was I had to buy Mario dinner in a restaurant of his choice. We ate in Vatican City in a restaurant frequented by the clergy, so I had to mind my P's and Q's. Mario said that if bishops and archbishops were dining there, the food had to be good, and he was right. He was a short, chubby little guy, and I recall his exact words after we had a big meal and polished off our second bottle of red wine.

He patted his tummy and said, "A man has to look after his stomach, Geovanni."

At my expense, of course, but I must say that those Roman Catholic higher-ups sure knew how to dine.

Rome was a real eye-opener for me. History was always my favourite subject in school, and when I was standing in the Coliseum, all I could think about was that from this great city the Roman Empire sprang forth and colonized much of Europe. It was no easy feat back then, and even today our English language is greatly influenced by their Latin. The ancient ruins, the buildings, the churches, the Vatican—everything was fascinating. Being a card-carrying Catholic, I was somewhat disappointed that I didn't have a private audience with the Pope. His loss.

The next day, I pointed the Volvo north, stopping at Milan for the night. I didn't have time to enter the Gothic Cathedral in the city; however, I thought that the exterior was just as impressive in its own right as the Basilica in Rome. The Italians started construction in 1386 and it was officially completed in January of 1965—five hundred and seventy-nine years later. They must have heard about my impending visit and put the pressure on the workers to finish on time.

From Milan, I drove through the Alps into Switzerland, passing through Lucerne, Zurich and Basil without any problems because the mountain passes were clear of ice and snow. In southern Germany, I was close to 4 Wing, so I stayed overnight to visit my buddies. That was one thing about the air force in the '60s. The wages weren't great but you could always count on a bed for the night if you showed up at a RCAF Station. And thirty days of annual leave was a nice perk. In Germany, the single airmen had an additional twelve dollars a month overseas allowance, and for the married airmen it was bumped up to over one hundred dollars a month. Along with the duty-free items, the fifteen-cent-a-litre gas and our pay in American dollars, we weren't doing too badly. At the time, the Canadian dollar was exchanging for a dollar and ten cents American.

HOLLAND, SPAIN, FRANCE AND ITALY—FOUR GUYS

In the spring, Dave bought an older model Jaguar Mark X that had seen better days. The body wasn't the greatest and the odometer had more than a few kilometres on it. Once, when we were returning from Bitche, France, the engine started to hesitate and buck as if we were running low on fuel. Dave knew it was the electric fuel pump because he had encountered the problem the previous week. He wanted me to ride in the trunk where the pump was mounted and tap it with a screwdriver while he drove. I declined, citing claustrophobia, so I drove and he did the tapping. Between the French and the German borders north of Bitche, there is a one-mile stretch of no-man's land. When we got to the German border I made sure I stopped and opened the trunk to show the border crossing guard that I wasn't smuggling humans. I tried to explain in my best broken German what the problem was. "*Kapute, nein benzine*," then pointing at the fuel pump "*Nicht gut*, TAP, TAP." He caught on right away as if this were an everyday occurrence and said, "*Defekte pumpe*," and waved us through. Dave's car problems didn't end with his defective fuel pump. A black cloud was hanging over the Jag, and a blue cloud was trailing behind. Bob Lake told him that he would be happy to give it a valve job, so, of course, Dave took him up on it. On the base, we had an auto club where they rented out the bays by the hour and also loaned you tools from the tool crib. Bob very meticulously ground the valves properly then put the engine back together, ready for the true test. Dave thanked him up and down then turned the ignition key, which resulted in this terrible sound that could only be metal on metal. Unfortunately, Bob had made one small error when re-assembling the engine. The timing chain was installed one hundred and eighty degrees out of phase so that the pistons smashed into the valves, which is never a good thing. Dave's Jag would never run again. The dream was over.

Shortly after that calamity, Dave bought an older model Chevrolet from an airman who was buying a larger, more reliable vehicle for his growing family. Some of the Canadians would install a second gas tank in the trunk so they could fill up with cheap gas on the base if they were planning a longer trip. The additional gas tank had been installed quite professionally, with a proper filler hose and gas cap alongside the original gas cap on the rear fender, but before he sold the car, the original owner removed all these additions except for the gas cap and pipe because he didn't want to leave a gaping hole in the fender. We were halfway to Amsterdam on the autobahn when we pulled in for a fill-up and a snack. We got a fill-up all right. The young kid working there opened the wrong cap—not his fault—and pumped about fifty litres straight into the trunk before we noticed what was happening. It was our chance to make history—a 1965 car bomb—but I wasn't too thrilled. We pushed Dave's car a good distance away from the pumps to a storm drain, removed the spare tire, searched around for a screwdriver, and then very careful punched a hole in the spare tire wheel well to drain the gas. The trunk carpet and our overnight bags were completely saturated. After half an hour, we carried on north with all the windows rolled down. Within the hour, the boys wanted to light up, but I quickly vetoed that idea. Even three days later on our way home, the car still smelled like a gas plant. The guys insisted on smoking, so we compromised, stopping every hour so they could get their fix outside the car.

Amsterdam was quite the town. Language was no problem because in the Netherlands the school kids learned four different languages, English being one of them. All the hotels in the canal district were tiny and consisted of a pub on the street level and, at most, twenty rooms above on three or four levels. Our favourite was the Play-Boy, not the *Playboy* of Hugh Hefner's empire. No bunnies in the Play-Boy, just one lonely bar girl. It was also a favourite of the Canadian army soldiers who were posted at Soest in Northern Germany. The owner/manager of the Play-Boy wouldn't allow the Royal 22 Regiment—the Van Doos—and the Black Watch into his hotel at the same time because they would wreck the place while they beat each other up. All in good fun, of course. We were staying in a top-floor room one New Year's Eve, and directly below us four soldiers from the Royal Canadian Regiment, the RCR's from Soest, were diving out their window into the canal. They then climbed up a rope secured to a bed in their room so they could dive in again. There was a city ordinance stating that if you fell into a canal in Amsterdam, the police had to hose you off with cold water in the street and then cart you off to the hospital. The canals in the '60s weren't much cleaner than a sewer.

On one of our trips to Amsterdam, a soldier with the Princess Patricia Canadian Light Infantry, the PPCLI, asked us for a lift back to Soest because he was flat broke and couldn't afford a train ticket. All this guy had in his overnight bag for a week's leave in Holland were two extra T-shirts, a few pairs of shorts and socks and a shaving kit. Since it wasn't too far out of our way, we drove him to his camp east of Dusseldorf and ended up staying in the barracks overnight. When we got to the mess hall for supper, I could see right away how much better we had it compared to the grunts. For starters, our friend had to beg, borrow, and practically steal the metal dinner plates and utensils for us so we could eat in the mess hall, and then it was our responsibility to clean them up after the meal. That evening the inter-regimental hockey league featured the PPCLI's versus the RCR's and it was a hard-hitting rough-and- tumble contest with a few fights to make it interesting. There were just as many fights in the stands as on the ice surface.

Amsterdam was a great city for walking and cycling but not the best for driving and parking. In order to pass parked cars on the narrow one-way streets, we had to drive up on the sidewalks. If we were lucky enough to find parking, we had to straddle the sidewalk. When I woke up the first morning, I couldn't find my car, so I told a Dutch cop that someone had stolen my car overnight. He said not to panic; it would have been relocated within half a kilometre and then he pointed to the parking signs. Due to garbage pick-up, on even days, parking was allowed on the right-hand side of the street and on the left on odd days. Sure enough, after two hours of wandering through Amsterdam in the rain, I finally found my car, none the worse for wear.

Unless it was the middle of the summer, it always seemed to be damp in the Netherlands. From light drizzle to wet snow, it played havoc with starting the Volvo after it had been sitting for a few days. Occasionally, I would have to take off the distributor cap and dry it out with a tissue instead of running down my battery trying to start the engine.

If you were European, probably the most popular street food in Holland was raw herring, when it was in season. Down the hatch. Once was enough for me and my fellow Canucks. We favoured *frites* smothered in mayonnaise instead of ketchup. The Amstel beer was only about three percent alcohol. One typical cold and wet winter day in a bar over by the central train station, I got involved in a card game with five Canadian soldiers. Interesting, but not too complicated. Each player was dealt a card, face down. The first one to draw an ace would order a drink, and it could be any combination, but it would never be good. Scotch and wine, vodka and rum. The second ace would taste it, the third ace had to chug-a-lug it, and the final ace had to pay for it. Play that for two hours, especially if you were catching the third and fourth aces a few times, and it could be very expensive on your wallet and your health.

On one excursion in the Netherlands, we went to a traditional Dutch village a little north of Amsterdam. It was on a Sunday, and we were most likely the only tourists there. Many of the folks were dressed in their traditional clothes complete with wooden clogs and were on their

Traditional Dutch villagers heading to church on Sunday

way to church. I was under the impression they didn't approve of us taking their picture I remember one older woman hiding her face behind her husband's head just as I snapped the picture. The town was very quaint with its colourful buildings, bridges over the canals and especially the windmills. From there, we went north then drove over the Afsluitdijk, a highway/causeway that goes for twenty miles and is a dike that keeps the North Sea from flooding the lowlands of Holland. Twenty-seven percent of the country is below sea level, and if the ice cap keeps melting it's going to take one hell of a lot of thumbs in the dike to save the farm land.

On August 1, 1965, the German Grand Prix was being run at Nürburgring, about two hours north of Zweibrücken. Dave followed Formula One racing, so he convinced us—his roommate Brian Cordinly, Mike Pierce and me—that it was a must-see. All the small towns surrounding Nürburg were joining in the big weekend by hosting wine tents for the occasion. Normally, in the summer months, Germany was awash in beer tents complete with Bavarian *oompah* bands. Not in the Nürburg area; it was well known for its vineyards. The four-piece *oompah* bands consisted of a tuba, clarinet, accordion and trombone, and if their loud brassy sound didn't give you a headache, you could count on the wine doing the trick. I'm not a big wine fan, but we had a good time the day before the race, arriving early in Nürburg so I could put the Volvo through its paces on the track. For ten Deutschmarks, a driver could take a car out for one lap, which was approximately thirteen miles. I didn't set any course records that day, but I did see what the Formula One drivers had to contend with: straight stretches ending with tight corners, and many, many trees that could stop a car in a hurry. Just after the start line, the race cars entered the *Sudkehre,* which is a really tight hairpin corner. Along with about fifty other spectators, we jumped a fence and had ourselves a ringside vantage point on that corner. Within a few minutes the *Polizei* showed up and sent us back to the safe side of the fence. "*Aus, aus, verboten, aus, aus!*" After thirty minutes, I thought the race was kind of boring mainly because of the length of the circuit and the forest of trees blocking the view. We would hear the cars, see them for a few seconds, then wait eight minutes until they came around again. Watching it live isn't all that it's cracked up to be. One of the top Formula One drivers of all time, Jim Clark of Scotland, won his sixteenth Grand Prix race that day and would go on to win nine more. Sadly, in 1968 in Hockenheim, Germany, he died in a racing accident after going off the track and hitting a tree. He was only thirty-two years old.

One of the more popular destinations in the summer months was Barcelona, Spain. When the temperatures heated up, it seemed that half the population of northern Europe invaded the Mediterranean shores, and we were only too happy to tag along with Dave Clarke providing the transportation. On the way down, we passed through the Principality of Andorra, high up in the Pyrénées and surrounded by France and Spain. Somewhere in our travels, Bob Lake and I picked up a stomach flu, which wasn't a great way to start a two-week holiday. We rented a cheap little cabana at the Laughing Whale, a huge beach resort about six miles west of Barcelona. On the first day there, Bob fell asleep on the beach and woke up a few hours later with a nice sunburn to go along with his flu. The Laughing Whale came highly recommended. I could see why with its miles of sand, warm water, decent restaurants and a lively discotheque right at the camp grounds frequented by the fairer sex from all over, even from New Zealand and Australia. If that wasn't enough, a short drive brought us to Ramblas Street, the older section of Barcelona that was alive with open-air markets, night life, cabarets, pick-pockets and bars. If you became bored wandering along Ramblas Street, something was definitely wrong with you. Late August was still quite hot, and I hadn't gotten over the stomach flu, so I entered a public washroom where I paid for six squares of toilet paper. I assumed that, dealing with all those tourists, the attendant would understand some English, but "sick" didn't register with him so I tried the German "*krank.*" Nothing. Finally, I caught on and handed over some more money.

He said, "*Enfermo?*" and passed me a few more squares.

I replied, "*Grande enfermo,*" and paid more money resulting in a more generous supply. At that point, I would have paid anything. You gotta love it.

Other than Barcelona, we didn't see much of Spain, and if truth be told we probably saw more tourists than locals, a direct result of staying at a resort campground. Even most of our meals were more northern European than Spanish. I guess the highlight would be the warm waters of the Mediterranean and the nightlife at the resort, and for some, the bull fights. But not for me. We, along with many other first-time visitors to Spain, bought cheaper tickets in the *Sol* line-up and fried in the late afternoon sun as we watched the massacre. To my mind, it was a cruel and senseless sport, the outcome of which was never in doubt. Matadors six, *El Torros* zero.

On the French Riviera we checked out Saint-Tropez, Cannes, Nice and Monaco. At Saint-Tropez, we ventured out onto the famous nudist beach where clothing is optional. All four of us wimped out and went with the optional. We parked ourselves fairly close to an attractive and shapely *mademoiselle*, and tried to look inconspicuous. That ploy didn't work because eventually she muttered something in French, and this big Frenchman sat up from where he had been buried in the sand and glared at us. After a few minutes of watching the seagulls soar overhead, we slunk off in disgrace.

I talked the boys into making a side trip to visit Pete and Silvia Mommi in Carrara. We stopped only long enough for a quick hand shake and a hug, and delivery of a care package of Canadian cigarettes and booze. On this trip, I was determined to see what I had missed the first time around, so we stopped at the Leaning Tower of Pisa before driving into Rome. Now that I was the official guide and not the driver, I wasn't minding the traffic so much, and we had four sets of eyes, much better than one. We made the usual tourist rounds and some new-to-me attractions like the Forum, Constantine's Arch and Circus Maximus where the Roman chariot races were held. I even pointed out the window of the room where Nero allegedly played his fiddle while Rome burned. At the Trevi Fountain, all four of us made a wish and threw a coin over our shoulder. I don't know what Bob Lake wished for, but I do know that within a year he was married.

From Rome, we visited the Republic of San Marino, which is another microstate in the centre of Italy, one hundred and ninety miles south of Milan. We weren't leaving Italy without visiting Venice, so following San Marino we made a beeline for the Adriatic Sea and the city of canals. Venice is a great little city for walking. We didn't ride on the gondolas. If I was going to spend that much money going down the canal in a gondola, I would rather it be with a nice looking *ragazza,* girl, than with my three buddies. We had lunch in a nice open-air restaurant, and everyone ordered a pizza, which was a big disappointment. Our favourite restaurant in Zwebrüchen was the Portifino, owned by Johnny, an Italian, who served awesome pizzas and killer escargots, if you and your friends didn't mind garlic breath. Every item on the menu was *numero uno,* and when the waiter presented us with the bill, he serenaded us. Now that was a restaurant.

We drove by Verona, the little Italian city that William Shakespeare put on the map, and then spent the night in Milan. The Principality of Liechtenstein, high up in the Alps and bordered by Switzerland and Austria, was our next port of call. That made three microstates in two weeks. At that time, Liechtenstein was reputedly the richest country in the world, probably because they didn't spend a large chunk of their budget on national defence. To wrap up our trip, we spent the night in Lucerne. The next day, we went on through Basel and back into Germany. What little we did see of Switzerland convinced us that sometime in the future it would be worth another trip to tour both Austria and Switzerland properly. I was thankful that we shared the driving, and everyone, including Dave, was surprised that his car survived the journey with hardly a hiccup.

In the fall of '65, Dave and I toured the war memorials in Normandy while the weather was still warm. On our way to Vimy, we visited a small village close to 1 Wing in Marville, France, where countless skulls and bones, victims of the bubonic plague in the 1400s, were neatly stacked up in a church tomb. I've been told there are upwards of forty thousand human remains in that tomb, but regardless of the number, it was a very sobering experience. Historians calculated that the bubonic plague/black death wiped out one third of Europe's population. Vimy Ridge was another sobering experience because no matter what you read about it, you have to witness it first hand to appreciate what our World War I veterans went through for us. We then drove up to Waterloo in Belgium where the Duke of Wellington defeated Napoleon on June 18, 1815. The Lion's Mound, the monument erected on the famous battlefield, was very impressive, especially when seen from a distance. It was ironic that the next day we drove down the Avenue des Champs Élysées in Paris where we saw the magnificent Arc de Triomphe, erected to honour the victories of Napoleon Bonaparte. We made the regular tourist stops like Notre Dame, the Louvre Museum, the Eiffel Tower, and the Moulin Rouge in Pigalle. My favourites were the Louvre and the Eiffel Tower. You could go through a few rolls of film up on the Eiffel Tower although I didn't climb all the way up because I'm not too fond of heights. The City of Lights was definitely something to see, but my lasting impression of Paris could be summed up in one word: rudeness. In a little kiosk in Pigalle, I tried to buy a roll of film for my camera. I encountered a very rude old woman. Maybe she didn't like my *anglais* or my feeble attempt at French, or perhaps it was the Charles de Gaulle factor, but I practically had to beg her to sell me more film.

My general impression of France was, first of all, the climate was like Goldilocks and the Three Bears—not too hot and not too cold—just right. And the cuisine was *numéro un*. Many of the small villages were run-down but definitely picturesque. The people were more laid-back than your average European. Next time I venture to France, I'll bring my own personal translator to experience the country properly. In the '60s, English wasn't commonly spoken outside of the tourist traps. I should have learned French when I had the chance.

REX AND THE SENATOR

Rex Rexin

A few rooms down the hall from me lived Robbie Robinson, an engine tech, who hailed from Truro, Nova Scotia, and Rex Rexin, a clerk admin type from Surrey, BC. Robbie, a confirmed bachelor and at least ten years older than the rest of us, was also known as the Senator. Some of his main interests were following the stock market and shooting pool. He could really handle a cue stick. Robbie commissioned another engine tech at 3 Wing, Moe Foote—a pretty decent artist—to paint a 20 x16 portrait. Robbie hung the painting in his barrack room, and in the frame, he looked very dignified and mature, dressed up in suit and tie, receding hairline and all. Once, while he was showering, I snuck into his room and attached a sign on the frame that read "Senator E. C. Robinson, Ret'd Cpl., RCAF, CDI." I don't think Robbie was all that impressed, but Rex thought it was a hoot.

They took a week's leave one summer to holiday in Barcelona, driving down in Rex's Volkswagen Beetle. After about six hours of driving, Rex was pretty exhausted and suggested to the Senator that he could take a turn at the wheel. Imagine Rex's surprise when Robbie confessed that he couldn't drive.

Rex said, "What do you mean, you can't drive or you don't have a driver's license?"

Robbie replied, "Well, actually, both, Rex."

"Nice of you to mention it now, buddy."

They left 3 Wing at five p.m. on Friday and pulled into Barcelona at five p.m. on Saturday, a full twenty-four hours later. By then, Rex was like a zombie, a very tired and angry zombie, who slept fourteen hours straight that night.

Later that same summer, Rex and I decided to drive in his vehicle to 4 Wing for the weekend. We were within fifteen minutes of the base, driving down the autobahn, when his engine seized up. After having it towed to 4 Wing, we headed over to the Airmen's Mess to drown our sorrows when who should walk in but Wally Litoski, a munitions and weapons tech whom we knew from 3 Wing. When Wally heard Rex's tale of woe, his eyes lit up because he had the perfect solution. A win-win solution as it turned out. Wally was into rally driving, and in his Beetle, he had an engine that was souped-up with bored-out cylinders and over-sized pistons. He had a line on a Porsche engine that would fit very nicely into his own Volkswagen, so after a few more beers, all three of us walked over to the base auto club to transform Rex's car into a super bug.

Wally was the chief mechanic, I was his assistant, and Rex handed us the tools. We finished around two a.m., and I was covered in grease. Not Wally or Rex. Wally had coveralls to wear and Rex just got his hands a little dirty. When the job was completed, Rex had a robust little Volkswagen, and when Wally had his up and running, he was a terror on the autobahns. Whenever we drove the autobahn you could always see headlights flashing one or two miles back, which meant that you had better stay in the right-hand lane because a Mercedes or BMW would be flying past you shortly. With his Porsche engine, Wally would cruise at ninety-five MPH until a BMW came up to pass him. Then he would step on it, leaving the BMW driver, mouth wide open, in his exhaust.

The world cup soccer championship was creating quite a buzz in late July of '66. Germany squeaked by the Soviet Union with a score of two to one in the semi-finals, and England defeated Portugal by the same margin. The final was to be contested in London at Wembley Stadium on July 30th. Rex wasn't much of a soccer fan, but he was definitely a bit of a shit disturber, so for the days leading up to the big match, he drove all over Zweibrücken and the base with a very professional-looking sign attached to the back of his car. The sign had a drawing of a soccer ball with the words *World Cup '66* written under it. Beneath that, in large letters, it read *Deutschland Uber Alles*.

One morning, the Commanding Officer of 3 Wing, Group Captain Don Laubman, was driving to the headquarters building when he noticed Rex's car with its controversial sign parked along the side of the road. He talked to the Station Warrant Officer and it was suggested that Rex should come in for a chat. The SWO told Rex that the sign was somewhat insensitive and inappropriate. He explained that while the phrase *Deutschland Uber Alles* (Germany above all else) was the opening line of a popular German song, it was also a rallying cry in WWII, closely identified with the Nazi regime. It was also mentioned that Group Captain Laubman was an air ace in the war, downing eight enemy aircraft in a three-day period. Allied war veterans didn't really care for that phrase.

Rex wasn't ordered to remove the offending sign, but he soon came around to their point of view and took it down. Career-wise it was never a good idea to ignore the suggestions of a first-class warrant officer. Group Captain Laubman was a well-liked and respected officer who made a great commanding officer. More than a few times I was on his start crew when he took an aircraft up on a sortie. He was always courteous and civil towards us lowly LACs, unlike some of the flight lieutenants who were rather aloof. But back to soccer. It was England *uber Deutschland* by a score of four to two in extra time.

The day after England's moment of glory in Wembley Stadium, I was in Ostend, Belgium with Rick Kell. Rick was an integral systems tech from Stellarton, Nova Scotia, and we worked together in 434 Squadron launching CF-104s and then parking and refuelling them after their sorties if they were serviceable. If the aircraft was unserviceable upon landing, it taxied directly to the line-servicing hanger for repairs and then eventually was towed back up to the squadron staging area. Rick was a tall guy who was really into karate, hence the nickname Killer Kell, or Karate Rick. Ostend was the European equivalent of Ft. Lauderdale, Florida, the favourite spring break destination for US college students, only in Ostend the break was during the summer months, and it was young English factory and office workers doing the invading.

Downtown Ostend was one big party with dozens of people joined together arm in arm walking down the main street chanting, "England won the coop, England won the coop," and it was likewise in every bar. The fans did their best to drink the town dry, yet we didn't see any fights or vandalism. This must have been before football hooligans were invented although I couldn't vouch for Rex's safety if he showed up in Ostend that weekend with his *Deutschland Uber Alles* sign attached to the back of his German-made vehicle.

At the end of '66, New Year's Eve, Rex had an interesting and memorable time ringing in the *Neues Jahr*. He and a German *Fraulein* were in Pirmasens, a larger city just east of Zweibrücken, celebrating with thousands of other folks when a bunny hop dance was organized. In a matter of a few minutes, hundreds joined the line. The leader bunny hopped through one door of the men's washroom, right past half a dozen men standing at the urinals, and then out the other door. The dancers didn't miss a beat nor did the guys relieving themselves. Only in Germany, you say.

GREAT BRITAIN

In early June of '66, three of us toured Britain. Dave had relatives just outside London, and Chris Brown, an aircraft electrician, had grandparents in northern Wales. As we were passing through Luxembourg, we stopped in at a sleazy bar for refreshments and a bathroom break. There were cut-up strips of newspaper hanging from a nail on the wall for toilet paper, a slight step up from the Eaton's catalogue used in the outhouses on the prairies during the Depression in my mother's childhood. We took the ferry from Calais to Dover where I had to learn in a hurry about driving on the "wrong" side of the road. I was doing fine until my first roundabout when I exited in the wrong lane, but we came to no harm. Right away we noticed that the Brits weren't as aggressive as the drivers on the continent. The Italians loved their horns, the Germans their speed. In France, many of the highways had three lanes instead of four. The middle lane was for passing, and the rule was the first vehicle in that

#10 Downing Street

lane had the right of way. But if the car bearing down on you was bigger than yours, you didn't worry about the rule book. You just got back into the right-hand lane. Being chicken was sometimes good. We all referred to the passing lane in France as the suicide lane. In merry olde England, many times the drivers would encourage you to overtake them by slowing down and then indicating with a hand signal when it was safe to pass.

We stayed at Beaconsfield, located twenty-five miles northwest of London. It was a beautiful town of about twelve thousand people, and it had a pub—the Royal Standard of England, which was the oldest freehouse in Britain at nine hundred years old. On the weekends, the pub was bursting at the seams, and the mini-skirt set was out in full force, which was a nice touch. In '66 in Britain, the beer wasn't refrigerated. It was served at room temperature, and you got used to it. I didn't complain because in the two weeks we spent in Britain, I don't believe that I ever woke up in the morning with a hangover. When we went into London from Beaconsfield, we used the rail system which was safe, convenient and cheap. One night in London, we had to hire a taxi to get home because we didn't realize that the trains shut down at ten thirty p.m. At first, the cabbie was reluctant to drive us "all the way" to Beaconsfield, and once under way I understood why. He was out of his comfort zone. It seemed forever to arrive at our destination. Although the highway was fairly straight, he didn't exceed forty miles per hour, and many times for no reason he would slow to twenty. Was he confused and thought that his meter worked on minutes instead of mileage?

In Britain, they have regulations regarding pub operating hours. To circumvent that, clubs have a scam where you can buy a "membership" in a "private club," allowing you to buy alcohol when the official pubs are closed. London is a great city for tourists, and we toured many of the must-sees while there. Dave's sister Sue flew over from Canada and was staying with friends in London at the same time. We rendezvoused in front of Big Ben one afternoon. Another day we had a nice drive out in the country to Stafford-on-Avon to watch a Shakespeare play, either Henry VIII part two, or Henry V. I can't recall, having lost my ticket stub, but regardless, we got our dose of culture that day.

And speaking of a different kind of dose, while driving north to

Liverpool after our London visit, I noticed that I'd developed an itch in the nether regions. Sure enough, while we stopped to gas up, I did indeed discover Phthirus Pubis, the dreaded crabs. It had to be that toilet seat in Luxembourg. I should have visited my good friend in the Luxembourg train station, the washroom attendant, instead of that sleazy bar. In Liverpool, we made a beeline to the nearest pharmacy, arriving there at five forty-five p.m., just before they closed up shop. There were four young shopgirls hanging around the counter, and the chemist was busy at his desk. Two or three of the girls asked if they could help me.

I said, "No, I'm just looking at these sunglasses on the counter," all the time trying to get the chemist's attention. Finally, he noticed me. I'm sure that he'd seen this many times in the past—a young bloke with a pained look on his face who would rather be any place other than his pharmacy. He very discretely inquired as to the problem, and I told him I had crabs.

"Crabs?"

"Yeh, you know, those nasty little critters, down there." That's when I noticed all the shop girls had very discretely disappeared. He told me they were closing in a few minutes, but that anytime after ten a.m. the next day I could pick up the appropriate cream that he would prepare. After applying the cream the following day, I thought at first that I was miraculously cured, but unfortunately it just slowed the critters down.

From Liverpool, we drove about fifty miles south to a quaint little village in northern Wales and stayed with Chris Brown's grandparents overnight. The next morning as I was shaving with my electric shaver, Chris' grandpa walked by wondering what that darn racket could be, so I showed him. I swear he jumped back two feet. He had never seen such an ungodly contraption in all his life. And I thought that I came from the backwoods. Chris stayed in Wales, and Dave and I turned around and headed north to Scotland. Just after we crossed the border into Scotland, Dave discovered that he didn't have his wallet, so we pulled into a police station where they phoned the station in the small English town where we had spent the previous night. The policeman drove over to the inn, and sure enough, there was Dave's wallet under the mattress. This was long before room safes became commonplace. Dave arranged to pick it up on our way south, so in the meantime he had to suck up to me because he was flat broke.

In Edinburgh, we found a cheap hotel close to Princess Street, the main drag. We saw Edinburgh Castle and Robert Louis Stevenson's home, but the highlight for me was walking up and down Princess Street and, of course, the pubs that we found there. In those pubs we heard the same jokes that we heard in England and Wales, only the nationalities would change depending upon what country you were in. It was Britain's version of the Newfie joke. In Edinburgh, the first line would be, "Did you hear about the English/Welsh/Irish lad who. . ." and in Liverpool it would be, "Did you hear about the Irish/Welsh/Scot bloke who. . .."

Edinburgh Castle

I quite enjoyed touring Britain. The people were friendly, and, in most cases, we could understand what they were saying or trying to say to us colonials. It just amazed me that such a small country had such a huge influence on the world. Military power to music to mini skirts, they were a force to be reckoned with. I'll pass on the cuisine, though. You can only eat so many fish and chip meals.

Once we arrived back at 3 Wing, I went on sick parade because I still had an itch. Wouldn't you know it, when I walked into the doctor's office, there was an attractive young female with an English accent, who looked like she'd just graduated from medical school yesterday. She asked me what the problem was, and I said, "Crabs."

"Crabs, what's that?"

Oh, no, I said to myself, not again. "You know, body lice, down there."

"Oh, right, CROBS, OK, let's have a look." She checked me out and said, "Sure enough, you have CROBS." She wrote me a prescription for a really strong-smelling ointment that had to be applied and left on for twenty minutes before showering. The only problem was, I had to get back on the road again and drive over to 1 Wing in France for three weeks' deployment. The runways of 3 Wing were being resurfaced, and my squadron, 434, would be operating out of Marville. After driving there and finding my room in the barracks, I decided that now would be a good time to de-louse because no one was there.

Into the showers I go with the ointment that had a smell strong enough to gag a goat. Half an hour later, I was drying myself off when I heard this big booming voice.

"Who the hell's got crabs in here?"

I walked out of the shower stall to find six airmen at the wash basins cleaning up after their shift. All eyes turned towards me. "I got it off a toilet seat in Luxembourg."

This big burly guy replied, "Ya sure, buddy. That's what I told my wife, too."

COLD WAR BRIDES, THE THREE STOOGES AND SPORTS

In '66, we saw less and less of Bob Lake unless we ran across him at work. Bob was always shy with the fair sex, like me, but in a small village close to Zweibrücken, he had met a young *Fraulein* who was consuming much of his time and attention. It appeared that Bob was head over heels in love. He was doomed. Ursula, the girlfriend's older sister, was about nineteen years old and a real looker. She probably spent most of her pay cheques on the latest fashions, make-up and hair. Bob and I double-dated with the sisters on two different occasions, both times on hot summer days at the outdoor swimming pool on the base at 3 Wing. Ursula could really fill out a swimsuit. She was way out of my league, and it didn't take me long to figure it out, especially when she mentioned that she was hoping to meet and marry an American who would be her ticket to Hollywood. Ursula honestly believed that she had what it took to become a movie star in the States. The swimming pool was a good start because 3 Wing was a nuclear base and had quite a few USAF M.P.s and bomb custodians posted there. She would never risk ruining her mascara or hairdo by swimming in the pool but would just spend the afternoon lounging on the grass and hoping for her ticket to stardom to show up. Opting out of the double-dating scenario wasn't heartbreaking for me because it seemed that Ursula would be very high maintenance with diminishing returns. I very much doubt that she got even a sniff of Hollywood, but if she did, in all likelihood she would not have made it much beyond the casting couch.

In August, Bob decided to get married. They had a civil ceremony in the village *rathaus,* the town hall, and the reception at the bride's home. Their home was in Germany, but in the past, it had been in France. With the history of wars in the area, the border was constantly shifting. According to Bob's father-in-law, at that moment, the house was smack dab right on the border, so the front door opened in Germany, but if you walked out the back door, you would be in France. Five of us from the base went to Bob's wedding, and he appreciated the support because he seemed overwhelmed by it all. At the reception, we were the perfect guests, sampling the cognac and trying a slice or more of each German torte that was offered. There were at least six different tortes, traditional German multi-layered cakes with whipped cream, mousses, jams and fruit. For Bob's sake, I hoped that *Frau* Lake was as handy in the kitchen as her mother was.

In order for a Canadian serviceman to marry a European, he had to have prior approval from the military, but I believe that Bob missed that one little formality. Just a few days after the blessed event, it was discovered that *Frau* Lake had some distant relatives living in East Germany. This was a no-no, especially since 3 Wing was a NATO base with nuclear capabilities. Within the week, Bob and his new wife were shipped back to Canada, ending up in Winnipeg. It must have been a real shock to her system, but at least it wasn't like the war brides of the '40s who found themselves trying to survive out on the wind-swept prairie, miles from civilization.

In late September, Dave Clark, Rick Kell and I wanted to see Oktoberfest, the famous Munich beer fest. We arrived early on Saturday afternoon, so we had a chance to tour the notorious Nazi concentration camp at Dachau, a few miles out of Munich. From the greeting at the main gate "*Arbeit Macht Frei*" (work sets you free), to the "River of Blood," to the ovens, it was a depressing experience, definitely not a highlight of my three years in Europe. Dachau was the crown jewel of the SS concentration camps, and it left us with a horrible feeling. I was ready for a few beers after that tour.

The beer tents on the Oktoberfest fair grounds were enormous and the *oompah* bands extra loud to compete with all the beer-guzzling, *lederhosen*-clad folks. Throw in the Bavarian hats, the *weisswust* and *knodel* dumplings, and the blonde *Frauleins* bringing the one litre steins of beer to your table, and you have a party, a gigantic one. Everyone told us that it was impossible to steal one of these beer mugs, but I was out to prove them wrong. I scored four that night, two for myself and one each for the guys. I worked the "stumbling drunk" move to perfection. I would approach the exit, weaving all over with an empty stein, take an imaginary sip, then stumble and spin around and with my back to the doorman, hide the stein under my jacket, regain my footing, then stumble out the exit. It worked every time. Once outside, I would hide the souvenir under a tent flap and then walk back in for another go.

It was getting late, so after a few beers and sausages, we left the fairgrounds and looked for a hotel. Good luck on an Oktoberfest weekend. Six to seven million people swarm into Munich for the beer fest; consequently, there wasn't a single room left to be had in the entire area. We had a two-man pup tent and sleeping bags, so we needed only a quiet place out in the country. I drove west out of Munich, turning left onto a road that looked promising. There was no moon, and the skies were overcast, so we would be pitching the tent in almost complete darkness. Rick lost the coin toss, so he ended up sleeping on the back seat of the Volvo. It was ironic and bad luck for Rick that the tallest guy would be occupying the smallest space to crash. Even though it had rained lightly earlier on, we had one heck of a time driving the tent pegs into the rocky ground. I didn't have a hammer. I was using the largest wrench from my tool box. Then Dave had the bright idea of using his Hofbrau beer stein as a hammer, the same stein that I'd risked life and limb to steal from Oktoberfest. Naturally, after a few taps, it shattered. Dave grabbed the next mug which happened to be mine. I cursed him and he reciprocated and then push came to shove with a few punches thrown in for good measure. It was like a scene from the *Three Stooges* with Moe and Curly fighting and Larry watching. On a couple of occasions when I hit Dave, his glasses flew off, so we had to call time-out, get down on all fours and locate his glasses in the dark. Without his specs, Curly couldn't see much past his nose. Finally, after a few of these "equipment time-outs," Larry, aka Rick, negotiated a truce before someone got hurt. I'm not one to hold a grudge for long, but Dave was pretty heated so he grabbed his overnight bag and disappeared into the night. All night long we could hear traffic close by, and sometimes we could even see the headlights of vehicles. The next morning in the daylight, we realized we had pitched our tent right in the middle of the east-west Munich autobahn, one of the busiest highways in Germany.

Two months later when Dave finally spoke to me again, he explained where he went that night. By thumb and by train he made his way over to 4 Wing, and early Monday morning he phoned Sgt. McLean in telecom labs where he was working at the time, and asked for a week's leave. Luckily he wasn't working for Sgt. Lewis in line servicing because Lewis wasn't a softie like McLean. At one point, Lewis threatened to put Dave on charge if he was late for work one more time. Alarm clocks and roommates just couldn't get Dave going in the morning. Finally, out of desperation, he placed a glass of water on his bedside table and gave me permission to drench him if he didn't respond. After two near-drownings he finally shaped up.

The base hockey team, the 3 Wing Flyers, was a top-notch team that played against the other two Wings and held their own playing teams from Germany, France, Belgium, Switzerland, and Austria. If an airman with the Flyers wanted to extend his tour in 3 Wing, he usually had no problem staying an extra year or two. One weekend, the Flyers were going up against Mannheim, a top German team. It was a home-and-away series with the first game in the Peter Cunningham Memorial Arena at the base and the following weekend game in Mannheim. Our number-one goalie was Tommy Bell, a big loud boisterous meathead who was a real showboat and even drama queen at times. If he was playing in the National Hockey League today, he would lead the league in two-minute penalties for "embellishment."

For some unknown reason, the German hockey fans just loved Tommy. Many of his teammates couldn't stand him, but he was a good goaltender. It was a real tight game, and after a scrum in front of the Canadian net, Bell was given a two-minute penalty for delay of game because he purposely dislodged the goalpost from its mooring. Of course, he protested vehemently to the referee, pleading his innocence. He put on quite the show and wasn't letting up, so a few of the German fans started to whistle, and pretty soon all the German fans were whistling. It was a sold-out game and at least fifty percent of the spectators in the stands were German. In Germany, when sports fans want to show their displeasure they never boo, they whistle, and it was loud. That's when Tommy raised his right hand and gave the Hitler salute to the fans. And then it really got loud in there. After the game, our CO, Group Captain Laubman, apologized to Mannheim's manager and told him not to worry about the game next week in Mannheim because Spike Martin would be in nets and they'd leave Bell back home in 3 Wing. The manager told the CO not to bother coming if Bell wasn't playing. That's how much they loved him. Luckily, he didn't pull that stunt today because in Germany that salute is now illegal and is punishable with up to three years in jail. If you're a neo-Nazi over there, you don't want to be giving the salute with or without the *Heil Hitler* or *Seig Heil in public.*

As far as my own sporting endeavours, I played inter-section softball every summer with the Telecom Air team. I was on the 3 Wing basketball team but soon lost interest because riding the bench wasn't my thing. We had three or four American airmen on the team and some of those boys could flat out play. If you're well over six feet tall and have been playing since kindergarten, chances are you are going to shine on a basketball court. Dave Brown, who was also on the team, talked me into trying out for flag football in '66 and the following year for tackle football. I quite enjoyed it although I had a lot of catching up to do. I was probably the only one on the team who had never played the sport before. I was doing some of the punting and place-kicking duties and trying out for wide receiver. In my first game, when the quarterback finally threw the ball my way, I hesitated just enough for the sure touchdown pass to sail over my outstretched arms, so that was it for my stint at wide receiver. I was banished to the offensive line where I didn't enjoy the game quite as much anymore. At one hundred and sixty-five pounds, I wasn't the ideal candidate to be in the trenches. When we took on the Americans, I always lined up against this two hundred and forty-pound defensive lineman who had a nasty habit of sacking our quarterback. I finally figured out that if I fell down when he hit me I could slow him down because his feet would get all tangled-up walking over me, allowing our quarterback to hand off or pass. Anything for the team, but like I said, not nearly as much fun as being wide receiver.

Maybe soccer would be a more rewarding sport. I was having a beer with Mike Pierce in the mess one day when we were joined by his workmate. Young Jonesy, an English kid complete with a Yorkshire accent, was playing for the base soccer team. He mentioned that they had a match that weekend, and due to injuries, they were short one player. Like a nice guy I volunteered my services. We played against the local side of a nearby village on a damp Saturday afternoon. Their average age was probably close to forty-five versus our twenty-five, but it was no contest. The final score was four to zero in their favour. It's hard to score when you don't have the ball. I guess it was another example of young legs being no match for skill and cunning.

CORPORALS, CASTLES AND LIZ TAYLOR

In '63, Paul Hellyer was the Minister of National Defence, and to keep the Defence budget under control, he was pushing hard to unify the army, navy and air force. By February of '68 unification was finally passed in Parliament, and soon after the armed forces were wearing green uniforms. I don't know if unification was a financial success, but I do know it wasn't much of a morale booster. It was partially reversed in August of 2011, and the pigeons got their blue uniforms back. One move that Paul Hellyer made in '66 had the rank and file's full support. At that time, it wasn't uncommon in the air force for a LAC to retire as a LAC because there were only so many corporal positions up for grabs. On October 1,1966, all LACs in the RCAF and the equivalent ranks in the army and navy were promoted provided they had four years service and had passed their trade board exams. No more career LACs. Now there were just a ton of corporals running around. All chiefs, no Indians, so eventually the new rank of Master Corporal was created to fill the first level of supervision over the LACs and corporals. On that joyous day in October, we all invaded the Corporals' Club and started whooping it up like we'd won the Irish Sweepstakes. Not quite, but the brand-new corporals did get a half-decent pay raise because of the promotion. Since they were now instant NCOs, Rex and Rick Kell were buying the beer that night. The original corporals weren't all that thrilled with this latest arrangement, but there wasn't a damn thing they could do about it. They had to share their cozy little home away from home with Hellyer's Corporals.

In the spring of '67, Dave's roommate, Brian Cordingly's civilian buddy from Canada, was hitchhiking around Europe and popped into 3 Wing for a visit. It was poor timing because Brian was on duty that weekend driving brass around Germany. His trade was Mobile Support Equipment Operator or MSE-OP, which is a fancy military term for vehicle driver. Dave and I were given the job of entertaining Brian's friend, or babysitting if you will, so we decided to check out a few of the castles on the Rhine River. We saw one relatively small castle on top of a steep hill overlooking the river, so we set out for a look-see. There were numerous trees on the hill, and when we finally got to the twenty-foot wall, it was quiet, so we assumed that the castle was unoccupied. There was a large tree very conveniently growing close to the wall, so I climbed it, and just as I was about to step onto the top of the wall, which was embedded with broken glass, this little German kid popped up out of nowhere and yelled *"Halt!"* and then, *"Vater, Vater."* I knew what *halt* meant and I was pretty sure that *vater* was German for father, so I made a hasty retreat down the tree. As we hiked back down the hill, I could hear some cursing from up above, and then a crashing noise because someone was rolling large rocks the size of cannon balls down towards us. We had to duck behind the trees until he re-loaded, and then we scooted out of his range, *schnell*-like. It was obvious that wasn't the first time that he employed this method to repel invaders, because he knew what he was doing. He had plenty of ammunition, but thankfully he didn't use boiling oil. After that experience, we decided to go over to Heidelberg Castle that catered to tourists although it wasn't as much fun. Between the castle and the old section of Heidelberg, I went through two rolls of film. Situated on the Rhine river, Heidelberg has to be one of the nicer cities to visit in Western Europe.

There was a nightclub in Saarbrücken that was quite popular with the single airmen at 3 Wing. Most likely some of the married guys too. Rick talked me into going one weekend because of an exotic French dancer whose claim to fame was that in 1958 she was a double for Elizabeth Taylor in the movie *Cat on a Hot Tin Roof*. Taylor had a scene where she was supposed to walk up a staircase partially disrobed, but she refused to do nude scenes, so that's where the exotic French *mademoiselle* came in. Her *derrière* doubled for Liz Taylor's *derrière*. We had to wait until midnight for her act to come on, and by then, there was a full house. She put on a pretty good show, and when she finished, she wasn't wearing much of anything as she flung her unmentionables out into the audience. One of her frilly garters ended up by Rick's feet so he quickly stuffed it into his pocket.

There was a break between the dancers, so Liz Taylor's double went backstage to grab a dressing gown and then came back out to gather her clothes. She found everything but the one garter, so she interrogated us. Of course, we pleaded ignorance. Backstage she went and returned with a big flashlight. By then, two mean-looking bouncers came on the scene because the next act was being held up. All three of them glared at us, but Rick wouldn't surrender the damn garter. I told him that the bouncers would lay a beating on us when we stepped outside the nightclub, but Rick was determined. Meanwhile, I'd noticed six tables across from ours there were a dozen meatheads celebrating something and being quite loud about it, either a stag party or else one of the boys got promoted that week. Our only chance of leaving that nightclub with all our teeth intact was to exit when they did. We bided our time and finally walked out with our new friends at two a.m. As we passed through the exit, the bouncers were staring us down, but they didn't dare lift a finger. What some people will do for a souvenir.

IRON TRIANGLE AND THE DEUX CHEVAUX

James Patrick Gannon was a supply tech from Edmonton who came over to 3 Wing after a two-year stint in Summerside, PEI. He was a short good-looking guy, and you didn't want to tangle with him because he spent much of his spare time in the gym working out. Dave, Jim and I had many friendly games of pool on the twelve-foot table in the mess. However, Dave and Jim's friendship eventually soured because Dave thought that Jim was too aggressive. One early Saturday evening, Rick and I had just sat down for a beer in the Papa Club when Jim came in with a buddy visiting from 4 Wing. Jack was a radar tech and a former teammate of Jim's on the base biathlon team in Summerside. He was also a gym rat, standing a few inches over six feet, but unlike Jim, he was easygoing. They wanted to see the bright lights of Kaiserslautern further north, so we decided to travel together in Jim's Opel. I left my car parked just off Ixheimstrasse. The city, affectionately referred to as K-Town, had a population of a hundred thousand and a huge U.S. army base nearby. Ten miles west was the USAF airbase of Ramstein and the largest military hospital outside the continental US at Landstuhl, so we knew in all likelihood that we would find a bar to wet our whistle. We ended up in the heart of the "Iron Triangle" where the majority of K-Town's bars were located, many of them much bigger than the bars on Zweibrücken's Ixheinstrasse.

Jim was normally a moderate drinker, but this night he was really knocking back the beers and getting quite loud. At one point in the proceedings, our waiter cut us off, so Jim got somewhat belligerent. We knew it was time to leave when the waiter started waving a beer bottle at us after he cut us off. By then, Jim was three sheets to the wind, so I took over the driving duties. We stopped in Ramstein for one more beer and then headed home. As we approached Zweibrücken from the west, this married Canadian gal, who Rick and I both recognized, passed us in her car. We had seen her once in a local beer tent with a girlfriend, without their husbands. They weren't there for the beer, if you get my drift.

Rick jokingly said, "There's your chance Jim," so Jim urged me to overtake her, and like a fool, I passed her and then pulled over. Jim jumped out and started waving his arms to flag her down and damned if she didn't pull over, parking just ahead of our car. There is no shortage of fools in this story. She rolled down her window and Jim struck up a conversation that lasted maybe half a minute. I don't know what he said, but it couldn't have been too nice or too flattering because she got out of her car in a hurry and lambasted poor Jim upside the head. She tried to hit him again, but Jim being the gentleman he was, didn't strike back. Rather, he put his hand on her chest and gave her a good shove. Bad timing James. At that very instant, a US Army MP car was stopped at a red light not half a block away, and the MPs witnessed everything. The MPs were from Detachment 307, a US Army supply depot on the northside of Zweibrücken. I yelled at Jim to get into the car, which he did, but I couldn't go because the woman now had both hands on the hood of the Opel and was screaming like a banshee. I revved the engine a few times, but that didn't scare her off, and I could see that the MPs now had a green light. Out of desperation I popped the clutch just to move an inch or two. It was enough because she jumped aside, and I roared down a few side streets with the headlights off and made good our getaway. The MPs had two choices. Chase after the Opel or go to the damsel in distress, and fortunately they chose the latter. We worked our way back to my Volvo, swapped vehicles and drove back to 3 Wing like nothing had happened. Had I been driving my car for the K-Town caper, all four of us would have likely spent time in the digger at the guardhouse because there was only one red 544 Volvo at 3 Wing. Rick and I were driving by the front gate at noon on Monday when we saw the woman's husband walking into the guardhouse, no doubt now part of an investigation involving the army MPs and the air force police. I imagine that the wife kept a pretty low profile for a few months after that.

That was Jim's second incident in Europe involving cars. The previous summer, he was driving a '56 Ford in southern France en route to Barcelona when he hit a Deux Chevaux on a curve, totalling the car. Jim wasn't really hurt, but he was kept in a hospital under guard for a week until the Canadian Embassy could spring him loose. The manufacturer, Citroen, didn't build a very safe vehicle. In an accident, doors and fenders would be scattered all over the road. The Deux Chevaux means two horses in French, but in truth, the car had more than two horses under the hood. It had between nine and twenty-nine, depending on what year it was produced, and the '62 model had a top speed of fifty-two mph, probably with a tail wind. The standing joke was that it could go zero to sixty in one day. Among the nicknames the Deux Chevaux acquired over the years were The Ugly Duckling, The Frog, The Goat, The Flying Dustbin, The Student's Jaguar, and noting the canvas roof, The Rag Citroen, to name but a few. Rumour had it that it was a mail-order vehicle that you assembled at home with sheet metal screws—and a prayer. I couldn't imagine the Deux Chevaux ever driving in the inside—suicide—lane or for that matter even passing another vehicle unless that vehicle had two flat tires and they were travelling downhill with a tail wind.

CENTENNIAL AND SARDINIA

The summer of '67 was a busy one because it was Canada's centennial year. On Canada Day, 3 Wing had a huge parade with every province represented with their own distinctive float. BC's float had two sea horses, totem poles and a snow-capped mountain. Nova Scotia entered quite a stunning replica of the Bluenose schooner, and Saskatchewan really nailed it with a twelve-foot high model of a Saskatchewan Wheat Pool grain elevator followed by a John Deere combine. Every Saturday, a different province would host a celebration in the Junior Ranks Club. The week leading up to BC's big night there were signs all over the base warning everyone to watch out for fallen rock. At the gala event, Chief Fallen Rock greeted us at the door. He was Gordie Geron, outfitted in moccasins, loin cloth and a Chieftain's headdress. His friend Rudy Faezzler, wearing an animal skin and packing a club, was Fred Flintstone. The Chief and his sidekick Fred kept us entertained that night. Rudy, a skinny little airframe tech, was a natural comedian who

Bluenose Schooner

didn't need cue cards to keep you laughing.

That same week, a squadron flying Canberra aircraft from RAF Station Brüggen, located in northwestern Germany near the Dutch border, came to 3 Wing for a week to fly with/against our fly boys. Their ground support technicians were a good bunch of guys, and they never said no to a beer—or a party, for that matter. We referred to them as Brits or Kippers, shortened to Kip, for their strange habit of eating kippers for breakfast. After BC Centennial Night wound up, Rex, Rick and I, along with six Brits, ended up in my room where I had a well-stocked fridge, soon to have echoes in it thanks to our new friends. Rex walked down to his room and came back with fresh supplies, and Robbie, unknowingly, donated a few cool ones as well. It appeared that the Brits were going to pull an all-nighter, so in the spirit of international friendship, Rick emptied out his fridge before we ran dry. At day break, we went up to the mess hall for breakfast. Then someone had the bright idea to go swimming, so off we went in the Volvo and the Volkswagen, all eight of us. Rick bailed on us; he had no stamina.

Rex knew of a depleted rock quarry thirty minutes away that had been flooded, and it made an ideal swimming hole. When we arrived at ten-thirty a.m., we found out how popular it was. Even on a Sunday morning, we had to search high and low for parking spots. I was reminded that as kids, three of us would go swimming, and we had all of Twin Lakes to ourselves. By two p.m., we headed back to 3 Wing because it was just too hot, the beer was too warm and we'd been up for thirty straight hours, give or take. Back on the road, Rex led the way, but after a few minutes we pulled him over and kicked him to the back of the bus, where he promptly fell asleep. One of the Brits did the driving. It was an exhausting weekend, but we looked after our visitors. We were good hosts. For Queen and Country and Commonwealth.

There was an open invitation to visit the boys up at RAF Station Brüggen, so a few weeks later, Rick and I drove up for the weekend. They treated us royally, and two things stand out in my mind. First, the big hit that summer was the song "San Francisco"—wear flowers in your hair—sung by Scott McKenzie and written by John Phillips of the Mamas and the Papas. At a popular bar just over the border into Holland, a few of the Brits, male and female, raided the flower beds and wore flowers in their hair and sang a great rendition of the song, a cappella.

The second thing that happened turned out okay but had the potential for a disaster. Most of the British airmen didn't own cars, so I made two trips to transport them from their base to the Dutch bar. After the second trip, I parked in a stall, locked up and joined the festivities in the bar that was hopping by then. A few minutes after sitting down, one of the guys asked me for my car keys because he wanted his jacket from the back seat, so I handed them over.

Ten minutes later, a Brit ran into the bar all excited and asked me if I was the bloke who owned that red Volvo. "It's in the ditch!"

We all rushed outside, and sure enough, there was my beautiful car sitting in the ditch. It was no worse for wear, and, fortunately, it had been a dry month, so the ditch wasn't filled with water as it normally was. With a few guys pushing, I had no problem driving it out. My guess is that my "friend" was going on a joyride and couldn't master the left-hand drive, was too drunk to drive, didn't know how to drive, or all of the above. He was nowhere to be seen. He disappeared along with his jacket, but at least he had the decency to leave my keys in the ignition.

I spent the entire month of September on temporary duty at Decimomannu, Sardinia on an Italian airbase where the RCAF and the Luftwaffe, the German Air Force, practised live firing and bombing. I was now fully qualified for comm and radar systems on the CF-104, so I joined a crew of techs from 3 Wing, along with the aircrew and their aircraft, for four weeks in the Mediterranean sun. It was a tough job, but someone had to do it. Basically, it just involved starting, parking and refuelling aircraft with the odd snag thrown in to make it interesting. I doubt if I replaced more than three or four black boxes in the entire month. We soon found out that if we wanted prompt service from the fuel tender, we had to keep the driver well supplied with Players filter cigarettes. We even had a little wet canteen by our barracks and the beer of choice, Ichausa Birra, which was brewed three miles down the road was surprisingly good.

Decimomannu, which was shortened to Deci and pronounced Dutchie, was twelve miles north of Cagliari, the capital of Sardinia, and the bus ride to the city was an adventure every time. The bus would hardly slow down as it made its way through the narrow streets of Elmas, halfway to Cagliari. The villagers would be sitting on their front steps with their feet on the pavement and enjoying a quiet cigarette and maybe even a glass of wine when their day would be rudely interrupted by a noisy, speeding bus spewing diesel fumes. They would curse the driver and shake their fists, and the driver would curse right back at them and take both hands off the wheel to give an arm gesture that was a gross insult to the villager's mother. Thankfully, the driver didn't insult the man's sister because that would have involved lifting his leg.

Cagliari had some beautiful sandy beaches, and we would go for a dip in the warm Mediterranean waters. The Sardinians thought that we were all loco for swimming in September. One of the guys organized a bus tour that took us to various places on the island such as ruins of ancient villages that had been excavated.

Rudy Faezzler brought his camper down for the month so his wife and three kids could have a holiday. When he wanted to go fishing but couldn't get anyone interested, I volunteered. I figured that if the fish weren't biting, at least Rudy would keep me entertained for the day with all his stories and jokes. Fisherman Joe would be our guide. We thought that with a name like that it had to be a successful fishing trip. A no-brainer. Joe used to work in the mess hall at the airbase, but the rumour was that he was dismissed for pilfering food. He had a wife and four kids to feed at home. Joe now made his living hanging around the main gate at the base, trying to peddle touristy items such as velvet wall hangings, tapestries, sea shells and sea turtle shells to military visitors. He knew two commercial fishermen who were happy to take all three of us on their boat. We picked Joe up early Saturday morning and drove for at least two-and-a-half hours over windy mountainous roads to the fisherman's hut where we found diddly squat. No fishermen and no boat. We hung around for awhile until it became obvious that the fishermen were either fishing already or else Joe had conned us. I'm leaning towards the latter. All was not lost though because he said that his friends wouldn't mind if we helped ourselves to the eels and the crabs. The eels were funnelled into traps where they couldn't escape when the tide dropped, and the crabs were just babies, measuring an inch across the shell at most. A tad undersized, you might say. I couldn't see the point in taking these, but then again, maybe I wasn't the visionary that Joe was. He filled up a few buckets, covered them with sea water, and off we went with our day's catch to Cagliari.

His house was on a rocky beach where he set up a hibachi. Joe suggested that a cold beer would be nice, so Rudy and I sent the seventeen-year-old son to the corner store, and he came back with a dozen Ichnusa Birra. I thought that I would need some Dutch courage to sample our catch, but as we found out, the barbecued eels were quite tasty. The baby crabs were something else again. Taking Joe's lead, we just popped them whole into our mouths, shell and all, and proceeded to chew on them until we got all the juices out, then spit out the broken remains on the beach. Naturally, we boiled them first, and they didn't taste all that bad. Much better than the ones that Dave Brassard and I caught back in the Falls and had to throw in the garbage.

Fisherman Joe, sons and eels

On average, the Sardinians are shorter than the mainland Italians. Joe's family was no exception. He was short, his son was about five feet four inches, and his daughters, aged twelve, fourteen and sixteen, and as cute as buttons, were all well under five feet tall. The fishing boat that didn't materialize had been a disappointment, but the other damper on that day was when we noticed that Fisherman Joe's wife started carrying on and sobbing uncontrollably. It dawned on us then that Joe had a serious drinking problem, and we weren't helping matters. Rudy and I felt bad about it, but when we left, at least all the beer was gone.

After an enjoyable month in the middle of the Mediterranean, a C-130 Hercules was supposed to fly us back to 3 Wing on a Friday, but it was grounded with engine problems which meant that our flight was delayed by two days. Normally, we wouldn't have minded, but Saturday was the grand finale for the centennial celebrations of all ten provinces back at the Junior Ranks Club in 3 Wing. We spent Saturday night in the wet canteen at Deci instead, watching geckos crawl across the ceiling above our sorry heads.

AUF WIEDERSEHEN DEUTSCHLAND

After Deci, I had less than three months to go and then homeward bound. Three years went by too fast. Rex cheated the system. He married an American school teacher who was employed at the dependents school at 307 Detachment across town and was granted an extension. Postings were announced in October. Both Mike Pearce and I got Edmonton, my second choice. Jim Gannon and Rick Kell would be going to Trenton, Ontario. Dave ended up with St. Hubert, Quebec, but it didn't really have much of a consequence because he wasn't re-signing after his initial five years. A big difference between the Canadian and the US servicemen was that we wanted a longer posting and they couldn't wait to get home to the good old US of A. Perhaps it was that on average, we were better paid, better treated and didn't have Vietnam hanging over our heads. Every toilet stall in every bar in Germany was covered in graffiti, and the common theme was "short-timer" as in "PFC Jim-Bob Murphy short-timer—23 1/2 days" or "S/Sgt L. Stevens short-timer—1 month, 4 days." Another serviceman who got a lot of mileage in Europe was "Leroy." "Leroy was here" had to be scrawled in every can of every *gästehaus* and bar within twenty-five miles of a US military base. Leroy had no rank and he wasn't a short-timer.

By mid-November, the Eat, Drink and Be Merry season, *Fasching*, was in full swing again in Germany. On a Saturday night, Jim, Rick and

I went to the large hall in Zweibrücken where it seemed that every able-bodied person in town had shown up. Unlike the average person there, we weren't wearing costumes, just masks like the Lone Ranger. Three tables over from us sat half a dozen Canadian school teachers in various costumes and disguises. The teachers had a real sweetheart deal with DND. They signed a two-year contract to teach in the school on the base, and a huge perk was not having to pay income tax. Almost like getting paid to see Europe. When I had a closer look, I thought that I recognized the person dressed up as Heidi, wearing a blonde wig with pig tails and a Swiss Alps type dress. When I had a closer look, I realized that it was Frank Canty, my least favourite teacher of all time. I went over to introduce myself and I had the distinct impression that Old Frankie wasn't too happy to see me again either. I had never made his top-ten list of all-time-favourite students. Now that he was in Germany, I didn't feel quite so bad about heading home.

In early December, time was running out, so Dave and Mike talked me into one last trip in Europe. It was one trip that I soon regretted. We drove up to Amsterdam for a few days. On our final night there, we had just walked out of the Penny Bar when a brand new shiny Citroen passed us on the narrow one-way street. These Citroens might have been related to the Deux Chevaux, but that's where the similarities ended. The newer models even had a switch that adjusted the suspension for heavy loads or rough roads. In Germany, many of the taxi cabs were Mercedes, and in France the cabbies' choice would be Citroens. As the car passed us, I tapped lightly on its roof. It was no big deal—it had happened to me numerous times with my Volvo. But in this case, the car came to a halt and out jumped this young guy, Dutch-Indonesian, who was trying to impress his girlfriend sitting in the front seat. First, he started screaming at me in a foreign language, and then he swung and kicked at me, but did not land any blows. My back was up against a building, dodging his wild swings, and within seconds, a semi-circle of onlookers, three deep, pressed in close. I had no trouble with his attempts to hit me because I was putting on my best impression of Muhammad Ali. "Float like a butterfly" and "Rope-a-dope" or maybe just plain "dope." Suddenly, out of nowhere, a fist came out of the crowd and connected with my mouth, breaking both front teeth. The body attached to that fist was short and built like a sumo wrestler with martial arts training. I was somewhat dazed, but fortunately a big Dutch cop appeared on the scene within seconds and told everyone, me included, to take a hike. The guy who nailed me was a compatriot of the Citroen driver, probably his buddy, and to his credit he knew how to throw a punch. When we caught up with Rick Kell in 3 Wing a few days later, he agreed with us that the guy was definitely into martial arts, and it was likely karate. For a day or two, I was on a plastic-straw, liquid-lunch diet. The only positive about our final European trip was that my car started right away the next morning instead of my normal routine of drying out the distributor with tissue paper. On Monday, when I checked in on dental parade, I was told that because I was now a short-timer, all they could do was make me a temporary partial denture which meant that I couldn't eat with it in place. Even laughing caused the temp to fall out, although, at the time, I didn't have much to laugh about.

A few short days after coming back from Holland, I headed west to Le Havre to ship my car to Canada. We had been warned not to leave anything of value in the car because chances were, when you claimed the car in Trenton, it would be gone, courtesy of either the longshoremen at Le Havre or Montreal or else the ship's crew. I left a cheap two-dollar emergency flashlight attached to the back ledge of the car and even that was taken. We were also told that smuggling alcohol and cigarettes into the country wasn't a good idea. I don't know if it was the truth or an urban legend, but apparently an airman filled up a one-hundred foot clear garden hose with vodka and stored it in his travel trailer that he shipped home. When the Canada Custom boys moved the hose, they noticed one tiny little air bubble in it which didn't bode well for the airman.

I dropped off the car in Le Havre then took the train back to Zweibrücken. Just before I took the bus to Marville to catch the service flight to Trenton a week later, a message came in informing me that my car sailed across the Atlantic twice, and was now back in Le Havre because of a wildcat longshoreman's strike in Montreal. That meant that I would be travelling to Vancouver for my two weeks' disembarkation leave, report for duty in Edmonton, and then try to find time to pick up my car in Trenton to drive it west. It was with mixed emotions when I boarded the aircraft in

Marville to fly to Canada. Happy to be going home but sad to be closing this three-year chapter in my life. Many of the airmen in 3 Wing I would never see again. I really enjoyed my stay in Germany. Zweibrücken's location was perfect because it was so central and accessible to many of the European countries. The countryside surrounding our base was mainly small farms in rolling hills, and I just loved the villages. After WWII, the Germans didn't waste any time building the country back up again. It was common to see *hausfraus* sweeping the streets in front of their homes. I liked the Germans—they had to be okay. My great-grandfather was born there. I had only two regrets: I never toured the Scandinavian countries, and I didn't take advantage of the ski hills in Austria and Switzerland. When we landed in Trenton, Rick collected me and drove me over to the transit barracks. He had returned three weeks before me and had already bought a car.

Dave Clarke had to remain in 3 Wing a few extra weeks to straighten out a car insurance claim with *Herr* Winter and Zurich Insurance. He had fantasized that his name was Jim Clark, the famous Grand Prix driver, and tried to beat his friend Mike Beard's time on the back road between K-Town and Zwiebrüchen. Mike won. Night time, windy road, wet conditions, unforgiving tree and a few beers resulted in Dave's Fiat totalled. At least he wasn't hurt, just his bank account.

BACK HOME

The day after I landed in Trenton, Rick was driving me to the train station when we went right by the compound where the overseas cars were stored. Rick glanced over at the compound and commented that I wasn't the only Canadian who drove a 544 red Volvo in Europe. On closer inspection, we noticed that the licence plate number was AF35178. What a coincidence. Then I got slightly hot under the collar because I was minutes from buying a train ticket to the west coast. It turned out that after approximately ten cars were unloaded in Montreal, the longshoremen struck, so the freighter sailed back to France with the remaining cars instead of waiting out the labour dispute. Talk about a serious lack of communication. Naturally, the battery was as dead as a doornail, so I had to get a boost. The longshoremen probably ran the battery down trying to start it and had to push the car off the boat and onto a car trailer, which wouldn't have pleased them. "We'll fix you," they most likely said, and then stole my flashlight.

Even though it was practically the middle of winter, the drive west was better than I expected. I was wondering what happened to all those snow storms that I'd encountered a few years previously while hitchhiking, but I certainly wasn't complaining. Once out of southern Ontario, and especially on the open prairies, compared to Europe, it seemed so quiet on the highway, almost like the country was on strike. In Regina, I stayed with Uncle Ian for the night. Uncle Archie was in Indio, California. Aunt

Marge gave me her son Gordon's phone number and address in Calgary and insisted that I stay overnight with him, but when I arrived in Calgary, there was still a bit of daylight left. Never having met this particular cousin, I decided to keep going. In Banff, I picked up a hitchhiker, and halfway between Golden and Revelstoke in the Roger's Pass, I hit a patch of black ice and spun around, damaging my back fender slightly on a guard rail. If not for that guard rail my story would have ended right there and then.

When I told the hitchhiker that Revelstoke would be it for me, he replied, "It's okay, I'll drive." I told him, "No thanks, pal. Black ice and night driving are a deadly combination." Finally, at the mature age of twenty-four I was starting to use some common sense. Other than that unsettling incident, the drive to Vancouver was uneventful. Mom and Dad were living on Old Yale Road in Surrey by then, having moved within the year. Dad took earlier retirement because of abdominal injuries he suffered in a mill accident in the early '60s during a big maintenance project on a paper machine. Lyle Green's father Woody, the leadhand, was operating an overhead crane that crushed Dad. Dad was flown to Vancouver for emergency surgery, and his stomach was never quite right after that.

My brother Don was now working for Crown Zellerbach as a mechanical engineer in its paper mill in Campbell River, and he also happened to be in Surrey on two weeks' holidays. They all wondered about my teeth, or lack thereof, so I told everyone that football sure was a rough sport, not for the faint of heart.

I was there less than a day when Don asked me to drive him to Whistler where he'd been skiing and had to leave his car due a transmission problem. Over the years, he was plagued with transmission woes on various cars. Don and automatic transmissions just didn't get along. By then, I'd had enough of my Volvo's starting problems in damp weather, so I dropped it off at a dealership in Vancouver. After almost three years of grief and two different auto mechanics in Germany, the mechanic found the fault in five minutes. With a bit of dye and an ultraviolet light, he detected a hairline crack in the distributor cap that wasn't obvious to the naked eye. A five-dollar fix—plus labour. Being in the car-repair business on the "wet" coast, they had no doubt run across that problem more than a few times.

While we were both in Vancouver, Don thought that it would be a perfect opportunity to visit Babe Wooley and his family in Coos Bay, Oregon. Babe, his parents and three brothers had come up to Canada where they ran their own logging show for a number of years in the vicinity of Ocean Falls. Eventually, the brothers and parents made their way back to the States, but Babe stayed on, logging with a cat and sometimes being helped out by Howie Smith and Ken Lessard. I played basketball two seasons with Babe, and although only five feet eight inches, he was built solidly and was hard to stop, especially in close. We also discovered that he wasn't one to get into a snowball fight with because he was deadly accurate and had a rocket launcher for an arm.

Since the trip was more than five hundred miles, we got an early start. I suggested that we would share any speeding tickets along the way. After three hours, Don took over the driving duties. Not five minutes later he was clocked at twenty-five mph over in a construction zone. I didn't mind the fine as much as the delay. We had to follow the state trooper ten miles off the interstate to a one-horse town and await our turn in court. We were lined up behind wife beaters, B & E artists, assault-with-deadly-weapon guys, you name it. Throw in a lunch break, and it was well over two hours before we could pay Uncle Sam and be on our way. Needless to say, it was pitch black by the time we rolled into Coos Bay. Babe lived outside the town on an acreage that had a small barn for his daughter's horses. He and his wife Peggy encouraged me to take their oldest daughter to the movies downtown, which I did. I don't recall what movie we watched or even what the daughter's name was, although Susan rings a bell. I can't be certain. We were only in Oregon for two days, just long enough to saddle up the horses, down a few beers, and talk about the good old days back in the Falls. That was the last time we would ever see Babe because a few short years later, he died in a tragic logging accident. An entire truckload of logs fell on him. Next to commercial fishermen, loggers have the highest rate of fatalities in North America. To top it all off, before Babe died, Peggy had developed multible sclerosis which was only going to get worse. At least she had relatives and in-laws in Oregon for support.

When we drove back to Mom and Dad's in Surrey, I hung around for a few days and then flew to Ocean Falls to spend Christmas there. John and Pat Riley now had two little ones, but they found room for one more, me, on the couch. Jack Cronin knew where all the parties were, so I was kept busy renewing old acquaintances and meeting new ones. It was at a late-night party that I was introduced to D, and we hit it off right away. She was three years behind me in school, so I hadn't noticed her back then, but she was very noticeable now. D was working in Vancouver but spending the holidays visiting her parents. We saw a lot of each other that week, but it had the makings of being a long-distance romance with my posting in Edmonton. Most of my old friends had moved, many of them to other pulp and paper towns scattered throughout BC. Even our faithful bootlegger, Harvey Werner, had flown the coop. There was no sign of Bozena around either, so it was probably another case of graduating from school and leaving as soon as possible before ending up married and never leaving. Roy Chernishenko, Dave Brassard, Archie Young, Lyle Green, all gone. Only John Riley and Jack Cronin were left of the old gang, and Jack would soon be moving to Prince George.

After Germany, the Falls seemed pretty dull and depressing. Ocean Falls was nothing to me now but youthful memories, and by 1980, it would be a ghost town. It was the people who had made the town, and in a few short years they would be leaving in droves. My time was running short, so I flew to Vancouver, stayed with my parents for a few more days, then purchased a set of tire chains for the drive to Alberta. Once again, Roger's Pass was a problem. With heavy snow coming down, I stopped by the restaurant/service station area of the pass to install the chains and have a quick bite to eat. By that time, the highway was closed until snowplows could clear a snow slide which completely covered all lanes. After a four-hour delay, I was underway again, and it was no picnic. I was stuck between two transport trucks in near-zero visibility, so I couldn't pass the lead truck. If I slowed down I was in danger of being clobbered by the truck following me. I was soon regretting my decision to get back on the road. Finally, I could exit at Golden. The distance was barely fifty miles, but it took over two hours and it was white knuckles all the way. That was the only occasion for which I used those chains, but they had been worth their weight in gold.

In ‘68, RCAF Station Namao was five miles north of Edmonton’s city limits. The runway was the longest in the British Commonwealth, and in the ‘50s served as a refuelling base for Strategic Air Command bombers of the USAF. The single men’s barracks were modern three-storey buildings which, thankfully, had only two airmen per room even though the rooms had four beds. My roommate was a quiet, older guy who worked in Communication Ground. His name was Stonehouse. I never did know his first name; everyone just called him Stoney. The first four months in Namao were spent working in aircraft maintenance. 435 Squadron had about a dozen heavy transport C-130E Hercules aircraft plus two WWII vintage C-47 Dakotas, sometimes called the “Gooney Bird.” The Dakota had quite a colourful and long history in the aviation world. It was the mainstay of the WWII British Army Air Support and flew the Burma Hump from India to China. It was heavily involved in the Normandy invasion on D Day in 1944 and was also a huge factor in breaking the Berlin Blockade with the multinational Berlin Airlift during the Cold War in 1948 and 1949. The Dak, acquired by the RCAF in 1943, was our main wartime transport and was finally retired from the military in 1989.

D and I carried on with our long-range romance via mail and telephone whenever I could find a serviceable pay phone. Initially, we talked about marriage, but that soon fizzled out. My first year in Edmonton, I had my fair share of courses to attend such as the Herc Comm course and various equipment courses, and they were all back east in Trenton. D had her doubts. Let’s face it, we only knew each other for a few days. Her grandfather told her to nip it in the bud if she had doubts, so I was now history. Grandpa was a wise old man, and I was still a free man. At first, when she told me to take a hike, I was somewhat bitter, but looking back I have to admire her for sticking to her guns. She did the right thing in the end.

HERCS AND VAN ISLE

In Herc Maintenance, we did all the scheduled aircraft inspections of various degrees depending on the airframe hours. These inspections could be between three days and up to five weeks for a major inspection. We could handle three aircraft at one time in our side of 5 Hanger, and if it was a slack period, some of us were sent home. The work could be as simple as swapping out time-expired electronic equipment to implementing complicated modifications on the five-week inspection cycles. In March, I spent the entire month back east taking the C-130 comm/radar course. One of my weekends in Trenton, Dave Clarke had some holidays, and after visiting his family in Acton, Ontario, he stopped at Trenton and drove me back to St. Hubert in South Montreal where he was posted. His five-year hitch was coming to an end, and he wouldn't be re-upping. At his apartment, we were just killing time until Dave could pick up his girlfriend at the Base Message Centre at midnight. He brought out his stash of marijuana and encouraged me to partake, but I graciously declined. I was a clean-living Canadian boy who didn't even smoke cigarettes. Then out came the hash and he started puffing away, so I weakened and tried it while listening to his stereo. I must admit that it was a weird sensation. My dilemma was whether to drive with Dave to the base and risk getting into an accident or to stay alone in his three-storey apartment. This was in the days when LSD was popular. Kids would get high and try flying off buildings, with predictable results. I opted to go with Dave, and if a traffic light turned amber, it seemed like ten minutes before we got to it. I was somewhat terrified. He was pretty mellow, and I was just yellow. That incident at St. Hubert was a one-off for me.

On my return to Edmonton, I was transferred to aircraft servicing which I quite enjoyed. I was part of a four-man comm/radar crew on a shift rotation of seven days on, three days off, then seven evenings on and four days off. Because the Hercs would be coming and going at all hours, there was a skeleton crew supplied by the day shift that worked midnights. After a long flight, the aircraft would land with multiple problems, especially the search and weather radar equipment, which we would have to rectify. In most cases, the equipment wasn't solid-state, which didn't help matters. We also did our fair share of parks and starts, refuelling, re-configuring the cargo area for either cargo or troop transport, towing, washing the fuselage, and my least favourite job, de-icing. One of my friends on the crew, Paul Ervin, an aero-engine fitter, was renting a two-bedroom apartment in Edmonton, and since his roommate was getting married in a few months, he said that I could take his spot, which suited me fine. Living in barracks was too structured for my liking although I could never complain about my roommates. None of them were drunks or slobs—or even drunken slobs like some of those my friends ended up with.

Talking about Paul, the Minister of National Defence, Paul Hellyer's brainwave to unify all three services came to fruition on February 1, 1968. First on the hit list were the rank designations which would now be army. No more flight sergeant in the air force. He was now a warrant officer, and a leading aircraftman a private. Even the commissioned officers were not immune to these changes. A flight lieutenant was now a captain, and a group captain a colonel. Later that year the new green uniforms would be phased in. The new ranks and new uniforms didn't do much for our *esprit de corps* in the air force.

Robbie's three years were up in 3 Wing, and he was posted to Edmonton, working in the engine bay. Probably because he was older than many of the single airmen, he was appointed Barrack NCO, which suited him just fine. He had a corner room on the ground floor that he didn't have to share, and even better, his room came equipped with a phone, good for his stock market transactions. The rest of the guys had to suffer with the pay phones. The few times that I entered his room, I noticed that his senator-like portrait which took pride of place on the wall was now being crowded out by his stock performance charts which he updated every day.

One Saturday night, I stopped in at the Rosslyn Hotel in north Edmonton for a quick beer and saw Mike Pierce sitting alone, so I joined him to shoot the breeze for awhile. After a few minutes I realized that I was doing all the talking and Mike wasn't responding, not even with an occasional nod. To this day I don't know how he managed it, but Mike had fallen asleep sitting straight up in his chair without falling over. I shook him awake and somehow got him to my car where he promptly passed out again. At the barrack parking lot, I couldn't rouse him so I had to sling him over my shoulder and carry him up to the second floor where he came to, thanked me, and made it to his room under his own power. Mike was no featherweight, and that sure didn't help my back.

In June, I took two weeks' leave to tour BC. First stop was Prince George where Jack Cronin was now employed in one of the pulp mills. Jack had just picked up his pay cheque, and no matter what we did or where we went, he wouldn't let me spend a dime. From golf balls at the driving range to a fancy steak dinner and all the beer that night, it was all on Jack. At that time, Prince George was booming, and the weekends were pretty wild, especially when the loggers came to town with money burning a hole in their jeans. Jack knew where all the "booze camps" were located—one was conveniently right next door to his apartment. The booze camps were Prince George's modern-day version of the speakeasies of prohibition, the illicit, unlicensed joints that stayed open as long as the customer still had money in his pocket.

If the cops busted the booze camp operators, it was no problem. They just paid the fine and started up again at a different address. In our wanderings that night, we crossed paths with Johnny Boucher, a steam plant engineer who also used to work in Ocean Falls. In the early '60s, he, along with Joe Desarmeau, was involved in a famous brawl that started in the Martin Inn and carried on right up Front Street past the hotel and the fire hall. Joe was a former professional wrestler who, a few years after that incident, tragically drowned while fishing at Twin Lakes.

I had to leave Prince George before Jack ran out of funds, so I drove west on Highway 16 to Terrace to visit Mary-Lynne and her growing family. By then my brother-in-law Tony, along with a partner, had started a company—T&T Sash and Door Co. Tony and Tommy. At Prince Rupert, I caught the BC Ferries boat down to Vancouver Island. Up until 1978 the southern terminus was at Kelsey Bay, about forty-five miles out of Campbell River. In 1978 a new highway was pushed through to Port Hardy at the northern tip of Vancouver Island where the southern terminus would be relocated. I don't think the Islanders missed their one-hundred-and-eighty-mile logging road that they suffered with for a number of years.

The ferry ride was overnight, so I had a cabin. I remember being awakened from a deep sleep the next morning by a P. A. announcement, "Would the owner of a red Volvo please report to his vehicle immediately." Then I realized that the boat wasn't rocking anymore, so I looked out the porthole and sure enough, we were tied up in Kelsey Bay. I quickly gathered all my belongings and ran out to the car, passing four other cars that couldn't go anywhere until I drove off. I was at the front of an elevated ramp, and if looks could kill I would have been a dead man. After driving off the ferry I pulled over to button up my shirt and tie my shoes, which allowed my new best friends a chance to pass me. All the drivers laid on the horn and shook their fists at me.

In Campbell River, I stayed at my brother Don's apartment for three days. Don could have used some of that good military discipline, both in his apartment and his car. He wasn't the tidiest of people. He was working until four p.m., so I drove out to Gold River on the west side of the Island. Gold River was a brand new "instant town" that sprang up in 1967 when a pulp mill was built, but the mill only operated for thirty years. If you're looking for inexpensive real estate today, try heading west on Highway 28 out of Campbell River. At that time, a section of the highway was being paved. Working on the crew was a character that I recognized. Chris "Shit" Sheppard was one of the flagmen, and he held me up a few minutes to shoot the breeze. Chris's father was the original "Shit" Sheppard back home. In England, he was a plumber, but when he came to Ocean Falls he became a pipe fitter in the mill. Young Chris soon inherited his father's colourful nickname. Back in Campbell River, Don and I had a quick bite to eat before we left for Cumberland where his softball team, including Ray Smith and Hank Modrass, also ex-Ocean Fallers, had a game. Cumberland's last coal mine had just shut down in '66, but in the late 1800s when coal was king, Cumberland was a going concern in the Comox Valley, dwarfing all the other surrounding villages.

After the game, we had no problem wetting our whistles because there were three licenced hotels in a two-block stretch on the main drag, Dunsmuir Avenue, in addition to a Legion four blocks further down. The next day, I was travelling to Nanaimo to catch the ferry to the mainland, when Don insisted that we have a round of golf in Courtenay before I left the Island. At Sunnydale Golf Club, I rented a set of clubs and a bucket of balls and proceeded to slice every second ball over the net and in amongst the parked cars until Don put a stop to it before I did some serious damage. Somehow, I survived the game, but I certainly didn't enjoy it. After living on the Island for two years, Don had became totally addicted to golf. It would take me thirty-five more years to acquire the affliction. I was just a slow learner.

Back at my parents' place in Surrey, I quickly became bored, so I phoned up an old classmate, Brian Hutchings, who was now a forestry engineer. We agreed to meet up at a hotel pub on Granville St. in downtown Vancouver that evening. When I drove there, all I found was a big hole in the ground. The hotel had burned down the year before. I gathered that Brian didn't venture out too often.

After my holidays, it was back to work and getting used to a whole new lifestyle of living off the base. No more room inspections and no more three squares a day at the mess hall, although I would weaken many times and buy a meal ticket. You can only eat so many beans and wieners and macaroni in a week. Paul's steady girlfriend, Bonnie, lined me up with her girlfriend, so we double-dated at an outdoor dance during Klondike Days. Marion was raised in rural Alberta, and how appropriate that her surname was the same as a farm equipment manufacturer, either McCormick or Comstock, I can't recall. We went out on three dates and she would call me John Deere, but I guess that I wasn't dear enough. There was no spark there, and it soon fizzled.

MISERICORDIA, MASKING TAPE AND TRENTON

In late September '68, I was in the Junior Ranks Club on a TGIF night having a beer with Pete Peterson. Pete was a skinny, six-foot seven-inch air frame technician who should have been into sports like volleyball and basketball, but he couldn't care less about athletics. His passion was cars, especially beaters, which explained the grease under his fingernails. Everyone thought that Pete was the shortened form of his surname, but actually it was from his first name, Peter. That night, on the club bulletin board, someone tacked on a poster advertising a dance sponsored by the Students' Union of the Misericordia School of Nursing in Edmonton. Pete wanted to go, and I decided to tag along. Friday, the 27th of September, would turn out to be the most important day of my young life because that's when I met Evelyne Dancause, a very cute, five-foot one-inch, shy and reserved first-year nursing student, who must have been impressed with my dancing skills because we were out on the floor a lot that night. Long tall Pete also hit it off with Brenda, a classmate and roommate of Evelyne's. Years later, Evelyne confessed that she wasn't even planning to go to the dance, but since it was a fund-raiser for the graduating class, the Students' Union docked the students' wages by the amount of admission to the dance, so she went just to get her money's worth. It's laughable to say wages. First-year students received a stipend of ten dollars per month, second year—twelve dollars and fifty cents a month and third year—fifteen dollars per month. It made my recruit monthly pay of eighty-six dollars look like a king's ransom.

The next night, I asked her out on a date to a football game, of all things. I picked Evelyne up at her parent's home shortly after supper so we would have a chance to buy tickets. With Hamilton playing, the game would probably be a sellout. The Hamilton Tiger Cats were a team that you just loved to hate. Evelyne introduced me to her family, and I quickly lost points for not speaking French. Darn. But I was back in their good books when I let it be known that I was raised Catholic. The family had moved the previous year from McLennan, Alberta, in the Peace River country so the kids could further their education after high school. Evelyne's father, Marcel, worked for Northern Alberta Railroad (NAR) for years and was finally rewarded by being granted a transfer to the big city when his children were coming of age. Evelyne was the oldest of seven kids, and eventually all four of her younger sisters would go on to university. I say eventually because her youngest sister Renée was still in diapers at that time. Both Renée and her four-year-old sister Carole were real cuties, but Carole, being shy, kept her distance. I picked up Renée and started bouncing her on my knee, which probably wasn't such a great idea because her diaper soaked through to my pants. I'd had worse things than that happen to me. Evelyne's mother, Germaine, was all embarrassed and tried to dry my pant leg, but I just laughed it off, hoping to earn some more brownie points. Those seven kids, Evelyne included, were as quiet as church mice. When she eventually met my family, Evelyne thought the two families were polar opposites. I always thought that we were fairly normal.

As we were leaving the house, Mme. Dancause handed me a large thermos full of hot chocolate for the game. I did manage to buy two tickets before the game sold out completely, but the seats were at least forty rows up where binoculars would have been handy. It didn't really matter to Evelyne because she'd never been to a live sporting event before and didn't have a clue what was going on even with my attempts to explain the game. All she knew for sure was that football was a brutal sport with everyone charging around on the field trying to maim each other. I wasn't paying too much attention to the game and don't recall what the score was other than Hamilton was really embarrassing Edmonton.

When I drove her home, we discovered the thermos bottle sitting in the car, unopened, so I emptied it out in the flower bed along the house on our return. I didn't want her parents to think that I didn't appreciate the hot chocolate. After we exchanged phone numbers and a kiss, I was on my way and already smitten, and I was hoping that it was mutual. It was looking like the coin that I'd flipped into the Trevi Fountain in Rome in 1965 was starting to pay dividends.

Soon we were dating fairly regularly, depending on my shift rotation. Every chance I had, I would take Evelyne out to get her away from the nurses' residence. Mrs. Casgrain, the house mother, kept a close eye on her charges. When I showed up at the residence, I would have her ring the floor phone for Miss Dancause. When it rang upstairs, there would be a mad dash for the phone, and whoever picked up first would holler out "Dancause," disappointing every other student who was expecting or hoping for a call or a visitor. Nursing students had to sign in and out in a log book, and if they returned after curfew, the house mother had them sign in with a red pen. There were consequences for infractions.

Shortly after Evelyne and I met, my roommate Paul and his girlfriend Bonnie were married, so I was looking for another roommate to share the rent. I signed up Rick Foreman, a young comm tech private—army ranks now—who was working in telecom labs. He was a tall, easy going, humorous guy who always saw the bright side of any situation. Perhaps because he worked straight days and I was a shift worker, but more likely because of his nature, we always got along well. Just three weeks after meeting Evelyne, Rick and I and two other comm techs had to attend a four-week equipment course in Trenton. There were more than a few tears, but the course was compulsory. I had to go. Orders were orders.

The other two techs were Noel Gauthier, an older master corporal, and Larry McGinnis, a young private who had gone through Camp Borden with Rick. Rick didn't know it at the time, but within a year he would be related by marriage to Larry. All four of us bunked together for the month, and if Larry wasn't in the classroom, you could always find him flat on his back reading a pocket book on his bed. Gauth soon nicknamed him "canvas back." He hardly ever even joined us for a beer in the Junior Ranks Club.

One weekend, Rick persuaded me to go up to Ottawa with him because he had promised a girl that he would be her escort for her Grade 13 graduation dance. After class on Friday, we caught a ride to CFB Uplands in Ottawa. Rick would be taking a bus on Saturday morning to a small town, forty miles away, so we had Friday night to kill. The Junior Ranks Club at Uplands looked pretty dead, so Rick suggested that we cross the river into Hull—now Gatineau—where all the good nightclubs were, and they didn't close until four a.m. One bus and a taxi took us to the area where we spent more than a few hours. Getting back to Uplands at two a.m., I noticed that one of Rick's shoes was falling apart. The stitching gave way, causing his sole to flap as he walked, or should I say stumbled. I steered Rick towards the line servicing hangar where I knew a skeleton crew would be on duty, and woke up the telecom tech for emergency shoe repairs. He unlocked his supply locker and I helped myself to Glyptal and masking tape and had Rick up and stumbling in short order.

The next problem would be getting Rick on the city bus just outside our transient barracks by eight a.m. I woke him up at seven and dragged and pushed him to the showers. As soon as I had pushed Rick out the door, I went back to bed for a few more hours. By seven fifty a.m., there he was out at the bus stop, hung over, unshaven, clothes all wrinkled (it had rained Friday night) and a shoe bound in masking tape. Once downtown, he transferred to a Greyhound bus and told the driver his destination, and before the bus left the terminal, he was fast asleep. On arrival at his destination, the driver had to go back to shake him. As he stumbled off the bus with a pounding headache and a seriously wrinkled suit, the only one to disembark, he looked around. An older woman got out of her parked car and asked if he was Rick. She explained that her daughter was at work and wouldn't be home until two thirty p.m. She drove him to their house, and after taking off his shoes, he made the mistake of lying on the couch where he promptly fell asleep for four hours, finally waking up when the girl came home from work. After supper, Rick escorted his date to her graduation dance and then stayed overnight with the family, returning by bus on Sunday afternoon to Uplands. I don't know if the mother was too impressed with Rick initially, but I'm sure that after his four-hour nap, he probably won her over with his wit and humour. Even with a splitting headache, he could always see the bright side. And on another positive note, Rick's shoe never flapped or even leaked again after that Glyptal job.

It was a happy homecoming when we landed back in Edmonton after a long month in Trenton. A surprising incident happened one evening when I showed up at the nurses' residence to pick up Evelyne. As I walked through the main entrance, who do I see waiting in there but Pete Peterson. I asked him what he was doing.

He said, "Waiting for my girlfriend. What are you doing here?"

Probably because we worked different shifts, neither one of us had a clue what the other guy was up to. Evelyne and Brenda were roommates, and each knew the others' boyfriend's first name only. That night, it seemed both guys arrived at the same time, so when the house mother called for Evelyne and Brenda, they went down the elevator together. No one had the faintest idea what was happening until the elevator door opened again on the main level. Two good friends were dating two roommates, and none had realized it. After that, there were frequent double dates.

After Trenton, Larry McGinnis introduced my roommate Rick to his cousin who was now in Edmonton. Gladys (we all called her Glad) was a tall, pretty, dark-haired young woman who had spent four years in 3 Wing as an air force brat; her father was a flight lieutenant in air traffic control. Rick and Glad were head over heels in love in a matter of days. Sounds familiar.

Once, when we went on a double date, Glad turned to Evelyne and me as Rick left the room and said, "Isn't he a hunk, a real hunk?"

Much to my disappointment, in December I was transferred to telecom labs. Now that I had taken the C-130 aircraft course and had a fundamental knowledge of all the systems, I liked working in servicing, especially the evening shift. On that shift, if all the departures had departed and all the arrivals were refuelled and de-snagged for telecom, the Sarge would send half of us home. Not so much with the engine techs because chances were that their problems were more involved and time-consuming, sometimes requiring engine changes and run-ups. In labs, I found it very frustrating to be chained to a bench for eight hours a day. To be honest, I wasn't the world's greatest telecom bench tech, and because the equipment wasn't solid-state, it wasn't all that reliable. Every morning we had a full cart load of radios to repair. It was easy to understand why the C-130s' communication and navigation equipment was duplicated, i.e. radio compass number one, radio compass number two,UHF transceiver number one, UHF transceiver number two, etc., etc. To make matters worse, the NCO in charge of the labs, Sgt. Ken Forner, wasn't the most likeable of persons. He was a tall, disgruntled man who no doubt had seen continuous service since WWII, and promotions had passed him by. We referred to him as "Lurch," but not within hearing distance. Lurch was the six-foot nine, scary-looking household butler in *The Addams Family*, a TV sitcom that was popular in the mid '60s.

At that time in the telecom labs, my back was really bothering me. Unfortunately, the military didn't believe in the merits of chiropractors, so I didn't endear myself to Lurch when I was granted sick leave for a week by the medical officer. The doctor prescribed pain killers and seven days of bed rest on a back board, which gave me very little relief. It would be another ten years before the air force came out of the dark ages and allowed servicemen access to chiropractors. For me, that made a world of difference, and except for the occasional relapse, my back pain is now manageable. When I showed Sgt. Forner the seven-day sick leave form, he came awfully close to calling me a malingerer but didn't dare because he couldn't argue with a doctor who was a major. A few months later, he got his revenge.

For Christmas Eve, I was invited to the Dancause family *réveillon*. This is a French-Canadian tradition where a large meal is served after attendance at midnight mass, and then the gifts are opened. With seven kids in the family, that's a whole truckload of gifts to hand out. As a guest, I was given the honorary Santa hat and the job of passing out all the presents. Evelyne's younger siblings could hardly wait to leave the table to gather around the Christmas tree, but I had no problem with the feast of turkey, *tourtière*—torture pie to you a*nglais*—and raisin pie for dessert. The food was wonderful but a lot to consume at two a.m. Madame Dancause was surprised when I insisted on helping with the clean-up in the kitchen. It was either that or fall asleep in the living room because it was three thirty a.m. before I could make good my escape. Evelyne reminded me years later that this was the only time I helped clean up after a meal at her parents' place. Once again, I was hoping to earn brownie points.

Twice in January, my service doctor, a navy major, paid us a visit in telecom labs. He was busy designing a prototype mattress full of styrofoam chips to treat people afflicted with back pain. Ken Williamson, our resident electronic genius in labs, built him a device to cut up the Styrofoam efficiently. The major would throw the mattress on the floor and have me lie on it and critique his brain child. He was even talking about eventually applying for a patent if it worked out. All this time, Sgt. Forner was lurking in the background, glaring at me and muttering to himself. He didn't dare say anything because majors always trump sergeants.

In February, Lurch really nailed me good. Because I was the only single comm tech corporal in the transport squadron, he submitted my name to go on temporary duty to Trenton to work in the light transport hangar for an unspecified period of time. The De Havilland Aircraft Company in Toronto sold a number of new Caribou aircraft to the Royal Malaysian Air Force, and Trenton was tasked with training the aircrew and ground crew from Malaysia. I thought it was a big joke because I was the only avionics type sent down from Edmonton, along with two airframe techs from Ottawa. Basically, it just meant that one out of the three servicing crews would have an extra comm tech—me. Just my luck. I meet the girl of my dreams and we would be separated by 2200 miles for who knows how long. Reality bites. The only good news was that the RCAF had just purchased five Boeing 707s, and every second day a service flight flew from Trenton to Comox, BC, with pit stops in Winnipeg, Edmonton and Vancouver. The next day it would fly back east again, and I could catch a free ride on my days off flying priority five, standby, which normally wasn't a problem. Because of shift work, every third weekend I would have four days off. It was an added bonus that Lurch would no longer be lurking over me.

I drove my car back east that same month so I would have wheels on my time off, and that trip seemed awfully long and damned depressing. And wouldn't you know it, it was another frozen trip across the Great White North. In Trenton, at least I wasn't assigned to transient barracks. I ended up in regular barracks in a large room with two others, and one of them, Stan, was a total piss tank. He worked in aircraft maintenance five days a week with every weekend off. His routine was to drink himself into a stupor every Friday and Saturday night and then pass out in the barracks, except sometimes when he wasn't too blotto, Stan would take a cab to his favourite Chinese restaurant in downtown Trenton. I saw him in there once, passed out face down in his chop suey. He never got the bum's rush from the owner because Stan was a regular and a good tipper. Maybe transient barracks would have been a better choice of lodging after all.

The Malaysian ground crew was a good group of guys, very friendly, very jovial, always kidding around, although I noticed that they didn't seem too friendly with the aircraft electrician. He was ethnic Chinese and the other six ground crew were Malaysian and Islamic. When they got tired of the mess hall food, Rick Kell and I would occasionally drive them into Trenton for Chinese food.

The odd time, I would see Jim Gannon when he wasn't either working straight nights or attending college in Belleville. After two years of college, he took his release and went back to his hometown of Edmonton where he finished his commerce degree at the University of Alberta.

The best part of being in Trenton was boarding the 707 on the service flight back to Edmonton. I had sublet my apartment to Don Feener, a young radar tech in telecom labs who was a friend of Rick Foreman, which meant that I had to sleep on the couch when I flew out west, but I wasn't complaining because I had the choice of either Rick or Don's car to borrow while in Edmonton. I saw Evelyne every chance I could, which was quite often. Naturally, we would drop in to pay a visit to Evelyne's family. When I spoke to Mme. Dancause, she would invariably ask me

"Why?" so I would explain "why" and then again another "Why?" and another explanation, and on it went. Finally, after about a year, Evelyne paid attention and clued in to what was going on. Madame's "Why?" was actually *ouais*, French slang for *oui*, much like our English "ya" for "yes." Everyone had a big laugh over that one. I had thought that she was a very inquisitive woman, and she was probably thinking that John is sure long-winded.

On one of my trips to Edmonton, Rick came in late one night and asked me if I could drive his Pontiac over to Sears at Kingsway Mall to have the alignment rechecked. Sears had just done a front-end alignment that day and it didn't seem right. He went to work the next morning with Don, so I drove his car to the service centre. To say that the steering was a little off would be a gross understatement. The car was pulling so hard left that it was all I could do to keep it on the road. Lucky that Sears was only about a mile or two away.

When the mechanic put the car on the hoist, he just laughed at me and said, "This car has been in an accident, buddy."

Talk about egg on face. Sure enough, that night Rick fessed up and said that the previous night on the St. Albert Trail, he drove through the traffic circle instead of around it, mangling a tie rod end on the curb.

In Trenton, winter soon turned into summer with no indication of when I would no longer be required to augment the Caribou/ Malaysian program. On a few occasions, I enquired about my status, and every time the master warrant officer said that I was definitely needed, which I knew was a complete crock. When the MWO went on leave, a warrant officer from 10 Hanger came down to fill in, and right away I marched into his office to see what he could do for me.

The first thing he said was, "Who the hell are you and what are you doing here?" So I explained my situation. He went back to 10 Hangar, had a little chat with the avionics officer, and when he returned he asked me, "Cpl. Forbes, when would you like to leave?"

I replied, "Today."

"OK," he said. It was that easy—no thanks to the MWO. I had my clearance form signed in record time and was on the road by two p.m. My goal was to drive to Edmonton before Klondike Days finished so I could take Evelyne out to the exhibition. I made it with two days to spare but had more important matters to attend to first. Back at my apartment, I placed a nicely wrapped gift in the fridge and suggested that she check inside for something cool to drink because it was hot that day.

Evelyne said, “What’s with this package?”

“It’s a gift for you. Open it.” When she unwrapped it, she found a beautiful musical jewellery box that I’d bought in Trenton. When opened, a little ballerina danced on a small mirror in the centre. Then the waterworks started because taped to the mirror was a diamond engagement ring. Am I romantic or not? I asked her to marry me, and between sobs, she said yes. Even I got teary at that point. Tears of joy. We headed over to her parents’ house and broke the news. Much to my relief, they gave their blessing, although they were concerned that Evelyne would not complete her course if we got married. Mr. Dancause had to leave school in grade six to help support his widowed mother and family, so he was adamant that a good education was important. Evelyne assured her parents that she would carry on with her nursing career. We hadn’t even talked about the timing for this blessed event, but I was hoping that we wouldn’t have to wait until Evelyne graduated in two more years.

TYING THE KNOT

I started work back in telecom labs, and things were looking up because my old nemesis, Sgt. Forner, was now retired—talk about tears of joy. Woody Grant took over as NCO I/C of labs. I knew Woody from 3 Wing and although he was "strictly by the book," at least you could talk to him. After Woody's tenure, Larry Bonin stepped into the position when he was promoted to sergeant. Previously, Larry and I had worked together on the radio equipment, and I found him now to be very flexible and reasonable while running the lab.

Just before Christmas, Rick and Glad were married, and I must say that it had quite a positive influence on him. It didn't take too long for Gladys to tame Richard. Another one bites the dust. I signed up Don Feener to replace Rick in the apartment. He was an easy-going down-homer, and we got along okay, although later on I didn't appreciate it when his younger brother started couchsurfing with us.

Evelyne and I decided that June of '70 would be the month to tie the knot, but first she had to get permission, not from her parents, but from the Director of Nursing. The policy stated that the nursing students must live in residence. The first question the Director asked Evelyne was whether or not she was pregnant, which was a negative. Reluctantly, the School of Nursing gave her the green light. They didn't have to be concerned about her marks because she was always near the top of her class. After

Evelyne's first year of nurses' training, the new Misericordia Hospital was built in west Edmonton. She thought that she'd died and gone to heaven because all the rooms in the new residence were single occupancy, and they even came with a sink.

In April when the snow melted, Evelyne's parents drove up to the Peace Country to visit relatives, namely *Pepère* Isaïe Houle, Germaine's father. We decided to follow them. Isaïe Houle, aged ninety-four, was living in a nursing home in McLennan and was quite the character. Germaine was the youngest of his sixteen children of whom seven had died either at childbirth or at a very young age. Even though he had lived most of his life in either Saskatchewan or Alberta, Isaïe spoke only French, except for the odd English word. When we were introduced, he noted my surname and asked Evelyne in French if Forbes was a Scottish name. When she confirmed it, he said that he hoped I wasn't a drunkard. Apparently one of his many daughters had married a Scot who was known to take the odd drink.

I asked Germaine why her father had a non-French speaking retired farmer for a roommate. She replied that it was to keep the peace. With previous French speaking roommates, he would invariably get into heated discussions about politics and religion. *Pepère* didn't care for one of the nursing sisters at the residence, so occasionally he would whack her across the back side with his cane when they passed in the hallway. Unfortunately, the old man died about six weeks before we married.

One of Evelyne's favourite aunts, Yvonne Lamoureux, lived with her husband, Narcisse, on a farm four miles from McLennan. He was originally from the tiny hamlet of Lamoureux, founded in 1872 on the west side of the North Saskatchewan River, across from Fort Saskatchewan, Alberta. Evelyne always got a kick out of the way our friends pronounced Lamoureux. It was "La-more-ay" to them, and not "La-moor-œ."

In the '80s, while high up on a ladder repairing his roof, Narcisse fell on his wife who was steadying the ladder down below. He survived the fall, but Yvonne suffered a broken back and was never to walk again, except very painfully with a walker. She was a very determined, feisty woman who was convinced that she would improve and walk again if she continued doing her physio exercises. After Narcisse died in '88, Yvonne lived alone for many years in her farmhouse. We attended a family picnic on the farm once in the '90s. She had cleared her backyard of all the wild shrubs, working on hands and knees, sometimes using her small chain saw. Later in life, Len Lamoureux, a WWII Army veteran who was in the battle of Ortona in Italy, would show up in her life and make things a lot easier for Yvonne. Len, a cousin of her deceased husband, had a truck camper and would drive her all over northern Alberta, visiting relatives and such. It was great to see Len treating Yvonne like a princess, carrying her up and down stairs, and helping her in every way possible. She never seemed to lose her spirit and kept trying to regain the use of her legs up until her death at age ninety. Yvonne was a lesson to us all, determined to the end.

One of Germaine's older brothers, Raymond Houle, had a potato farm that was fifteen miles south of McLennan by the tiny hamlet of Guy. Hands down, he was my favourite uncle-in-law. He was a natural storyteller with a memory like an elephant. Fifty years after the fact, Raymond could describe a neighbour's cabin and family to the smallest detail. That would include the dimensions of the log cabin, all the kids' names and ages and who died in what year and from what illness. And that was when good Catholics had huge families. Since the Peace River country is so far north and gets substantially more sunlight, crop yields are much higher. Raymond's potatoes dwarfed those in southern Alberta, but he always had to contend with early frosts. If the frost was severe, he could lose his entire crop in a heartbeat. It was a hit-and-miss operation. Finally in the late '70s, after too many misses, he sold his farm and moved down the road to Valleyview, where both he and his wife Bernadette found work. They bought a house trailer and moved onto their son Ron's acreage where Ron and his wife Irm had built a house. The couple now had three boys. In '79, all seven of them packed up and moved west to Victoria. Ron spent some years in the RCAF in the mid '50s but didn't really care for the life. He wasn't a "lifer" like I would be. Before Prime Minister John Diefenbaker scrapped the Avro Arrow project at Malton, Ontario, Ron was involved in the program as an aircraft electrician.

In early May '70 I was sent to Fort Irwin, California, for six days as ground support for the C-130 Hercs that were airlifting Canadian troops and their armoured vehicles to train with the US Army in desert warfare. Fort Irwin is basically in the middle of nowhere—the Mojave Desert—about twenty-seven lonely miles north of Barstow. The Hercs used an ancient dried-out lake as a runway. The four turbo props on the aircraft created quite a dust storm on Bicycle Lake on landing and takeoff, and that, coupled with the heat, didn't make for a very enjoyable time for the ground crew. After four days of eating dust, we were going stir crazy, so we took the military bus into Barstow and rented a car, heading south on Interstate 15. An hour and a half later we ended up in Ontario, California, where we downed two cold beers each and then drove back to Barstow. That was a lot of time and money to quench our thirst. We should have stayed put in lovely downtown Barstow. My lasting impression of the place was that of a run-down small city with miles and miles of railroad track for the numerous trains that rolled through there day and night.

Back in Edmonton, Evelyne and I were preparing for our nuptuals on the 27th of June. Her mother sewed a beautiful satin wedding gown with a long train and twelve-foot veil. In the spring, the Feener brothers moved out—Don tied the knot, and Don's friend Mike took his spot in the apartment. I'm beginning to see a pattern here. First Paul Ervin's roommate married, then Paul, followed by Rick Foreman, now Don and soon to be John. I swear that Mike only owned two pairs of socks that he rotated every day, throwing one pair into the corner and wearing the other pair. When Mike moved back to barracks in early June, I ended up with three rooms of furniture for our new apartment. Part of the monthly rent was for the rent-to-own furniture, and over the years, I and my roommates had paid off about ninety-five percent of it. It wasn't our first choice of furniture, but for thirty dollars extra, we weren't about to get too picky.

At seven p.m. on the 27th of June 1970, I was standing at the altar of St. Pius X Catholic church with my best man, cousin Neil Gourlie, along with Mike Pierce. Traditionally, the bride is a little late, but in this case it was the priest, Evelyne's uncle, Father Arthur Houle. He was visiting from Montreal and hadn't been given a key for the regular priest's office, and so there was no Bible or Office of the Sacrament of Marriage available. After a stressful few minutes, my father-in-law-to-be ran back to his house two blocks away and saved the day by bringing back the family Bible.

Father Houle attended seminary in Hales Corner, Wisconsin and spent his entire ministry in Quebec. He had never performed a marriage ceremony in English before. Finally, at seven ten p.m., Marcel was walking Evelyne down the aisle accompanied by bridesmaids Brenda, her former roommate, and her sister Rolande as well as little sister Carole, flower girl, and little brother Gilles, ring bearer. Understandably, Evelyne's uncle was a little nervous during the ceremony.

At one point, he asked, "Evelyne, do you take John to be your lawfully wedded wife?" Years later I would kid Evelyne and say that due to that gaffe we were not legally married. Half of the folks in the pews hadn't noticed that mistake, but they did when he asked her to repeat, "In sickness and in death." Then there was a lot of tittering going on, but like a trooper, Father Houle carried right on and got the job done. Out of four airmen who attended the Misericordia Nursing Students' dance that fateful day in September of '68, three of us would eventually marry three of those nursing students. Must have been a trap, but I didn't put up much of a fight.

For the wedding reception, we had rented the neighbourhood community hall that easily accommodated the one hundred and twenty guests. Eight of my relatives from Saskatchewan were there as well as two cousins from Trail, BC, and, of course, my immediate family. I was especially happy to see Aunt Margaret and Uncle Em make the trip because they were special to me. I had also invited some of the guys that I worked with in telecom labs. Evelyne had a ton of relatives there from all over northern Alberta, and it seemed like half of McLennan. A cold buffet was served at nine p.m., and I was responsible for providing the refreshments for the bar. Later, when the bar was getting low, Marcel somehow found more beer and wouldn't let me pay for it. Evelyne's parents couldn't do enough for us. There was always a stash of money under the floor boards in the front hall closet of their house "just in case." Just after midnight, we left the hall as Mr. and Mrs. Forbes, Evelyne looking fabulous in her new "going away" outfit and me still in my sharkskin suit that I'd purchased in 3 Wing. Ten years later she insisted I get rid of it in favour of a more updated look, which broke my heart. Pete Peterson and Marcel Bertrand did one heck of a job attaching the tin cans under the car because it wasn't until the next morning, when I wasn't wearing my suit, that I managed to crawl under the back end to cut off the cans with side cutters. The "adornments" had made a hell of a racket in the underground parkade. I had booked a room at the Chateau Lacombe just off Jasper Avenue, and when we rode up the elevator with two other just-married couples—the brides still had their wedding gowns on—there was an uncomfortable silence as we all stared at the floor numbers lighting up. I had tried to book a honeymoon suite, but none was available. I'd left it too late, and the Chateau was a favourite of newlyweds.

The next day, we had the gift opening in the early afternoon at our new apartment in the west end. Family and close friends were invited, and, thankfully, not everybody showed up because pretty soon the suite was wall-to-wall with people. At that time, fondues were the latest rage, so it was no surprise that we ended up with a few—five to be exact. We eventually re-gifted three of these fondue sets to some of our lucky friends. I still remember the discussion that my father and Evelyne's father had about how they were now related. They had to be in-laws, but it couldn't be fathers-in-law, so they finally settled on parents-in-law and shook on it.

On Monday morning, we left Edmonton, heading to Vancouver for our two-week honeymoon. The weather was good, the forecast great, and I had this wonderful woman sitting beside me, alone at last. Life was good. We stayed at my folks' place in Surrey because they were taking their truck camper into Saskatchewan to visit relatives. After spending her whole life on the prairies, Evelyne fell right in love with the west coast. If only she would learn how to swim. What she wasn't too thrilled about were the slugs that came out at night after sunset. In the slug world, the grass is always greener on the other side of the sidewalk. Evelyne absolutely refused to budge from the car if we came home after dark. Every night I had to give her a piggy-back ride down the length of the sidewalk from the garage to the back door. What I wouldn't do for my princess.

We met up with Pete and Brenda Peterson and took in some of the touristy things together: the Capilano Suspension Bridge, Grouse Mountain Gondola, and Crescent Beach in White Rock. We even got a chance to meet the wacky woman who christened Peterson, Peter. When my parents got home, Mom invited her two sisters and a brother from the Vancouver area to dinner and to meet her new daughter-in-law. Evelyne didn't know what to make of my Aunt Anne, a very devout Catholic and probably stricter than two of Evelyne's aunts who were Catholic nuns. Just before she died in her early nineties, Aunt Anne was still volunteering in the gift shop in a Vancouver church.

Anyway, after dinner all the women were in the kitchen cleaning up when out of the blue Aunt Anne looked at Evelyne and asked, "Evelyne, are you on birth control?"

You could have heard a pin drop. Everyone, especially my lovely wife, was flabbergasted. Aunt Fran, bless her heart, came to Evelyne's rescue with, "Frankly, Anne, it's none of your damn business."

After the honeymoon, it was back to work. I continued on in telecom labs and Evelyne worked the remainder of the summer in the operating room at the Misericordia, basically as free holiday relief for the regular staff. It was a real bargain for the hospital because Evelyne's wage that summer was twelve dollars a month.

The following June 20, the Class of '71 graduated. There was a white formal banquet and dance on Friday night at the Royal Glenora Club, and the grad ceremonies were held at the Royal Jubilee Auditorium on Sunday afternoon. The graduation at the Jubilee was a gala event that caused more than a few tears to be shed. The nursing grads looked fantastic in their white uniforms with the contrasting dozen long-stem red roses. Unfortunately Marcel missed seeing his daughter receiving her diploma because he spent half the time outside trying to console three-year-old Renée. She had gotten quite a fright when she woke up from a deep sleep to see a nun, Evelyne's aunt, in her black habit sitting beside her. She started screaming and wouldn't settle, so Marcel had to carry her to the car.

FIRST HOUSE/LAST MORTAGE AND ADOPTION

After her graduation, Evelyne stayed on at the Misericordia and worked on the gynecology unit. She found the work rewarding. However, she soon tired of the Head Nurse's authoritarian regime, so she resigned to take a position at the Edmonton General Hospital on the general surgery and thoracic unit. The General was located on Jasper Avenue, just a few blocks away from the original Misericordia. We then moved to a nicer two-bedroom apartment on Stony Plain Road, a fairly short bus trip to work for Evelyne.

The following summer, 1972, my cousin Neil phoned us mid-morning on a Saturday with a request. He wanted us to take over entertaining our relatives who were visiting from Saskatoon. Neil and his wife Marion, along with two kids—soon to be three—lived in PMQs at the army base in Greisbach, and they were worn out by Uncle Clem, his wife Kathy and two rambunctious teenage boys, my cousins. Clem was Uncle Em's younger brother, and Kathy was my mother's youngest sister. Keep it in the family. When they showed up at our apartment for lunch, I could see right away that we were in for a long day. Clem made a beeline to the couch, by-passing the kitchen table, and, ready for some serious imbibing, set his half-empty bottle of vodka on the coffee table.

There was only so much to talk about, especially when these folks were virtually strangers, so Clem suggested going to a pub after supper, which we did, leaving the boys alone at the apartment. When we got back home at nine p.m., it didn't look good. The main entrance downstairs had a large plate glass door, and four equally large glass panels alongside the door. The glass panel beside the door had a crack in it with a piece of skin attached, approximately nose height for a fourteen-year-old kid. There were drops of blood on the stairway, and I had a sick feeling that those drops would lead us directly to suite 304, which they did. Inside was one battered looking, shaken kid with a brother who was looking somewhat guilty. I assume that they had been horsing around, chasing one another when Miles, I think that was his name, had a violent encounter with the panel. I guess it was easy to do because my mother bumped into the same glass panel months later, but she was walking and there was no damage done. Shortly after we got home, there was a knock at the door. It was the building manager who had also followed the trail of blood to our suite, and he wasn't too happy. There was a shouting match with my uncle who wasn't about to back down from anyone.

The manager threatened to sue Clem, and Clem said, "Be my guest because I'll counter-sue in a heartbeat", but before things really escalated, the manager checked his building insurance policy and discovered, much to everyone's relief, that he had coverage, so they kissed and made up. Clem was due back at work in Saskatoon on Monday where he drove city buses, and we weren't too sad when they left the next morning.

That same summer I sold my trusty old '65 Volvo to Ken Williamson in telecom labs—it must have been cramped with his wife and their four kids—and I bought a '68 four-door Volvo sedan from another comm tech, Arlo Stade. Just after I bought the newer Volvo, Evelyne wanted me to teach her how to drive. The car had a stick shift and she was a little uneasy about the clutch pedal, so I was trying to talk her through it.

"OK, dear, push the clutch all the way to the floor and select the reverse gear. Now slowly, very slowly, let up on the clutch and give it a touch more gas. You can do it."

It was a short lesson because there was only one solitary tree in the apartment parking lot, and Evelyne backed the car right into it. End of lesson. On her next days off she went to a driving school where she learned on an automatic transmission and then mastered the stick shift in an empty shopping centre parking lot. Less stress for everyone involved.

Later in the summer we drove to northern BC to visit Don in Prince Rupert, where he worked in the new pulp mill. Then we headed back down the Skeena River to stay at Mary-Lynne's place in Terrace. They had originally come north where Tony found employment when the Eurocan pulp and paper mill was being built in Kitimat, and that's where he learned the carpentry trade. On the outskirts of town, Mary-Lynne and Tony had a small acreage that was big enough for their house and a smaller rental house plus room for a horse named Red, a cat, two dogs and, of course, my three favourite nieces, Debbie, Angela, and Lynette.

Sister Mary-Lynne with Debbie, Angie and Lynette

Tony loved his dogs. He found it hard to drive past an animal shelter or the SPCA When I went outside I noticed some green stuff on the sidewalk that I didn't recognize so I picked it up. Imagine my horror when I realized that it was dog poop. Hector, the German Shorthaired Terrier, was apparently helping himself to the horse feed, and the girls neglected to inform their uncle. The following summer poor Hector was dog-napped, but it didn't take too long for Tony to come home with a replacement mutt.

That horse was something else. My sister took an apple pie out of the oven and placed it on the kitchen window sill to cool, and Red happened along. I guess he figured if Hector could eat his food then he could chow down on real food—he had good horse sense. Red got a couple of decent bites in before the pie went flying into the kitchen sink.

While we were visiting in Terrace, Mary-Lynne searched high and low all over the house for her roaster so she could cook a turkey. Finally, in frustration, she yelled out the window, "Has anybody seen my roaster?" Dead silence.

Then Angela piped up, "Wed's dwinking out of it."

We bought a soft-top tent trailer and drove up to the Peace River Country to visit Evelyne's relatives. In the town of Peace River, we saw Evelyne's Aunt Annette and her husband Scotty Anderson as well as Uncle Eldège and his wife Jeanette. Then we set out to see her Aunt Yvette and Uncle Max at their farm, fifteen miles off the beaten track. It had poured buckets the night before, and the farther we got from the paved highway, the worse the driving conditions became, and the rain wasn't letting up. I was driving on what they call Peace River gumbo. The mud was so thick that soon the small trailer tires would no longer rotate, and eventually Evelyne had to sit on the car's trunk for traction, but her 108 pounds didn't do much good. I was travelling at a snail's pace and to top it off, my radiator started to boil over two miles from Max's farm. At that point, I turned the engine off and walked down the road to a farmhouse to ask for water. I should say half a farmhouse because the people who were homesteading there ran out of money after digging their foundation, and they were living in the basement with just a sub floor for a roof. When a woman emerged from the basement I explained my problem, and she said she would be happy to give me some water, and then she looked over my shoulder and burst out laughing. I looked back and there was Evelyne, struggling up the driveway in the gumbo, barely making any headway because her size seven shoes were now at least a size fifteen. She looked like one of those circus clowns with the oversized shoes, soaking wet, with mud up to her ankles. Even Evelyne had a good laugh over that. We pulled into her aunt's farmyard at least two hours after we were expected and had to wait until the following afternoon when the roads dried out enough to get back to *terra firma* and civilization.

During that summer, I was involved in two different military operations. The first one was in Thule, Greenland, called Operation Boxtop, lasting two weeks. Our Hercs were flying fuel and supplies around the clock into Alert on Ellesmere Island, the most northern permanent settlement in the world. The ground crew worked twelve hours on, twelve hours off doing parks, starts, refuelling and de-snagging. After he finished his shift, Noël Gauthier, now a sergeant, caught a ride via Herc up to Alert to visit his brother whom he hadn't seen in years. He was a communications research technician, nicknamed spy, because he spent his entire shift listening in on the Soviet Bloc countries, mainly the USSR. He had taken a yearlong Russian language course and then was posted to Alert for six months at a time. Alert was officially known as a "signal intelligence collection station." Gauth must have had quite the reunion because he was passed out in the back of the aircraft with his arms wrapped around Babette when he returned. Babette was a seven-and-a-half foot styrofoam cross between a playboy bunny and a giant rabbit. We couldn't figure out how he managed to smuggle his "girlfriend" out of the combined mess because it certainly wasn't under cover of darkness with twenty-four hours of daylight in the summer months up there. When the airlift was finally completed, we had a big windup celebration with a few games involved in the barracks. I didn't enter the arm wrestling competition, but I did go home with the Indian leg wrestling championship.

The second operation was Operation Strong Express, a NATO exercise that involved transporting Canadian troops and their vehicles from Trenton to Norway. My lasting impression of that operation, other than the de-snagging of aircraft, was the enormous amount of fuel that we had to pump into the fuel tanks for the long flights across the pond.

That winter, I started carpooling with Paul Durant who lived in a high-rise in downtown Edmonton. He was the master warrant officer in charge of the telecom, electrical and instrumentation labs on the third floor of 5 Hangar. Paul really encouraged me and my good friend Dennis Coughlin, an instrument tech, in woodworking. It was about that time that Evelyne and I decided that it would be nice to buy a house and build up some equity instead of throwing away rent money every month. And an apartment was no place to be raising a family. When I mentioned to my co-workers in labs one day what we were planning on doing, Wayne Kubala, a very opinionated master corporal, went ballistic. He told me in no uncertain terms that to be even thinking of buying a house would be the dumbest and most foolhardy act of my entire life. I should be renting a house in PMQs (Private Married Quarters) at the base like Wayne and his wife because the monthly rent was so cheap. Get a grip, he told me.

The next morning, he came to work with all the facts and figures to support his argument. Wayne must have been up half the night because he even found amortization charts to wave in front me. Two weeks later I brought in the signed real estate contract to show him the house we had just purchased. He just rolled his eyes and walked away.

The house had a lot of character and was well maintained, a craftsman style built in 1905. We had the hardwood floors refinished and then moved in four days before Christmas. On Christmas day, I found a flashlight and crawled up into the attic where I discovered a treasure trove of goodies. We had purchased the house from an estate, and the two adult children of the deceased owner divided up just the furniture and didn't bother checking out the attic. There were framed paintings and portraits. Also left behind were circa 1920 French boudoir dolls with silk dresses, one doll from the late 1800's, along with many old books, personal letters, blueprints and even detailed expense accounts of numerous houses, a hotel and an orphanage that the deceased owner's father, an Irish contractor, had built.

The letters we found told a sad story. The owner, Elsie Hall, and her husband, James Templeton Hall, a newspaper columnist for a Calgary daily, were separated when WWII began. He enlisted in the RCAF after lying about his age—he was too old for active duty—and became a tail gunner on a bomber. Then we read letters from the war office informing that his aircraft was shot down. A little later, the authorities thought that he was a POW. Later still, the Governor General wrote Mrs. Hall saying his whereabouts were unknown. Finally, at war's end, a letter from the Queen stated that James Templeton Hall was officially declared dead. After reading that last letter, Evelyne and I were both in tears. Three years later we looked up Mrs. Hall's son, who owned a pharmacy in southern BC, and gave him the bundle of letters, photos and portraits. He must have been shocked when he read all the letters because we found out later from one of our neighbours, Mrs. Cairns, that the kids weren't aware their parents had been legally separated before the war. Anyway, that was one Christmas day that we would never forget.

In our little old house, besides the beautiful oak doors and trim throughout, the other great feature we appreciated was the heating system. In the basement was a huge boiler, dated 1903, that originally was coal but later on was converted to gas. It ran a low pressure hot water heating system which was quiet, steady and toasty warm even at forty below zero. The wiring in our little house consisted of the turn of the century knob-and-tube system, which was pretty basic, so I decided that an update was in order. By then we were good friends with the couple across the street, Wenda and Reiny Lux. Wenda's younger brother Bob was an apprentice electrician who showed me the basics, and along with the help of the "Electrical Code Simplified" booklet for residential wiring, I figured out the rest and modernized our house. Evelyne was forever grateful that she could use the toaster in the morning with the kitchen radio on without blowing a fuse. Next up on the agenda was a project to create enough space in the basement to operate a table saw. With the assistance of my next-door neighbour, Andy Sinkovics, we eliminated a few posts and installed a weight-bearing beam that made a big difference. Andy was always willing to help or advise me. He already owed four older rental houses that he was forever working on, and he had a ton of experience. It didn't hurt either that he had tickets in both welding and plumbing.

With room to work in now, I was becoming more and more interested in woodworking, so I enrolled in a few cabinet making courses in the evenings at Northern Alberta Institute of Technology (NAIT). Then I bought a new table saw for the basement, but what really helped was when we flew out to Vancouver on the service flight, my dad insisted that I help myself to his carpentry tools. At that time, he was rapidly losing interest in the tools and instead would just walk around Surrey for hours on end, sometimes even getting lost for a bit. This was probably the early stages of Alzheimer's before the condition's name became commonplace. I knew one of the transportation techs, Hoppy Hopkins, who worked at the Air Movements Unit check-in counter at the airport in Vancouver. We had met in Marville, France in 1966 when I was on temporary duty in 1 Wing. Officially we were allowed forty pounds of luggage on the service flight, but I showed up at the terminal with a huge wooden trunk that Dad had built years ago, and it must have weighed two hundred pounds because it was packed full with tools. Hoppy didn't even hesitate. He quickly just put the trunk on the conveyor belt and winked at me. The following year when he was transferred to Edmonton, I paid him back in spades. I lined him up with a very attractive nursing aide who worked on the same ward as Evelyne at the General Hospital.

When I was in the car pool with Paul Durant, I mentioned to him one day that I felt that I had done my penance in labs and wouldn't mind a transfer to aircraft servicing. Just like magic, within a month I was transferred. It never hurts to have friends in high places. Shortly after moving into the house, we adopted a puppy from the SPCA. Duchess was the runt of the litter, a Heinz 57 variety who looked like a smaller and chubbier version of a German Shepherd. Over the years she was a great pet. When she was about four months old, Duchess darted out into traffic unexpectedly and was knocked out cold by a car. I carried her home thinking she was dead, but after thirty minutes she came back to life, with no apparent ill effects. Our street, 127 Street, became quite busy, so the neighbourhood organized and pressured city hall into making it one-way with numerous four-way stops, which made a huge difference in the traffic. Our argument was that 127 Street was mainly residential with three elementary schools and a hospital. Thankfully, the traffic engineers agreed with us.

In 1973, we contacted social services and applied to adopt a child. Final approval usually took at least one year. On April 29, 1974 at four p.m., I was flying out to Victoria and then to Abbotsford, BC for Waincom Deployment which involved airlifting soldiers from Victoria and Chilliwack to Wainright, AB for an exercise. That morning, social services asked us to report to their office in a west end shopping centre because they had matched us with a baby boy. We were ecstatic. At the office, a social worker brought in a tiny two-month-old boy in a plastic laundry basket, complete with an empty bottle of colic medication. He was pale and anemic-looking, and Evelyne thought that he looked more like two weeks old than two months. Social services wanted an immediate yea or nay from us. Would we accept this little guy and take him home? It's difficult to put into words how we felt, but we were so excited that after counting fingers and toes, we gave them a yea. Now we had an instant family. We signed the adoption papers and entered the baby's new name on the form—Colin John Andrew Forbes. Colin slept all the way home like a little doll, and I didn't see his eyes open for another six days because I had to fly out right away for deployment. Before I boarded the Herc, I'd bought a bunch of cigars to pass out to the guys. When we finally checked into a motel in Victoria four hours later, I phoned Evelyne and her situation didn't sound too reassuring. Shortly after my departure, Colin woke up and there was nothing that she could do to settle him down. Evelyne was near tears and Colin was inconsolable and appeared to be in pain. That evening, my in-laws came over to meet their first grandchild, and Marcel was pressed into duty, holding Colin and walking him around. That eventually did the trick, and Colin slept for awhile.

Evelyne had to resign from the General Hospital because at that time, social services insisted that adoptive moms be stay-at-home moms until the final adoption papers were signed. This took a year. We bought her an older model Ford so she could get out and about. Those long and cold Alberta winters would give anyone cabin fever. Just for a lark, I stuck a large decal on the driver's side door that read "Chevrolet." More than a few guys pointed out to Evelyne that her car was actually a Ford. She would give them a shocked look and say, "Are you sure?"

To say that car was a beater was putting it mildly. In order to survive winter driving in Edmonton, you needed a good heater, and this car definitely lacked one. It leaked, so I pulled the heater core out and soldered it up but it still leaked, so I installed one from the auto wreckers. It lasted all of a month before it failed like the previous one. There was Evelyne driving around town in sub-zero weather with all the windows rolled down so the glass didn't frost up, Duchess hanging out the window, and both she and Colin bundled up in layers of winter gear when a city cop pulled her over.

He asked her, "Was your husband stunting in the west end last weekend?" Apparently, they'd had a report and the description matched her beater.

She replied, "Are you kidding? In THIS car?"

HIGHER EDUCATION

I was intrigued and mystified by what a university education might be all about. My high school track record was pretty dismal, but I put that down to pure laziness and lack of trying—read "caring." Bob Scott, my grade twelve English teacher and school principal, always said that I was the equal of my brother who had a mechanical engineering degree from UBC. I knew three aircraft techs who were working towards engineering degrees at the U of A even though they were married with a household full of kids. So I enrolled in Psychology, Ancient English Literature, and Canadian History courses for the spring semester. I could attend classes during the day while working either afternoon or midnight shifts in aircraft servicing. On the afternoon shift, the sergeant would send half of the crew home if all the aircraft were down and serviceable. If it had been a long flight when the aircraft touched down in Edmonton, we would expect a long list of telecom snags, especially with the search and weather radar system. The midnight shift was just a skeleton crew that was there in case of late night arrival or departure of a scheduled flight, or the launch of a search and rescue mission. Many a night I brought my sleeping bag in and found a quiet place to sleep, normally on the bunk in the Herc flight deck if the aircraft was parked in the hangar. I quite enjoyed my university experience although Evelyne wasn't so thrilled. She had her hands full with trying to keep Colin quiet in a tiny house, mostly in the dead of a frigid winter while I was either trying to sleep or study. After three weeks, I dropped psychology because I wasn't enjoying it and couldn't really see the point. My classmates were just out of high school, so I had ten years on them. I wasn't about to waste my time; whereas, some of those kids in the class appeared to be satisfied with a passing grade and nothing more. Some seemed to be coasting, but I was there to prove a point, to myself that is. Of course, I had the advantage of a light course load and was supposedly more mature, not partying every weekend.

I always liked history, and my final mark was a seven out of nine. I found the English course very interesting. We were studying material that had been written 600 years previously, which made it not only entertaining but also historical. The course was Chaucer's "Wife of Bath" from *Canterbury Tales*. Our professor was wonderful. She could speak with the Olde English dialect of the 1400s. I was pleasantly surprised when I pulled down an eight for the course. In June, the Department of English sent me a letter inviting me to come in for an interview in regards to applying for the Honour's English program. I did have that interview, and my professor tried to encourage me to apply because she thought I had potential. I promised to give it serious thought over the summer. I basically took that one semester at university to see what it was all about and also to find out what I was capable of. Two of my friends attending the U of A faithfully stuck it out, and both graduated with engineering degrees. The third guy, Doug, tragically developed a brain aneurysm and died during his course. He was in his mid-thirties with a wife and two kids.

While living in Edmonton, I had taken two different aptitude tests, and they clearly showed that I probably would be a lot happier in a non-technical trade such as a social science teacher, a printer like my uncle Archie, a realtor, or of all things, a musical performer. That last one really surprised me. I scored low in the basic interest scales for mathematics, science and mechanical, and high in recreational leadership, social services and writing. It was plainly obvious that electronics would never be my strong suit. After the second test, I went with Evelyne to be interviewed by the university guidance counsellor, and he asked me how I would describe our relationship. He got a good chuckle out of it when I thought about it for a few seconds then said, "I lead," paused, then looked at Evelyne and said, "but she pushes." By then I was in my twelfth year of service, so if I could stick it out for eight more, I would draw a pension, and even though our wages weren't great, the Treasury Board had started to throw the odd decent pay raise our way. To make a long story short, that was my university career—one semester. I just wanted to see what it was all about and if I was capable, but unfortunately, I was sadly lacking ambition, and I didn't relish the thought of spending the next four or five years in a classroom.

After the year was up and we signed Colin's final adoption papers, Evelyne decided to go back to work part-time. It was only a five-minute walk up 127 Street to the Charles Campbell Hospital. The hospital had originally been a federal tuberculosis hospital for northern residents but gradually morphed into a general hospital, serving northern Alberta and the Territories. Child care worked out well because we were always on opposing shifts, except for the odd time when we needed coverage if our system didn't mesh perfectly. In those cases, we would drop Colin off for an hour or two with the local United Church Minister's wife who lived on our block. Evelyne worked there for only about a year because she thought that it was run more like a hotel than a hospital, and she found it quite frustrating to be chasing after patients to provide treatments while being short-staffed. Many of the patients were long-term, and they understandably developed a social community. She ended up back at the General Hospital in a part-time position.

In late '75 I transferred to Herc Maintenance where the aircraft had scheduled maintenance from three days up to five weeks, totally dependent on the airframe hours. We had a large crew of eighteen comm and radar techs with Sgt. Dave Kitching in charge. Dave was an ideal boss, in our opinion. Fair and easygoing—one of the boys. We worked Monday to Friday with every weekend off, and when we came in on Monday morning, if the workload was obviously going to be light that week, he would send half of us home for Monday, Wednesday and Friday and the other half Tuesday and Thursday. We did regular maintenance, changed time-expired equipment, fixed chronic problems that aircraft servicing didn't have the time or manpower to solve, and installed wiring and equipment modifications.

The man in charge of all trades in maintenance was the not-so-popular CWO Norris, replacing CWO Blackwood who was transferred to 7 Supply Depot. Old Blackie was quite a character. In 1968, the Canadian Airborne Regiment was formed, based at the Griesbach Barracks Army Base in north Edmonton. The paratroopers' jump school was continually using our aircraft for training. Once in the late '70s, the Regimental Sergeant Major of the Airborne, Dick Buxton, was taking a shortcut through the maintenance hangar between the aircraft when a booming voice came over the P. A. system. It was Blackwood. "CWO Buxton, stop right there, freeze. Remove your boots and report to my office immediately." Blackie really gave him hell for walking into his hanger with steel blakeys on his boots. "This isn't a parade square, Buxton," he said. The issue was that the blakeys could create a spark near aircraft loaded with jet fuel. In '71, Buxton died after jumping out of a Herc. He was using an experimental parachute, and when it didn't open properly, he deployed his reserve chute which, unfortunately, wrapped around the main chute. My cousin Neil who worked in the Greisbach pay office told me that it's a wonder that the parachute lines didn't all melt because Buxton had a reputation for cursing worse than a sailor. A memorial plaque was erected close to where he thundered in, and the field was re-named Drop Zone Buxton.

ACAPULCO

The first week of February we decided to take a two-week vacation in Mexico. Friends of ours in the neighbourhood, Don and Jackie Campbell, had moved the previous summer to a large farm ten miles north west of Edmonton. Don was a locomotive engineer for Canadian National Railroad, and both he and his wife had farming in their blood. Jackie agreed to look after Colin while we were away. They had five kids of their own and two foster kids, so one more wouldn't be a problem.

We scheduled a three-day stopover in San Francisco, and wouldn't you know it, although that city had had only four days of snow in the twentieth century, February 5,1976, the day before we arrived, was one of those days. Fortunately by the time we landed, most of it had melted away but not before half thc kids in the city made snowballs and placed them in their freezers. They were excited, but we, not so much. We checked into an older hotel downtown called the "Hotel California" just like the name of The Eagles rock hit that was released that same February. Years later, I read that the inspiration for the song came from the Hotel California in the small town of Todos Santos in Baja California Sur, Mexico. In the song, Don Henley sings, "It could be heaven, it could be hell." It was more the latter. In the first room we rented, the overworked cast-iron radiator was leaking steam and water all over the floor. The second room was marginally better except for the street noise.

The next day as we strolled down Broadway, I saw the billboard with the name Carol Doda over the Condor Club. She was featured more than a few times in *Playboy* magazine, and the Condor Club claimed to be the world's first topless bar. The Doda Bird was one of the pioneers in the silicone enhancement period of the '70s. The doorman was calling out, "No cover charge, no cover charge," so I asked him what the catch was.

"Just buy a drink," he said, so I suggested to Evelyne that it was time to get out of the rain and have a beer. She asked who Carol Doda was. I told her that she was a famous dancer, neglecting to mention exotic—an honest mistake. When we sat down in the near-empty bar, I ordered a beer and Evelyne a coke. Within a few minutes, the lights dimmed and the music started up, and from an opening in the stage ceiling, a large white piano slowly descended with the Doda Bird perched on top. As she got into her dance routine, there was a lot of hooting and hollering and whistling and clapping going on behind us. I turned around, and there must have been at least 15 US Navy sailors sitting towards the rear of the club. They must have come in just as the show started. That was the final straw for Evelyne. She said that she was leaving with or without me, so I followed her out the door, not even finishing my beer.

That piano was involved in a tragic accident seven years later. In the early morning hours after the club had closed, Jimmy the bouncer was making out with his girlfriend, exotic dancer Theresa Hill, on top of the piano. For some unknown reason, the hydraulics were activated and the piano raised up, trapping the amorous couple against the ceiling. When the janitor discovered them the next morning it was too late for poor Jimmy, but at least Theresa survived the ordeal.

In Acapulco, we checked into a hotel that was in the busy part of town. When we went for a walk, we witnessed a hit-and-run accident involving a teenage boy who was jaywalking in front of the hotel. He was unresponsive and was bleeding from a laceration on his forehead. We were concerned that he was going to get hit again, so I went out between the traffic lanes to try and direct the cars around him. That was scary because most of the vehicles hardly slowed down. Evelyne risked life and limb to walk out there to check his vital signs and found that he had a weak pulse. After about ten minutes, two cops showed up, parked half a block away and then slowly walked towards us while talking to a few people along the way, perhaps looking for eye witnesses or maybe just discussing the weather or the upcoming soccer match. At least they radioed for an ambulance, but I was hoping to be relieved of my traffic duties before I was run over. After a few close calls, I scampered to the safety of the sidewalk and indicated to the cops that I was going off duty. Not even a *gracias.* That was our introduction to Mexico.

The next day we checked into an older hotel on Caleta Beach. It definitely wasn't where the rich and famous stayed, but at least it was on the water. At that time, Acapulco was the number-one resort destination in Mexico. A few short years later, it fell out of favour and Cancun took over. We met two guys from Cleveland, both in their early 60s, who had been coming down in January and February for a number of years. They were married but their wives went on separate vacations. After a few days, Wes, one of the Cleveland boys, said he and his friend Evan wouldn't be so foot-loose and fancy-free anymore because their Montreal girlfriends were due to arrive anytime. The girls were also married. The husband of one of the girls was in a wheelchair, and the other one didn't travel for some vague reason, but that didn't stop the wives from vacationing in Acapulco every winter.

Evelyne and I overdid it at the beach. After three days, our lily-white skin took on a pinkish tinge, so we decided to take the bus to Mexico City where it would be cooler with less sun because of smog. The night before we left for Mexico City, Wes and Evan and their Montreal sweethearts wanted to show us what they claimed was the best nightclub in the city. We took two cabs and entered a large courtyard with fountains and tropical trees and a lit parking lot. The club was complete with armed guards who might have been city cops. There were two dance floors and a first-rate band playing. What the boys failed to mention was that the nightclub was basically a house of ill repute. When I was going to and from the gents, I had to run the gauntlet of numerous working girls. But it was a decent nightclub, and even the drinks were reasonably priced. Evelyne and I didn't stay too long because we had to catch the seven a.m. bus to Mexico City. At three a.m., I woke up and made a mad dash to the bathroom because I had a serious case of the trots. I knew that it couldn't have been the alcohol because I only had three beers at the nightclub. I was in there only a few minutes when Evelyne started frantically pounding on the bathroom door. She was sick also. We had been warned never to drink the tap water in Acapulco, but we had been ordering salads in our favourite restaurant and that lettuce was probably washed in that same tap water. The result was Montezuma's revenge, the old Aztec two-step.

We were a sorry-looking couple boarding the bus at seven a.m. The bus company advertised air conditioning and a hostess to serve cold drinks as we travelled for seven long, hot hours through the mountains. Not quite as advertised, however. The air conditioning was on the fritz, so we had to open the windows, and the cold drinks were served warm, *sans* ice. Half an hour into the trip, I noticed this pretty *senorita* across the aisle and one row up who was peeling a huge orange. It looked so good. I had declined breakfast earlier. When she slowly started eating each segment one by one, I mentioned to Evelyne that that was a form of torture and should be outlawed by the Geneva Convention. She had almost finished the orange when out of the blue, she threw up all over the man directly in front of her. This was serious projectile vomit and in that hot bus, the stench was positively revolting. Right away the woman ran to the back where the washrooms were. The poor victim of her onslaught, who was covered in vomit from his head to his collar, also bolted for the back. I was right behind him, but unfortunately for me he got the last washroom. I was heaving, but somehow managed to hang on to my stomach contents. Not a real highlight of my Mexican adventure.

Twice on the trip we were stopped by the army who ushered all the passengers off the bus as they searched for weapons or maybe even drugs, I'm assuming. The squad commander, *el capitan*, was paying a lot of attention to the pretty *senorita.* I doubt that she was a suspected terrorist—he was probably after her phone number.

When we finally arrived at the bus terminal in Mexico City, we took the metro to the heart of the city, the Zona Rosa. There we found the Hotel Geneve recommended by our Acapulco friends. It was an old but very classy hotel with reasonable rates. Within a few days, Evelyne's stomach discomfort seemed to clear up, but I wasn't so fortunate. For the reminder of our Mexican holiday, I didn't walk by too many bathrooms.

We spent three days in Mexico City, seeing all the touristy places such as the pyramids, old monastery, market places, and the famous Our Lady of Guadeloupe shrine. By then our sunburns had settled down, so we decided to head back to the lower altitudes and hotter temperatures of Acapulco.

Getting out of the Zona Rosa to the bus terminal turned into a real ordeal because it wasn't a simple matter of a quick ride on the metro. As we were about to board the train, a city cop stopped us in our tracks and pointed at our luggage. He didn't speak English or French and we only knew a smattering of Spanish, but a local man translated for the cop, explaining that nothing larger than briefcases and backpacks were allowed on the metro. Suitcases were definitely *prohibido*. I guess I could have attempted bribery but I didn't want to risk spending the rest of my holidays behind bars. By then it was three p.m., and the afternoon rush hour was just beginning although it seemed that every hour in Mexico City was rush hour. We tried hailing a cab at the curb. Most already had passengers, but two or three took one look at our luggage and carried on after initially slowing down. Evelyne doesn't travel lightly. Eventually, three different cabs stopped for us, but before we could hop in, someone else would beat us to it, virtually stealing our ride. The fourth cab driver who stopped, bless his soul, kicked out the guy who jumped the queue and loaded our luggage.

In Mexico at that time, the law stated that every cab must have a meter; however, there was nothing to say whether or not it had to be in working order. It was common practice for the cabbies to rip out the wires and disable the meter, which meant that you had to haggle for the tariff before you got underway. Our driver must have spent some time at Our Lady of Guadeloupe that day because he quoted us a very reasonable price without the regular song-and-dance of haggling. The bus terminal was at least five miles away, and he drove us there safely without running any red lights or taking any unnecessary chances, which was a bonus. We were so grateful that we gave him quite a hefty tip.

The bus company had a reservation system that wasn't ideal. Basically, it wasn't a system at all. You couldn't reserve for a specific time. After we bought our return tickets to Acapulco we had to sit and wait our turn which turned out to be five long hours. I ate my fair share of tacos before we got underway. The trip to the coast was much quicker than our first bus ride, mainly because the Mexican army didn't have their checkpoints set up as before. Terrorists and criminals down there have a strong union and don't work at night.

After a few more days of wandering in Acapulco, we noticed a tiny little hotel up the hill in a quiet neighbourhood. So being firm believers that the grass is always greener on the other side, we changed addresses for a final move. I could only tolerate so much beach time and lying around reading a book in the hot sun. We signed up for a midnight cruise out in the bay. It was a beautiful night for a cruise—all nights are beautiful in Acapulco—and there was a lively crowd on board. The mariachi band was top notch, which really got everyone up and dancing. Of course, the drinks were included, and the way they mixed ours I'm sure that in Mexico coke is more expensive than rum. Evelyne would have preferred a glass of wine, but her choice was either beer or rum so she choose the latter. The bartender really skimped on the mix, and after two drinks, she was pretty tipsy for the first time in her life. When the cruise ended at one thirty a.m., we had to walk up the hill to our little hotel. That was quite the adventure with Evelyne weaving all over the road. A few locals were walking down the hill as we were going up, and they must have wondered about us *gringos.* By then, I was pushing her up the hill and telling her to walk straight because it was damn embarrassing, and she just kept giggling. She spent the night in close proximity to the porcelain bowl, and the next morning she wasn't feeling all that chipper, but she couldn't blame it on the water and Montezuma's revenge.

When our holiday was over, the Air Canada stewardesses were on a rotating strike, and for some reason the airline wouldn't fly into Mexico, so we ended up with Air Mexicana to Los Angeles. Unlike our bus trip, we had no complaints with the service. The air conditioning worked just fine, and the drinks were cold. Back to Edmonton and reality. Two more months of snow and ice.

DAVE CLARKE, MOM AND DANIELLE RENÉE

In late spring of 1976, Dave Clarke stopped in for a visit. He was on his way from Acton, Ontario to Whitehorse in the Yukon. Dave was driving an old pick-up truck with an even older camper on the back and was accompanied by a dog and two cats. He had already been to Whitehorse earlier in the year. A handyman/carpenter promised him a job if he came back. I gave him some of my surplus tools like framing squares and hammers because heaven knows, Dad was pretty generous when he told me to help myself to his tools. Dave left his dog in our fenced backyard, which annoyed Duchess to no end as she was confined to the house. When he let his cats have the run of the basement, she was restricted to the main floor.

One afternoon, we went downtown to shoot some pool and have a few beers just like old times, and we topped it off by sharing a large, greasy pizza. Big mistake. At two a.m., I was rolling around on the bedroom floor in considerable pain. Evelyne had Dave drive me to the Charles Camsell Hospital, but by the time I was admitted to Emergency the pain had subsided. The doctor was pretty sure that I'd had a gall bladder attack. That was my one and only time and once was enough. When Dave was packing up to leave for the Yukon, he loaded up his dog and only one cat because the second one must have found a good hiding spot in the basement crawl space. Dave couldn't locate it. I told Dave that he wasn't leaving without it because my dog was about to have a nervous breakdown. So he had another go at it and finally emerged with the cat, but not before suffering more than a few scratches and bites on his hands. That damn cat thought that Edmonton was as far north as he wanted to go.

I was hoping that Dave's new career as a carpenter's helper would pan out because he wasn't what you would call an ambitious person. He had worked for awhile as a Vancouver cab driver. Up north, his helper's position didn't last. He eventually signed on with the Whitehorse Transit as a bus driver, which was also a short career, but he didn't starve or freeze to death because by then, Dave had met a school teacher who didn't mind supporting him. I was under the distinct impression that Evelyne was glad to see Dave leaving our happy little home. She thought he was leading yours truly astray.

On Mother's Day, May 9, 1976, Mom had just finished a load of laundry and sat down in her easy chair with a cup of tea when she suffered a stroke. Dad was out in the yard puttering around, and when he walked in the back door, she was gone. Only 62 years old. She got the short end of the stick. Her sister Anne died at age 98 and sister Frances at age 92. Two other sisters died relatively young of cancer, and Mom was always concerned that she would succumb to it as well. As it turned out, during the autopsy it was discovered that she in fact had cancer of the lymph nodes. Maybe it was a blessing that Mom went so quickly and didn't suffer.

Mom was a softie and wasn't a fan of corporal punishment, which in many cases, I probably deserved while growing up. She never interfered in our marriage, and Evelyne thought that she was a great mother-in-law. We flew to Vancouver for the funeral, and when we arrived at the Catholic church in Surrey, my siblings and I were surprised to see Father Jim Fagan, formerly of St. Margaret's Catholic Church in Ocean Falls, there to celebrate the funeral mass. He had seen the obituary in the Vancouver paper and had arranged with the local priest to celebrate the mass. After the funeral, he came over to Dad's house on Old Yale Road where he entertained my relatives and had his fair share of wine. At one point during the wake, I had to drive over to the liquor store because we were running dry. Reverend Jim and Don had a good long discussion about sports. In his younger days, the Reverend excelled in hockey and softball, and when he left Ocean Falls, he took up golf. It was the Reverend talking to "The Rev" because shortly after we moved to the Falls, Bruce Gilchrist started calling Don "The Rev" after the Reverend Forbes who ran the United Church missionary boat that plied the West Coast.

The next day, we siblings got together to decide where Dad would live because it was obvious that he couldn't manage alone due to his dementia. He agreed to move up to Terrace in northern BC to live in a small rental house that my sister Mary-Lynne and her husband Tony had on their property. Don and I drove Dad in to New Westminster to sign some legal documents and then arranged for the house to be listed with a realtor.

When we flew back to Edmonton, we were hardly in the door when our next door neighbour, Mrs. Cairns, phoned us to tell us that social services had been looking for us for the past few days. We quickly got in touch with them and then drove over to the Royal Alexandra Hospital where a bundle of joy awaited us. The authorities had a two week old baby girl born with hip dysplasia who was now being treated with a large splint around her hips, and they preferred to have a RN as an adoptive parent. Were we willing to take her? Dumb question. Evelyne's heart, and mine too, just melted when we saw this baby. Of course, we said yes immediately. Never in her wildest dreams did Evelyne think that she would have a fair-haired, blue-eyed girl. We named her Danielle Renée. She was the first adopted child in northern Alberta, Red Deer and north, to go directly from the birth mother in the hospital to the adoptive parents. The previous policy had the baby, as had Colin, stay at least six weeks with foster parents before permanent placement. Danielle was a great baby, very alert, and it wasn't long before she was sleeping through the night. When she was six months old, x-rays

Danielle 9 mo. and Colin 3 yrs.

of her hips determined that her splint was no longer required, that she could manage with quadruple cloth diapers. Over time, this seemed to be effective, although it entailed a lot of laundry.

Up in Terrace, Dad's mental state was rapidly deteriorating. He barely lasted three months living on his own in the little house on Mary-Lynne's property. One of the neighbours reported that they saw Dad over by the highway, and sure enough, when Tony drove over, he found Dad hitchhiking to Vancouver, eight hundred and fifty miles away. Mary-Lynne convinced Dad that he should be in the Skeena View Psychiatric Hospital where she worked. Since he was a volunteer patient, Dad could come and go as he pleased, and a few times he wandered off to the other side of town. He even told some people that his daughter kicked him out of his own house. For his own safety, the doctors certified him, so Dad ended up on a locked unit. Tony signed him out once and drove him over to the local pub for refreshments in the afternoon. Tony ordered two draft beers, gave the waiter a dollar, and the waiter left twenty cents in change on the table which Dad quickly pocketed. For the second round, once again Dad scooped up the change, and after they downed that one Tony asked if he would like another beer.

Dad replied, "Hell no, if you're too cheap to buy a round, let's get out of here."

JUNIOR LEADERS AND DREAM POSTING

In June of that year, I decided that with the summer weather upon us, it would be a good opportunity to replace the asphalt shingles on the roof. Norm McNeil, a comm tech I worked with in aircraft maintenance, volunteered to give me a hand on the weekend. The forecast was predicting warm temperatures, but that didn't materialize until Monday. The problem was that the first part of the roof was a low slope which required a shingle that didn't come with the self-adhesive tar. We had to paint on a strip of tar with a brush, but because of the cool temperature it wasn't an easy task. All we accomplished on the weekend was the low slope area of the roof, which wasn't very much. What we needed was a way of heating up the tar. I had a propane torch, but I didn't want to risk burning down the house to get a new roof on. After supper on Sunday, I drove my car with a utility trailer up on the boulevard grass out front to load up the old shingles to haul to the dump. Not only was it cold, but by then it had started raining sideways. As I was loading up the trailer, a city cop came along and told me that I couldn't park on the grass. He wanted me to park on the other side of 127 Street where parking was permitted.

At that point, I was wet and cold and stiff all over, and I almost lost it. I said, "Look, Officer, this grass that I'm parked on, I water it, I fertilize it, I cut it, and I control the dandelions—I'm not about to wreck it." He got the message and drove on. The next Friday was a light schedule at work, so

Sgt. Kitching gave a few of us a day off to finish the roofing. We assigned a young private, Mike Upham, as our foreman because he had roofing experience before joining the military. It was a pretty straightforward job because the normal slope shingles were self-sealing and the roof was a simple design with no valleys. The only problem we had was with the weather—this time it was much too hot to be up on a black roof all day. Evelyne put in a few miles that day between the kitchen and the ladder bringing the boys iced water. They didn't dare have a beer until the job was done and they were back on the ground.

Later in the afternoon, Norm was feeling a little off, so he probably had a touch of sun stroke. By supper time, we were finished except for the cap on the roof peak. After we fed the guys and sent them home, I went back up the ladder to nail down the cap. It was half finished when I noticed a car and tent trailer parking across the street from our house. Uncle Clem's married daughter Cary and her family were visiting from Saskatoon. Poor timing. We welcomed them into our home and then I excused myself because I had noticed some dark clouds rolling in from the west. On the prairies, if you have a really hot day, there is an excellent chance, like a ninety-nine percent chance, of thundershowers that evening. Any camper or golfer in Alberta would swear to that. Sure enough, within a few minutes, the skies opened up. I started pounding in nails like I was in the finals of a nail driving contest in the Carpenter Olympics. When the cap was nearly finished, there was a tremendous thunderclap followed by a scary-looking lightning display. Of course, Evelyne realized what was taking place outside by then, and she came running out to the backyard, ordering me off the roof in no uncertain terms. I wasn't about to argue with her. I flung the lightning rod hammer into the garden and scampered down the ladder, drenched to the bone. You had to witness a prairie rainstorm firsthand to understand the damage they could cause. I guess there's a reason why prairie farmers spend a fortune every year on crop insurance.

Later in the year, Evelyne took skiing lessons at Rabbit Hill in South Edmonton with Gerry (don't call me Geraldine) Gannon. After Jim got his business degree from the U of A, he articled for a year and then wrote for his Chartered Accountant's exam but, unfortunately, failed on his first attempt. By then, he had met and married Gerry, a divorcée who had young twins, a boy and a girl. Gerry was a first cousin to Mark Messier of Edmonton Oilers fame. Rabbit Hill was appropriately named because it was basically a bunny hill, ideal for beginners. In February, Evelyne and I scheduled a five-day ski trip to Banff. Friends of ours knew of a young couple, strapped for funds, who would be willing to stay in our home during that period and babysit the kids. The husband was attending university with aspirations of becoming a church minister.

He and his young wife, Julie, had a six month old baby, and they came across as quite capable and confident. As Evelyne was giving her last-minute instructions, Julie told us not to worry, to go and enjoy Banff, and when we returned, she would have Colin toilet trained and everything would be in order. We drove to Banff and really enjoyed ourselves—for two days anyway. The weather was ideal, the snow perfect, and the accommodations and meals just great. On the second night, we had just walked into our hotel room after dining out, when we received a long-distance call from Edmonton. Our sitter was overwhelmed because she couldn't cope with three kids, especially when one was hyperactive. Would we please return immediately, if not sooner? The next day we got home to a very relieved and exhausted Julie. There were a few loads of diapers to launder, and almost every dish that we owned was either stacked in the sink or on the counter, unwashed of course. And Colin was definitely not toilet trained.

In February of 1977, I had to go on the Junior Leaders Course (JLC) for five weeks in Penhold, a few miles southwest of Red Deer, Alberta. Penhold was formally a pilot training base and was currently used by the air cadets for glider school. It was mandatory to pass the JLC if corporals were hoping to be promoted to master corporal. All the students on the course were air force, but the sergeant basically running the show came from the Princess Patricia Canadian Light Infantry (PPCLI). Sgt. Lewis was a disgruntled NCO who, I gathered, had some sort of disagreement with his superiors while on UN duties in Cyprus, so he was now just playing out the string until retirement with not much hope for promotion. He was stuck with babysitting fifty pigeons who thought that the JLC was a waste of their time and energy. I agreed that the course definitely had its merits in an army environment where you had NCO's leading the troops in battle, but most of us air force types were technicians who repaired aircraft in a controlled environment. If it was broke, fix it. None of this nonsense about having group meetings and appointing #2 I/C's and #3 I/C's.

The best part of the course was that every weekend except one I could drive home to Edmonton. The worst part was the camping out in tents in the middle of winter. Each student would take a turn being the leader of a squad and assigned tasks such as figuring out how to transport a stretcher across a creek or putting out perimeter guards. Nothing to do with fixing aircraft, but we just had to grin and bear it for five weeks. Sgt. Lewis tried to be gruff and tough, but actually I kind of liked the guy. If you screwed up, his favourite expression was, "You know, anyone with half an eyeball and an arsehole could figure that out."

In the barracks, I was surprised to find my old roommate from 3 Wing, Bob Emmerson, once again assigned to my room. He was stationed with the Search and Rescue Squadron at Comox on Vancouver Island. He wasn't going home every weekend like some of us lucky ones. We were four to a room, but one safety systems tech had barely made his bed when he decided that he couldn't handle the JLC, so he withdrew. I never did know his name because he was in our room all of twenty minutes. We thought that he was being a bit dramatic about it, passing up a future promotion, especially when the JLC turned out to be a walk in the park, literally. Maybe he stressed out over fear of the unknown. The known was that he would be stuck in rank until he passed the JLC.

Once a week, the Commanding Officer, accompanied by Sgt. Lewis, would walk through the barracks, inspecting us in our dress uniforms and, of course, inspecting our rooms. *Déja vu,* basic training. One of the guys down the hall from our room, Ed Simmons, an aero engine tech from Edmonton, had just spent six months on UN duty in Cairo, and he had a bad case of gypo gut, the Middle-Eastern version of Montezuma's revenge. Just before the inspection party entered his room, Ed developed a serious bout of stomach pain along with gas, and you can guess what happened. Accidents happen. Unfortunately, by the time Ed ran down the hallway to the bathroom, it was too late. The CO asked Sgt. Lewis what was going on. Sgt. Lewis, who had done tours in the Middle East should have said, "Anyone with half an eyeball and . . .," but he bit his tongue this time. Our final exercise lasted twenty-four hours, during which they had us setting up command posts and doing fun things like crowd control and repelling demonstrators at the gate. Anyway, after five weeks, we all passed the course and went back to our home units where it was highly doubtful that we would be putting much of our newly learned leadership skills to use unless we re-mustered into the army.

By early 1978, I had been in Edmonton for ten years already, and since we weren't planning on adopting any more children, I expected a new posting in the spring. At our annual personal evaluation report, PER, we had three choices for preferred postings, and I always requested Edmonton, Comox, Trenton, in that order. That year, because Comox was everybody's first pick, I thought that there wasn't much chance of a transfer to Comox, so I requested Edmonton, Trenton, and Comox. Imagine our surprise when the message came from Ottawa granting us our dream posting, Comox. Because there were quite a few transfers that year, the Telecom Air Section organized a get-together in the Junior Ranks Club on a Friday afternoon. Even the telecom captain and the senior NCO's attended the beer call. I ended up sitting with Larry St. Denis, a co-worker, and it was apparent that he had a head start on the rest of the guys. Larry had been trying for a west coast posting for years, but he was going east to Trenton. When I mentioned that I was off to Comox even though Trenton had been higher up on my wish list, he got some agitated to say the least. Since I was still a corporal and Larry a master corporal, we were on different lists, but regardless, he didn't seem too happy for me.

I had to leave the club by five p.m. because my in-laws and Eugène and Delores Bachand, good friends of my in-laws, were taking us out to a fancy restaurant on the south side of the city. As I was warming up my car in the parking lot, I noticed Larry stumbling out, three sheets to the wind by now. I watched as he fumbled for his keys, and then he decided to take a leak beside his car before getting in. In the process, he dropped the keys. He then had to get down on all fours and sift through the by-now-yellow snow before finally locating them. Lucky, he only had four blocks to drive to his PMQ. When he finally got underway in his Carmen Ghia Volkswagen, he pulled out too wide onto the street, and collided head-on with a car in front of the Senior NCOs' Club. I could see that at that slow speed there were no injuries so decided not to be a witness but get out of Dodge promptly before the MPs showed up. I drove up by the hangar line and then down the main street and out the main gate by the guard house. As I made good my escape, I glanced over my shoulder to see Larry talking to the MPs, who were in the process of arresting him for impaired driving. Rumour had it that a few months later he got a second impaired driving citation in Trenton, issued by the Ontario Provincial Police.

After two days on the market, we received two identical offers for our house, both at the listing price, which was probably a good indication that it was underpriced, but since we had tripled our money in four years, we weren't complaining. We had to choose between a real estate agent who would likely flip the house and a young drywaller with a wife and new baby. The family won the lotto. In late February, we dropped off the kids at Campbell's farm and flew to Comox for a house-hunting trip. At that time, the civilian air terminal at the air base was about the size of a double wide trailer, and the luggage from the aircraft was dumped into the back of an old pick-up truck. We took a taxi into Courtenay to a second-rate motel. Evelyne found that five-mile drive quite depressing with the wind, the rain and the darkness. All we could see was a forest of tall evergreens. She was thinking, "What has John got me into, and is there time for me to back out of this deal?"

The next morning when we drew the curtains, she was greatly relieved to spot a Safeway store two blocks up the street and said, "Thank God, civilization!" For the next few days, our realtor, Al McKenzie, drove us all over the Comox Valley in our quest for the perfect house. There wasn't much selection, but we narrowed it down and selected a two-year-old house in Comox, two blocks up the hill from Brooklyn Elementary School. It was a typical Comox box with a partially finished walk-out basement, quite common in the Valley due to the water table and the hardpan in the soil. Thankfully, house prices were fairly stagnant and hadn't caught up to Edmonton's market, so we were able to pay cash and be mortgage free. And to think that five years earlier Wayne Kubala was adamant that we would be damn fools to take out a mortgage and buy a house instead of renting. That summer we had enough money left over from our real estate dealings to buy a decent boat.

409 SQUADRON, BOATING AND CAMPING

In late April '78, after our furniture and effects were packed away in the moving van, we said good-bye to family and friends and our wonderful little heritage home and looked forward to the next chapter in our lives. I bought a utility trailer to haul items like paints and stains and house plants that the moving company wouldn't transport. The trailer was originally the box of a 1941 Ford truck, and it paid for itself many times over the years. Duchess and I took to the highway and met up with Evelyne and the kids at the Vancouver airport. After a few visits with relatives in the area, we caught the ferry to Vancouver Island and drove to the Comox Valley and home.

I was attached to 409 Squadron that flew CF-104 Voodoos with nuclear capability. The Voodoo's role was to intercept and destroy enemy bomber fleets by detonating the nuclear warhead at high altitudes. We worked either the day or evening shift with every weekend off except for Quick Reaction Area (QRA) duties. The ground crew and aircrews worked twenty-four hours on, twenty-four hours off for two weeks, ensuring that two Voodoos would be airborne on short notice—five minutes. On the day shift, we would launch a number of aircraft for training, refuelling and de-snagging as required. In the afternoon, we would do a second launch and then go home when the evening shift took over at three thirty p.m.

Comm/radar technicians had it made working on the Voodoo because we had only six systems to worry about, and the serviceable rate was pretty good, especially when the antiquated ultra high frequency (UHF) radio transceiver was replaced with a state of the art solid-state radio in 1979. It hardly ever failed. Many a night we went home early after helping with the refuelling and aircraft towing and maybe a snag or two; whereas, the engine techs and the armament system techs (AST) might still be at work until one or two a.m. They couldn't leave until twelve Voodoos were serviceable. The armament system was comprised of the nuclear delivery system, the missile system and the infrared radar, among other things, which totalled over eighty-five black boxes that kept the seven AST boys hopping most nights. In contrast, the comm/radar crew had only three techs, and that was close to being over-staffed.

Along with Voodoos, 409 Squadron had three T-33 jet trainers that we serviced as well. Every Tuesday morning, Captain Gary Takach would take a T-33, affectionately called a T- Bird, on a PACE flight, flying over three different radar stations in BC: Holberg on northern Vancouver Island, Baldy Hughes by Prince George and Mount Logan by Kamloops. His mission was to check out the serviceability of the Tactical Air Control and Navigation (TACAN) and the Identification Friend or Foe (IFF) of those radar stations. It seemed that almost every time he landed back at Comox, Captain Takach would write up in the log book that his aircraft TACAN was unserviceable. And almost every time we couldn't find a problem—No Fault Found (NFF). Eventually, Captain Takach deservedly earned the nickname Captain Tacan. I believe that other than the Tuesday morning PACE flight, the main reason that 409 Squadron had T-Birds was to allow the desk-bound pilots their required flying hours so they could draw their flight pay.

One summer, one of the T-Birds was experiencing more than its share of radio compass problems, so we decided to ring out the entire system. We didn't have hanger space, so we were de-snagging the aircraft out on the hot tarmac. I removed the loop antenna on the aircraft belly so we could do continuity checks, and I was just cooking under there. A young airman, Private Kevin Binnie, was helping me out. After a few hours in the heat, we went inside the servicing section for a much-needed break. We weren't inside two minutes when the airframe sergeant, Frank Ross, told Kevin to mop up the oil spills on the hanger floor that were created when the aero engine techs changed a Voodoo engine. I explained that we were taking a break from the heat.

His reply was, "Private Binnie will do as I requested and you will help him."

I refused and then said that I didn't answer to him but to the comm/ radar NCO, Sgt. Robertson.

He blew up at this point and yelled, "You're refusing a direct order. That's a chargeable offence," and stormed off to MWO Bud Cameron's office. Eventually, I found myself in that same office, on the red carpet so to speak. The MWO was a well-respected boss, very fair and reasonable in his position. He emphasized that he didn't want to put me on charge, but I couldn't escape punishment for disobeying a superior's command, so he asked if I would accept two Saturdays in a row of Orderly Corporal duties in lieu of having a charge on my record. I had my pride but agreed to his alternative as long as I didn't have to mop up the hanger floor. By then, of course, Kevin had taken care of the oil spots.

The Orderly Corporal had to stay on the base for twenty-four hours performing duties such as issuing room keys for transient personnel, selling meal tickets in the mess hall and closing up the Junior Ranks Club, making sure to empty every ashtray into a butt can. The first Saturday it was really windy as I parked my '68 Ford pick-up at the mess hall. At one p.m. when my ticket selling duties were over, I went outside to find the truck now sitting in a shallow ditch by the parking lot. I had left the truck in first gear and foolishly didn't use the parking brake, so likely the wind started it rocking and somehow knocked the transmission into neutral. The truck rolled right across the parking lot, miraculously missing three parked cars on its journey to the ditch. My lucky day.

A year later Frank Ross was transferred to Chatham, New Brunswick. At his going away party, which I didn't attend, the airframe techs presented him with a boot attached to a board by a long screw through the toe, symbolizing Frank's tendency to spin a lot and get nowhere fast.

Because our house was only a few years old, there was no maintenance to worry about, but I did have to finish the rec room. We soon found out the following winter that baseboard electric heat wasn't the ideal way to heat a house in a damp climate. It didn't help that the aluminum frame windows were always sweating buckets of water, so I had a guy install an external chimney for a wood stove. The logging company sold firewood permits for five dollars, and you could take as much as you wanted as long as it was the hardwood like alder, maple, and wild cherry and not cut the softwood such as fir, hemlock, spruce and cedar. The wood stove made a big difference to our comfort and hydro bill. Of course, nothing good lasts forever. Years later the logging company stopped issuing wood permits and barricaded the logging roads because a few idiots would park under a freshly stacked pile of timber and lop off a truck load of valuable fir.

I would go out with my neighbour, Ken Boody, a young RCMP constable. He borrowed a truck, I hauled my utility trailer and we spent a few weekends stocking up for the winter and in the process trying not to write ourselves off. By then, Evelyne had put in a few shifts working in the ER at St. Joe's, and she was forever telling me that the only accident worse than a motorcycle accident was one involving a chain saw. Ken wasn't the only cop living in our neighbourhood. We didn't have a lot of speeding on our streets because there were at least seven RCMP members living close by. Across the street from us was a superintendent and within three blocks were two RCMP helicopter pilots and two regular members. Living beside Ken's house were the Wisemans, Brian and Joanne and their two boys. We became close friends.

Shortly after moving to Comox, we had money left over from the sale of the house, so we bought a used twenty-two-foot Starcraft boat powered with a Mercruiser inboard/outboard engine from Captain Floyd. He was a navigator in 407 Maritime Patrol Squadron who was transferred to Winnipeg. Before I signed the transfer paper, Floyd took us out for a test cruise, and the boat was quite sea-worthy with plenty of speed. I remarked to him that it was equipped with six life preservers, a nice anchor, an engine manual, and best of all a berth in the Comox Marina. He said he would throw in the life preservers, and if anyone asked, "Just say that you are Captain Floyd because the berth is paid up for the rest of the year." When I took possession, I found two life preservers, an anchor without the two hundred-foot rope and no engine manual, so I phoned him up.

His reply was, "What's the problem. I threw in two preservers, that rope was a gift from my father-in-law, so I can't very well give it away, and that manual didn't come with the boat. I had to buy it and it cost me thirty dollars."

I imagine that he really needed those items on the prairies. A week later, I was just tying up the boat at the berth when a lady walked by and asked who I was. "Captain Floyd," I said.

"No, you're not," she replied. "He was my next-door neighbour, and you're certainly not him." It turned out that she worked in the marina office and she gave me fourteen days to vacate the berth. I asked her to put me on the wait list for a berth. "Good luck," she replied. The wait list was between two and four years, so we ended up tying up at the wharf where it wasn't unusual to have three or four boats tied up alongside your own, and sometimes they were large fishing boats. That meant that the crews would be crawling over our boat to get to the wharf. This was far from being an ideal situation. *Caveat emptor.*

When we were transferred to Comox, we thought that nobody would visit us because of the distance and the ferry crossing, but that wasn't the case. Those Albertans were just waiting for an excuse to holiday on Vancouver Island, so most summers it was like running an unofficial B & B with a steady stream of family and friends visiting. Naturally, we used the boat quite a bit and were moderately successful with fishing. After a month of using the wharf, I bought a trailer that I hoped would be the answer to my lack-of-a-berth problems. If I had another guy on board, I had help getting the boat on the trailer, but if it was just Evelyne and the two kids--two and four years old—it was a real problem. Normally in the afternoon the wind picked up, and with Evelyne being short and a non-swimmer, it was stressful to say the least. We decided to sell the boat the following spring before someone drowned. I found out first hand that it's true that a boat is indeed a big hole in the water into which you keep pouring money. During the winter, the engine needed some repairs, and I swear that the same part on a marine engine was at least double the cost of a similar car engine part.

That spring, Evelyne insisted that I build a fence to enclose our backyard because Duchess was running around to the front door every morning to bark at the mailman. We also had to contain Danielle who was forever wandering down to Wiseman's house to peer in their basement windows looking for their cat and dog. I talked to both neighbours, and we all agreed on a weave fence with yellow cedar posts and red cedar boards that I bought from Field Sawmill. I rented a post hole auger that was totally useless because the auger would catch on the numerous rocks and roots and spin the engine and handles around, smashing into my hips. I ended up digging all the holes the old-fashioned way—pick and shovel, axe and pry bar, and a hand auger. Neither neighbour lifted a finger to help me, nor did they pay their fifty-dollar share. Lesson learned.

Because I was new to 409 Squadron and the CF-101 Voodoo, I had to attend a month-long aircraft and equipment course in Bagotville in northern Quebec. The data link system, which was a UHF communication system that couldn't be jammed, was still classified as secret, so we couldn't take notes or bring any of the written material back to the barracks to study, which was fine with us. No exams, no failures. There were only two others on the course with me. One guy was stationed at Chatham, and before he re-mustered to comm tech he was a comm research tech—spy. He was a real bullshit artist who knew everything, had done everything and had been everywhere. The other classmate was a young private stationed in Bagotville. He owned a car and didn't mind driving us around the area; otherwise, we would have died of boredom hanging around the barracks and Junior Ranks Club for a straight month.

At that time, Bagotville and surroundings seemed to me to be somewhat separatist. In one pub in a small town they wouldn't serve me unless I ordered in French, so my two buddies had to coach me through the basics. And it also seemed that every bar had strippers performing. The "spy" remarked that one gal had some nice moves and looked great. I suspected that "she" was probably a "he" and told him so.

"No way," he said. "I'll bet you a beer."

"Okay, you're on."

At the end of the act when the big reveal happened it was obvious that the stripper was indeed a guy. At least my friend was quiet for awhile—all of ten minutes, anyway.

The usual trick for the military was to transfer a family to a new base and then promptly send the member on course for months and let the spouses try to manage in a new community, settle the children in new schools, look for employment, etc., by themselves. Evelyne was much relieved when my Voodoo course was completed. The kids were getting to be a handful, and she was also working part-time on the medical and surgical floors at St. Joe's. Later she enrolled in an ICU course to qualify for shifts in ICU and ER and later still worked permanent part-time in ER, Diabetic Day Care and Home Care. During one of her home care visits, she was sitting on the couch while taking the patient's history when she suddenly felt something warm crawling up her leg. Glancing down, she realized it was a large tarantula. She claims not to recall how she reacted, but her patient said she shrieked, jumped over the coffee table, and bolted out the front door.

"Oh, there you are George," he said. The tarantula had escaped from his aquarium three days earlier.

Evelyne went straight to her boss and declared, "You can replace me or fire me if you like, but I won't be going back to that place." There was a reason the nurses were instructed to always leave their shoes on during home visits.

During our first summer on the Island, a fellow comm tech, Scott Teasdale, along with his wife Sue and two kids, drove out from Edmonton for a visit, towing the thirteen-foot travel trailer we had left behind. Now that we had our trailer, we could see a lot of the Island, especially the northern parts and some of the small islands on the inside passage. One night on one of those overnighters, we were rudely awakened from a sound sleep by a loud crash. Colin had fallen out of the top bunk. Lucky for him Duchess was sleeping directly below him on the floor, breaking his fall. Not so lucky for Duchess. No one was hurt, but after that Duchess slept under our bed. One weekend, we went with the Wisemans to a large campground at Tribune Bay on Hornby Island. Danielle had just turned four and wasn't riding a bike at that time but was showing interest, so I was helping her out with some positive encouragement.

Finally, I gave her a push, let go and yelled, "Peddle Danielle, peddle, peddle."

She caught on and went non-stop for at least forty minutes. The road circled the entire campsite, so every five minutes she would cycle by our trailer with a big grin on her face, not daring to stop because she hadn't mastered the starting process on her own yet.

Tribune Bay was a wonderful location, horseshoe shaped with plenty of sand, similar to what you would see on a postcard. Just around the corner was Little Tribune Bay, but it was out of bounds to me because, apparently, it was a nudist beach. The kids just loved camping, but Evelyne not so much. To her it was a lot of work, with meal preparation and making sure that Colin and Danielle weren't either drowning, getting lost in the bush, or being attacked by wild animals. What was most annoying to her was that she couldn't relax in a nice hot bath in the evening. One day I found the perfect bumper sticker that I stuck on the trailer's back window for her. It read, "Are we having fun yet?" Echoed her sentiments exactly.

The following summer we drove up Island to take in the three ports: Port Alice, Port McNeill and Port Hardy. We really enjoyed that camping trip. We being myself, Colin, Danielle and Duchess. Evelyne, trooper that she was, tolerated it. A week was a long time to go without a hot soak. At Port McNeill, we parked the car and trailer, took our bikes and boarded the ferry to Cormorant Island for a short ride over to Alert Bay to see the totem poles. There are two reservations on Cormorant Island, and they have quite a collection of totem poles; however, by the time we completed our bike tour and re-boarded the ferry for Port McNeill, poor Duchess was a nervous wreck. So were we. It was all about containment, or lack thereof. No fences and no dog leashes, which meant that within minutes of our landing at Alert Bay, every mutt on the island was hounding Duchess—no pun intended. I found a big stick alongside the road which helped to keep the hounds at bay and give Duchess some breathing room. As soon as the next ferry came in, we were on it, not even stopping to check out the museum because, of course, pets weren't allowed inside.

Morton Lake, Van Isle

On one of our camping trips to the North Island, we stayed for two nights at Woss Lake, halfway between the Comox Valley and the end of the pavement, Port Hardy. Woss Lake had a huge logging operation that involved logging trains with railway tracks going every which way. I don't know if the area was logged out or if the logging company was switching to truck logging, but they were in the process of ripping up all the tracks while we were there.

Everyone in the campsite was helping themselves to souvenirs including railway spikes that were in forty-five-gallon barrels. I noticed a track switch that was just begging to be pilfered. It would make a perfect gift for my father-in-law, Marcel, who was soon retiring after forty-one years with the NAR and CN. The switch was still attached, so I got out a hack saw to try to liberate it. After twenty minutes working away in the hot sun, Colin came along and right away suggested that if I took off one bolt and then slid this rod over that bar it would be free. He was right. In five minutes, I had it in my trunk and discarded the worn-out hacksaw blade. He saved me a lot of grief that day. It was apparent that the lad was more mechanical than his father. Later that year, one of Evelyne's sisters, Irène, hauled it back to Edmonton in her little Volkswagen. It must have weighed over 100 pounds. And many years after that, I conned Danielle into hauling it back to Vancouver Island in her car when Evelyne's parents were selling their house and moving into a seniors' residence.

During our second year in Comox, Colin celebrated his fifth birthday, so we enrolled him in Beavers. Late in the season, the older kids were moving on up to Cubs, and all the families were invited to the graduation ceremony at the hall. During the evening, I noticed that a cute-looking woman kept glancing at me throughout the proceedings. Later, as we were preparing to leave she came over and asked me if my name was John and if I had been stationed at 3 Wing in 1966. I admitted as much, and then she asked if I drove a red Volvo while I was posted overseas. I said yes, and I then asked her if she had ever ridden in that Volvo. It turned out that she had because we had dated a few times fourteen years previously. I couldn't place her until she mentioned her name, Lotta. I met her through Mike Pierce at a Christmas celebration in Hornback, a village close to the base. Small world. More coincidences: it turned out that she was married to Warren Brinkley, a master corporal radar technician with whom I worked in 409 Squadron, and Lotta was a good friend of our neighbours Bruce and Kathy Clague.

PURPLE COWS AND THE BONE YARD

Between 1978 and 1982, I was on deployment with 409 Squadron five different times. Twice to Cold Lake, Alberta for the Maple Flag Exercise that served as realistic training for various aircrews flying fighter, bomber, aerial refuelling and electronic warfare aircraft. Two or three NATO nations would send a contingent to take part in the exercise and make use of the huge air weapons range north of the base. The very competitive aircrews relished the idea of getting some action and maybe picking up bragging rights in the bargain. For the ground crew, it was just more of the same: starts, parks, refuelling and de-snagging along with sleeping in barracks and eating mess hall food. Naturally, both deployments were in late fall, just to remind me what I was missing, weather-wise, in Comox. And what are the odds—both times Alberta was in the midst of a province-wide beer strike. Before leaving Comox, we were forewarned, so along with our spare parts and tools, we packed up more than a few cases of beer to help us survive the two weeks in Cold Lake.

One afternoon when flying was finished for the day, a few of us were down on the flight line putting decals on foreign aircraft. These decals had a picture of a nighthawk—the squadron's mascot—with 409 and a nuclear bomb printed on it with the words "NUKEem in the NUTS."

When we approached a USAF jet, this big black master sergeant appeared out of nowhere and asked, "What y'all doing? I don't want no dee-cal on ma airplane."

No one was going to argue with him.

When cabin fever hit, we would all pile into the van at night and drive half an hour to Pierceland, Saskatchewan to the local bar that had a good supply of beer. In Pierceland, there was a corner store called the Purple Cow. On the porch, it had two four-feet-by-eight-feet plywood sheets cut out in the shape of a cow, painted purple, naturally, that advertised what they sold—milk, bread, ice cream, etc. The guys thought this would make a very nice war trophy, something to hang up inside our hanger back in Comox, so I told them to park the van around the corner out of sight, and I'd have a look-see. The cow wasn't nailed down, so under cover of darkness, I quickly stowed our trophy in the back of the van, and back to the base we went. Unfortunately, the American ground crew heard about this, so not to be outdone, the following night they descended upon Pierceland and scooped up bovine number two along with a bunch of the Christmas decorations that the town had strung up. By then, the folks in Pierceland had had enough—you can drink our beer, but no looting, please. They sent the RCMP to the base to chat with our respective squadron commanding officers who suggested, in no uncertain terms, that we return the war trophies.

As our deployment came to an end, the beer that we had flown in also came to an end and we had a lot of empties to unload. The bottle depots in Alberta wouldn't take them, so our sergeant and a few guys filled up the van and drove over to good old Pierceland to cash them in, but even there they were backed up with empties, being so close to the Alberta border. So the guys carried on down highway 55 for over an hour before finding a depot that would accommodate them. The guys had nothing better to do anyway because our Hercules transport wasn't due in for another day.

On another deployment, I was part of the TOPGUN competition held in Bagotville. CFB Comox and CFB Chatham sent Voodoo aircraft to compete against the local Voodoo Squadron in Bagotville. It was another example where wet and mild trump snowy and cold. Comox or Bagotville, what should I choose? On the base, there was a building that I had never seen before. After the day's flying was completed, everybody could mix socially. All ranks. A lowly private could sit down and have a drink with the squadron commanding officer if he so desired. It was military tradition that commissioned officers didn't fraternize with non-commissioned types like myself. They didn't know what they were missing. This mixed mess was really buzzing on Friday night, and Don Buchanon, an aircraft electrician in 409 Squadron, was up to his old tricks. Don was a real shit disturber from way back, and this time he convinced a few women in the building to enter a wet T-shirt competition he had organized. Don almost pulled it off, the competition, that is, when a female captain from the base control tower pointed out that it was a disgrace and they were being exploited, so the women bailed out just as Don was soaking the T-shirts with warm water in the washroom sink. The good captain didn't get too many popularity votes that night. I hope that someday Don writes his memoirs because if you believed half of what he had said and done, it would make for a very interesting read. My other memory from that trip was that a young pilot from our squadron took the honours in the Top Gun competition, and the Bagotville engine techs won the trophy for changing an engine starter in the shortest time.

The final two deployments were more or less R & R trips down south to reward us for working through the rainy season. They happened in the late winter, one in Tucson, Arizona and the second one in Reno, Nevada. In Tucson we stayed in a motel about five miles away from Davis-Monthan Air Force Base where our Voodoos were flying against the Air National Guard jets. We were given a tour of the famous "Bone Yard," the largest outdoor aircraft storage facility in the world. Because of the dry desert climate, it was ideal for storing and preserving both military and commercial aircraft of all types and sizes. Jet fighters, trainers, bombers, transports, in-flight refuellers, helicopters, commercial airliners, anything that could fly. Forty-four hundred in total were there. Ironically, a few days after the tour, our airframe techs had to make another trip to the bone yard because one of our jets, flying at thirty thousand feet, lost a landing gear door. They went with a USAF technician to a line of mothballed Voodoos in the desert to "rob" a replacement door. The USAF tech told the boys to stay in the van for a minute or two while he went up to the aircraft and pounded on the fuselage a few times. He then stepped back explaining that he had to wake up the scorpions and rattlers and give them a chance to crawl out before the guys could safely go about their work. Other than being the wrong colour, the door was in perfect condition. Now that's what I call a good supply system. Instant gratification. You see what you need, you take it, and the best part, no paper work required.

On Saturday afternoon, eight of us drove seventy-five miles directly south of Tucson to the Mexican border city of Nogales to do some shopping. As we parked the van on the Arizona border and walked into the city, the sun was going down. While we strolled through the downtown streets looking for bargains, one of the guys pointed out that a gang of shady looking characters had been following us for over thirty minutes, always keeping a discrete distance of half a block behind, so we quickly vamoosed back across the border before we had a chance to spend any more money or possibly get mugged. Thirty or forty years later, it's a whole different ball game. Just recently the US State Department issued a drug violence directive, warning that Nogales was among several Mexican border cities that were experiencing numerous public shootouts daily.

The following year, our reward was to spend ten days in Reno, Nevada, "The Biggest Little City In The World." We stayed in quite an old hotel/casino two blocks from the strip. It was ideal because we were practically the only guests staying at the hotel. They had recently lost their gambling license due to some violation, so it was as quiet as a funeral home and didn't smell like an ashtray, like most casinos. Our aircraft were flying out of the Reno-Tahoe International Airport with the Air National Guard, and we were normally finished for the day by four p.m., which left us plenty of time to take in what downtown Reno had to offer. Willie Nelson was performing, but at the time I wasn't a big fan of country music, so I passed on that and have regretted it ever since. Back then, the casino restaurants were practically giving meals away just to attract people. Another bonus was in the currency department. Our money exchange wasn't favourable, but some of the casinos were taking our Canadian dollars at par. They didn't make any money off me because I was no gambler, but a few of the guys fell in love with the one-armed bandits. One of our radar techs, Gary Ward, didn't drink, smoke or gamble, and I doubt if he even cussed. He had a good scam happening that he pulled off in the casinos. His house mortgage was up for renewal, so every night he would exchange the maximum allowed, one hundred Canadian dollars for one hundred USD that he would exchange back into Canadian currency when he got home. On the weekend, we drove to Silver City, a near-ghost town, and then went by Lake Tahoe. Before we knew it, our “holiday” came to an end, and it was back to reality on Vancouver Island.

DREAM HOUSE WITH A VIEW

Our house in Comox was a plain Jane functional house commonly known as a "Comox Box." Definitely not our dream home. We were hoping to build our dream home some day. We eventually purchased a lot on Stafford Avenue. At the time, it was the highest developed area in Courtenay with a view of the mountains and the Comox Glacier. An added bonus was a glimpse of the ocean at high tide. Evelyne researched numerous house plans and designs for ideas, then we sketched a rough floor plan for the main level and had a draftsman draw up a design and blueprints. With those in hand we talked to a small contractor who liked a challenge. Lou wasn't into building Comox Boxes. He was a free spirit with a pony tail and a positive attitude. He and his two helpers made for an interesting crew. One helper was known as "Egghead," a wiry guy who built houses only in the summer months because he attended classes at UBC the rest of the year, hence the nickname. We never did know his real name. Brad was helper number two. He was a skinny little guy who likely weighed in under a hundred and forty pounds. Before hooking up with Lou, he worked as a reporter for the Georgia Straight, a Vancouver-based underground newspaper that started in 1967 and is still going strong today although it is now more conventional than it was in its beginnings. I was reading the local obituaries in 2015 and noticed that Brad had passed away. For a number of years, he lived in Malaysia in what he termed "self-imposed exile."

To raise the capital for our new home, we sold our house on Hillside Avenue in Comox and rented a row housing unit at the air base. We referred to the unit as our chicken coop. It was a long nine months before we could move out. In May of 1982, Lou arranged for Val Hornby and his cat to dig a hole for the foundation, and we were underway. Because the lot was on such a slope, the front foundation wall had to be higher and thicker than normal, which added to the expense. After the foundation was poured, the crew took a month off to finish another job, and so I asked Brian Wiseman to help me strip off the shiplap boards that would be used later for the sub-siding. Once the main level sub floor was built, Lou said that protocol dictated that we have a flooring party, so we brought hibachis and plenty of beer to celebrate a milestone. We bought fir beams from a demolished warehouse in Port Alberni which we used in the twenty-foot high ceilings in the living room, saving one for our fireplace mantle. In Victoria, Evelyne found an old-fashioned clawfoot tub for the main bathroom. At the antique auction in Cumberland, we had the winning bid on a huge armoire that would serve as our hall closet.

Once the crew had the house built to lock-up, we had another milestone party, and then we were on our own. We had the wind-up celebration at Lou's shack in Merville, fifteen miles north of Courtenay. It was an ideal summer day for an outdoor feast, and a feast it was. Lou's girlfriend, Lynn, served a beautiful three-course meal, topped off with a very tasty cheese cake. Aren't they all tasty? My mother-in-law, Germaine, visiting from Edmonton, was somewhat shocked when, after the meal, Lou put all the dirty dishes and pots on the ground so his dogs could lick them clean, all nine of them—dogs that is. There was a litter of seven pups, plus the two Golden Labrador adult dogs. In no time the hungry mutts ate every scrap, every morsel of the leftovers, and the pots and plates were looking pretty clean. Evelyne's mother was initially shocked but soon got into the spirit of things and had a good chuckle over the unorthodox way of dishwashing. Six of the pups were a beautiful golden colour, but one was jet black, which was very odd indeed. Of course, the kids wanted to take one of the pups home—Danielle was a real animal lover like most girls her age—but Duchess vetoed that idea. After we ate, we had a nail driving contest where I came in a distance third. We played a game where we had to reach out on the ground as far as we could with a bottle of beer in each hand. Then, using the bottles, we had to drag ourselves across the dirt back to the starting line without touching the ground, except for our toes, of course. I was the champ that day, but the next morning, I felt more like the chump because I think I overstretched every muscle in my abdomen.

We didn't go home-empty handed that day. One of Lou's neighbours had a litter of long-haired Himalayan kittens that were being weaned, so naturally the lady plunked one into Danielle's lap. It worked every time. A foregone conclusion. Now we had a frisky little kitten to drive Duchess bonkers.

Three years earlier, when we were still living in Comox, we drove to Surrey to visit my sister where the first "cat in the lap" trick happened. Mary-Lynne handed Danielle, aged three at the time, a cute little orange tabby kitten, and Danielle wasn't about to surrender it anytime soon, so we brought it back to Vancouver Island with us.

As soon as she saw the kitten she said, "Dat my puzzle cat," because Danielle had a twenty-piece jigsaw puzzle that looked much like our soon-to-be new family member.

Puzzle had his moments in the short time that he lived with us. He had the annoying habit of munching on birds and mice that he dragged in from outside, always into our bedroom closet, and always at night when we were trying to sleep. When Puzzle started chowing down on a garter snake in the closet, Evelyne was very tempted to take the cat on a one-way trip to the SPCA In the wee hours of the morning one winter, we could hear him meowing outside our bedroom window. I checked out the front door to see three inches of fresh snow but no Puzzle. Next, I went on the sundeck at the back of the house where I couldn't see him but I could certainly hear his meowing, loud and clear. I hauled a stepladder up from the basement and checked the roof where I found plenty of cat tracks in the snow but still no Puzzle, so I shook the cat food box and lured him from the front roof close enough to collar him. It was not a fun night. There I was, shivering on a stepladder in a snow storm, barefoot with only a pair of shorts on. The SPCA was looking pretty good at that point.

If it wasn't for Danielle, I might have made that trip. When we decided to build, Puzzle didn't survive the big move into PMQs at the base. He was so stressed out, like us, that he parked himself on top of the armoire, refusing our offerings of food and water, and by the time that I dragged him out, it was too late. The vet clinic determined that his kidneys had shut down, so we had to have Puzzle euthanized.

The father-in-law of an air force buddy of mine down island in Deep Bay sold me top-quality hand-split cedar shakes for the roof, which I installed with much help from Evelyne. In late August, I finally installed the two sky lights. All summer long, we hadn't had a drop of rain, but to be safe, I had fastened a double layer of poly over the skylight openings once the roofing was in place. That evening after I nailed the metal flashing around both sky lights, I used Windex to clean the panes, but no matter how much I rubbed with my cloth, there were still spots that I couldn't get rid of. Then I realized that those spots were in fact a gentle rain that had just started. It soon turned into a regular downpour. I was fortunate that I hadn't left that task for another day because as I discovered, the sun had eaten away at the edge of the poly and any rain at all would have resulted in a lot of serious water damage inside.

Now that we were waterproof, we could start on the wiring. I had planned to do it myself; however, as we weren't really enjoying our accommodations in PMQs, we decided to hire someone who actually knew what he was doing to speed up the process. Al Tomlinson was a retired radar tech who had an electrical licence, and it was agreed that I would be his helper/apprentice. He was quite the character. Al was tall and quite clumsy. More than a few times he fell off saw horses and ladders.

Evelyne nailing on shakes

Once, I was up in the garage attic pulling a wire through all the holes I had drilled when it jammed up, so I yelled down to Al who was by the wire reel, “Pull back on the wire a bit, Al.”

“OK,” he said, then promptly took out his side cutters and sniped off the wire at the reel. Did I mention that Al was a tad deaf also?

Regardless of his short-comings, the job was completed with no major problems, and he saved us a lot of time.

My MWO in 409, Bud Cameron, told me a funny story about Al when they were both stationed in Trenton together. The Sgt. and Warrant Officers Club had a planeload of lobster flown in from the Maritimes for a fancy mess dinner one weekend, and a lady sitting directly behind Al was complaining that she didn’t know what to do with her lobster. He reached over with his big meat-hooks-for-hands and grabbed the uncooperative crustacean off her plate. He put it on the floor where he promptly stomped on it with his size twelve shoes, then put it back on her plate and said, “You’re welcome.”

While we were working on the roof, a couple of the guys from the neighbourhood came around to offer their expertise. Cal was retired air force and Wayne was retired army, and their rates were very reasonable. Wayne was a down-homer from Nova Scotia with a colourful accent. We always referred to him as “Newf.” The guys nailed on the cedar siding, and we were happy with the result: they were meticulous, very slow, but we didn’t care because they weren’t getting paid by the hour. It always amazed me that Cal never used a normal framing hammer that was between twenty and thirty-two ounces. Instead, his weapon of choice was a twelve-ounce finishing hammer. Later on, Cal helped me with the clear cedar on the twenty-foot ceiling in the living room, and he also built our kitchen cabinets out of alder hardwood.

Cal and his son-in-law, Peter Paus, were real godsends in helping us finish the house. Peter was a first-rate house builder who was in between jobs, so he and his helper tacked up all the drywall. We were really impressed with their workmanship. If a stud was bowed out or twisted, they took the time to either replace it or plane it before screwing the drywall sheet on. The drywall taping and mudding was a different matter altogether. We had three estimates and naturally took the lowest one, which turned out to be a big mistake. The drywaller was a sleazy little guy who looked like he spent his spare time in the bar. As it turned out, he *was* spending a lot of time *above* the bar at the Arbutus Hotel in Courtenay. Once he'd finished the initial taping, he would only spend about an hour a day working at our house, then he was off to the Arbutus where he had a contract to re-do all the hotel rooms. I had just finished all the plumbing, and we were waiting for the walls to be finished so we could move out of the chicken coup and into our new home.

Finally, one morning, Evelyne's patience wore thin, and she decided to confront him as he was unpacking his tools on a Monday morning. She told him that if he wasn't going to spend the entire day working on our place, then he could just pack up his tools and leave, and furthermore, not to bother coming back. That caught his attention. He stayed and the next day he had a helper with him. The whole sanding job was completed by the weekend. We were glad to see the backside of that guy. Out of all the workers and subcontractors we hired for our house construction, that was the only bad experience we encountered. His work was decent, but his attitude was terrible.

When I finished all the plumbing and painting, we said goodbye to the PMQs and recruited a few friends from work to help with the move. There was still a lot of landscaping that had to be done, a huge deck to be built, some flooring, door and window trim and baseboards along with a thousand minor jobs just to keep us from getting bored. When we moved in, the only place in the entire house that we could utilize for cleaning up, both bodies and dishes, was the bathtub in the basement. A few months after we moved in, in late spring, we were rudely awakened at six a.m. by a loud reverberating noise that sounded like we had a serious plumbing problem. I couldn't pin-point where the noise was coming from, so I frantically ran all over the house flushing toilets and opening taps while looking for water damage. After fifteen minutes the noise stopped, but the next three mornings, we awoke to the same hammering, always at approximately the same time. As a precaution, after finishing the plumbing, I had rented an air compressor to test all my soldering joints on the copper pipes before finishing the basement ceiling with drywall. I had hooked up the compressor to an outside hose bib, cranked up the pressure to eighty PSI and left it on overnight with no apparent loss in pressure. All was well, I thought, but now, a few months later, it appeared that I had a problem that was driving us nuts. I went back to the experts at the plumbing supply store for their opinions, and twice flagged down plumbers who were driving by to pick their brains. Three different theories, but no solutions, so it looked like I would have to tear up the ceiling to inspect my workmanship. Plumbing leaks behind drywall would be a nightmare, so I was losing sleep, awake before the alarm went off, waiting for a pipe to burst.

One fine day, just before six a.m., I was lying in bed wide-awake when I thought I heard something on the roof, so I very quietly made my way out to the street to check the roof. It was a damn woodpecker pecking away at the flashing on the roof. The noise resonated throughout the attic, loud and clear, driving us crazy. Apparently, that's what woodpeckers do in the spring to attract a mate. I threw a rock at the bird, just missing it. He flew away, never to return, and that solved our "plumbing" problem.

I installed six-inch tongue and groove alder flooring in the entrance way and living room, which turned out to be a real chore because many of the boards were warped. The only way to get them in place was to nail down one end then use a car jack to straighten the board in order to secure the other end. We saved money going with the alder, but it took forever to install. It would have been easier to carry on with the oak flooring that we used in the kitchen and dining room. More money, but a lot quicker, which brings that old adage to mind: "Time is money." There was so much alder left over that Cal used it for the kitchen cabinets.

When we were living in PMQs, I scrounged a large number of old bricks from the base dump that we cleaned up over the winter and which our talented bricklayer, Mitch, turned into a beautiful fireplace topped off with the fir beam as a mantel. I installed a small box fan in the living room floor that drew up the heat generated from the wood stove in the basement family room. We burned about five cords of firewood a year, and more than a few badly warped alder flooring boards. A '68 Ford 150 purchased from my former neighbour in Comox, Bill Cole, was worth its weight in gold both for construction and for gathering firewood. Every time I headed out to the bush, I thought about Evelyne's warning regarding chainsaws. "Weekend warriors," they were called, all those inexperienced guys out in the bush with deadly chainsaws slashing and mangling their thighs when the saws "kicked back."

The truck also came in handy for a camping trip one weekend, a good diversion from house building. I had bought an old truck canopy that I fixed up and made reasonably waterproof, then from my neighbour across the street, Len Mallet, I bought a beautiful cedar strip canvas-covered canoe. Evelyne was working that weekend, so she very lovingly packed a suitcase full of clean clothes, pyjamas, towels, soap, toothbrushes, etc., as well as a box of food for us to survive on in the wilderness. We took the logging road all the way to the end of Comox Lake and then over a beat-up rickety wooden bridge to Willemar Lake where we had the whole place to ourselves for two days. The kids, Colin especially, just loved that canoe. He spent hours out on the lake, and the only rule we had was that life preservers were mandatory. We ate our share of beans, wieners and marshmallows that weekend and somehow survived. When we pulled into the driveway on Sunday night, Evelyne just shook her head when she saw us because it was obvious that we should have left the suitcase at home. It was never opened. Roughing it. That's how we did it when I was a kid back in Ocean Falls.

During the summer of our "dream home build," one Monday after work I walked into our PMQ at the base and told Evelyne that I had been transferred, but before she fainted, I added that we didn't have to move because I was going to nav-comm labs, just upstairs from 409 Squadron. I wasn't really overjoyed about working in labs, but at least we weren't moving from Vancouver Island. I much preferred working on aircraft compared to being chained to a bench for eight hours trouble-shooting a radio. If truth be told, I wasn't an "ace" as far as electronics went. I would much rather be woodworking, creating a piece of furniture, something tangible, something that I could see and feel, as opposed to electronics where you had to put your faith in electrons doing their "magic." As it turned out, my position in labs would be in nav-comm stores for three years, which, thankfully, was anything but technical. The job just involved ordering and receiving parts and equipment to keep the lab running smoothly. I quite enjoyed most of the people working there.

Even the senior NCOs were okay to work for. Our warrant officer, Gerry Fleming, was a cross-country skier, and every spring he would organize a seven-man team to compete in the Mount Washington Snow to Surf relay race. It started with a downhill skier who handed off to a cross-country skier, then two different runners, then a cyclist who handed off to two canoeists paddling down the Puntledge River and across the bay to ring the bell at Comox Harbour, the finish line. I was in the final leg and had a reservist, Frank, with me in the canoe. Our team finished in a respectable position. Frank and I had practised during noon hour off Air Force Beach a number of times to get in shape—and sync—for the big race.

The following year, a young corporal in labs, Harold Peacock, thought that he deserved to be in the race because he was regular, not reserve, and was much younger than Frank, thus theoretically giving us a better chance of winning. I never could talk Harold into practising with me on the water. His idea of a workout was to play darts in the Junior Ranks Club until closing time, well lubricated with draft beer. On race day, Bernie, our cyclist, handed off to us in a respectable time, and we set off on the easiest portion of our leg—down the river, going with the current. Even before we hit the ocean I could see that young Harold was quickly running out of gas. Within sight of the finish line I noticed two competitors about to overtake us, so I suggested that we pick up the pace. Big mistake. Harold took a mighty stroke, his hand slipped off the paddle and his loss of balance and abrupt motion tipped the canoe, putting both of us in the drink in full view of all the spectators on shore. Right away my gumboots sank to the bottom of the harbour. Talk about *déja vu* and the Twin Lakes of my youth. At least this time I had a mandatory life preserver on, and a rescue boat was there to haul us in. I and the rest of our team weren't too thrilled with the dunking, nor was Evelyne, who happened to be on duty in the ER that afternoon. Someone who had seen the whole debacle came in and informed her that her husband was in the drink.

Reminiscing about the Snow to Surf race and Harold reminds me of another Harold story. He was renting a house trailer about six blocks from our home, and he wasn't too ambitious in the landscaping department, so he hired Colin to cut his lawn every few weeks. It was more like keeping the weeds in check. I had modified a wagon so Colin could haul our lawn mower the few blocks to Harold's. More than a few times after the weeds were knocked down, Harold was either low on funds or else he would disappear, which meant that I ended up paying Colin. I would then have to hound Harold at work to pay up. I found the best way to recoup the money was to bring up the subject at coffee break and embarrass Harold in front of all his co-workers. The next summer, it didn't take me too much to convince Colin that that was one job not worth his efforts.

MT. WASHINGTON, FRANCOPHONE SCHOOL AND FETAL ALCOHOL SPECTRUM DISORDER

The Comox Valley was a great location because on some days in the winter you could ski or golf or, for that matter, even fish. Our first winter there, we skied at Forbidden Plateau where I did a number on my knee one day, going over a small cliff that I hadn't expected or seen because of heavy fog. Since it was still early in the day, Evelyne and Colin didn't want to pack it in yet, so they set me up in the bar with an ice pack and carried on, *sans* John. That year, 1979, was pretty well the last hoorah for Forbidden Plateau. Mt. Washington had just opened and was at a much higher elevation with deeper snowpacks. Eventually, numerous lifts were built and the road there was paved. Only a forty-minute drive from our front door meant that for a number of years we purchased family passes, and the kids developed into pretty good skiers, Colin especially.

Once, Evelyne was going up the chair lift with a stranger when he blurted out, "Where the hell's that kid's mother?"

She looked down to see a young kid who had just wiped out on a black diamond run. Poles, goggles, tuque and one ski were scattered all over the moguls. As the kid rolled over onto his back, he waved at Evelyne and called out, "Hi, Mom!" We enrolled him in the Mt. Washington Junior

Ski program that met every Saturday. If we didn't feel like skiing that day, we could put him on the ski bus with his equipment and a lunch, and he could ski safely to his heart's content under adult supervision.

Every winter the Army Command in the four Western provinces would send a number of soldiers to Comox for a R & R ski trip, and there were always a few spots open for us local airforce types. One year, I applied and was accepted. I was on "temporary duty" for seven days, attached to the army on a week's ski holiday. I, along with my airforce buddies, had always joked about the "grunts", but I found them to be a good bunch of guys that week. We would normally have group lessons for part of the morning, and the rest of the day we were on our own. Teams were drawn up for a competition on the final day where we could be timed skiing around poles. We had a Calcutta organized with sums of money involved, but unfortunately before the big race and while getting in a few practice runs, I wiped out on some icy snow, wrenching my other knee. With physiotherapy, my knees really improved, but years later I would be paying for those ski mishaps. Live and learn.

Whenever Evelyne phoned her mother long distance in Edmonton, she spoke French. Danielle would be listening to the conversation, and she kept saying she would like to learn French so that she could "hear" Grandma. Although she was only seven, and she would have to cross a busy road and take a bus to school, we enrolled her in the federal francophone school on the base. She didn't seem too frustrated, and by Christmas that year she was quite fluent. She had good friends at school and excelled there. Colin's success in school was a different matter. He was very smart and had a great memory, so he did well until grade three where it became impossible to memorize everything. He had a short attention span, was easily distracted and had problems expressing himself, which led to frustration, blow-ups and fights at school. One of the local "experts" declared that Colin had dyslexia, which could explain his reading, comprehension and writing difficulties. I had noticed myself that he always mixed up right and left, which is part of being dyslexic. Numerous times he saw a psychiatrist in Vancouver for assessment and follow-ups. Unfortunately, none of the doctors at that time—1986—recognized Fetal Alcohol Spectrum Disorder (FASD). In 1973, two researchers at the University of Washington Medical School in Seattle had researched and finally labelled FASD and the harm caused to the fetus in women who consumed alcohol during pregnancy. News of this remarkable discovery didn't travel north for a number of years, which was a shame because it could have made a huge difference for Colin. In the meantime, the situation at school was rapidly deteriorating. None of the teachers nor the principal understood Colin's frustration and resulting behaviour, although some really made an effort and tried to work with him. When Colin was twelve years old, he was scrapping with another boy in class, and when the principal tried to break it up, he was kicked in the ankle for his efforts which resulted in Colin's expulsion, not only from his school but all schools in the district.

Evelyne had a good friend, Marianne Fiendell, a teacher and member of the Adoptive Parents' Support Group, who agreed to tutor Colin a few mornings a week. She was wonderful, but we knew it couldn't be a permanent solution. We decided that if Colin was going to have any chance at all, we were going to have to move to a larger centre where there were more resources. I sent a memo to Ottawa requesting a compassionate posting to Edmonton, stating all the reasons for my request including the support we would have with Evelyne's family still living there. My career manager in headquarters responded by transferring me to Downsview in Toronto. He also said that a compassionate posting meant that I would be forfeiting any chance of promotion. That didn't bother me, but we didn't relish the thought of living in PMQs again. Housing in Toronto was not cheap. I was told there was absolutely no chance of ending up in Edmonton, even though there were probably at least half a dozen master corporal comm techs there who would give up their right arm and firstborn to move to Comox. Awhile later, Evelyne happened to mention our transfer woes to her friend and colleague Leona. Ray Skelly, the NDP MP for the North Island, was a friend of Leona's, and Ray knew the Conservative Minister of National Defence. Unbeknownst to us, Ray talked to the Minister, and, lo and behold, before the end of the week, my transfer was changed to Edmonton. It was such a relief when we got the news. Not only for Colin's sake but also for my job prospects because I was now forty-two years old and had to be thinking of my future once I retired from the military.

The Comox Valley was a wonderful place to live; however, employment opportunities left a lot to be desired. Edmonton offered diverse prospects as far as opportunities for a different career.

When I initially got the ball rolling for a transfer, the house still wasn't completely finished even though we had been living in it for three years. I had to buckle down and do all the little jobs before we listed it for sale. On a Sunday night, I was working on a final little job, the last piece of the puzzle, installing the baseboards in the master bedroom. When I cut the very last baseboard, I miscalculated and cut the board too short. Was it measure twice and cut once, or measure once and cut twice? Anyway, it was nine p.m. by then and the mitre saw was loud and not very conducive for sleeping kids, so I decided to complete our four-year project on Monday after work. On Monday morning, I went to work and was greeted with the memo from Ottawa for my initial transfer. We listed the house with a realtor and didn't have any problem finding a buyer, thanks to the mountain and glacier views, unique design and being woodpecker-free.

In Edmonton, I would be attached to 440 Squadron, a Search and Rescue unit flying Twin Otters, so in late May I was sent to Edmonton to take the aircraft course. On the long weekend, I stayed with our friends Pete and Brenda Peterson in St. Albert. They had spent a number of years in Moose Jaw, Saskatchewan, and the previous year Pete was transferred back to the C-130 Hercules Squadron in Edmonton. On Sunday, the base was hosting a huge air show, and Pete had to work the whole day supporting the show. Pete and I left St. Albert early in the morning. The plan was that after I dropped him off at the base, I had the use of his car for house hunting in the city for the rest of the day. To call Pete's Toyota a beater would be kind. It was more like a wreck on wheels. He was never one to spend much money on vehicles. Before we even got to the base, it ran out of gas right on the gravel road lined with all the "no parking" signs posted for the air show. The fuel gauge wasn't working, and Pete probably figured there was enough in the tank until good old John could fill it up.

We hitchhiked to the guardhouse where he phoned Brenda and asked her to grab a funnel and the five gallons of gas in a jerry can in the garage and drive me back to his car before she went to church. She picked me up, but by then the Toyota had been towed to a compound back in St. Albert. Once we liberated the car and Brenda rushed off to church, I was on my own, but I had a hell of a problem with the car. It was either stalling or bucking like a bronco. We found out later that Brenda took the wrong jerry can, the one outside without the cap that consequently had rain water mixed in with the gas. I didn't get much quality house hunting done that Sunday or Monday. After my Twin Otter course was finished, Evelyne flew to Edmonton for the official government funded house hunting trip, complete with rental car and decent accommodations downtown. We found a house to our liking, a four-level split, about ten blocks northwest of our original house on 127 Street.

EDMONTON REDUX

In early July '86 we said goodbye to the Comox Valley and drove to Alberta, convoy style. Evelyne and the kids drove in our Honda and I and our Himalayan cat Colette followed in the Ford half-ton. Duchess was old and in pain, and we didn't think she would survive the move, so we had her put down before leaving. For the past year, she was slowing down to the point where she wouldn't even chase sticks, her life-long passion, and she would basically sleep for hours on end. Like most dogs, she got stressed-out in vet clinics, so we gave her a pain-killer/tranquilizer before taking her in. Within half an hour of taking that pill she was back to her old stick-chasing self. Now I really felt bad about having her euthanized. She was a wonderful pet, and I wouldn't wish that chore on anyone. Once on the mainland, we stayed with our former Comox friends and neighbours, the Wisemans, who had just moved into a new home in Langley. Brian and I spent half of one day installing a garage door while Joanne and Evelyne caught up. A few years later, Brian retired from the RCMP, and they moved to Penticton where I ended up installing another garage door in another new home. He owes me big time.

Driving through the Rocky Mountains on the Trans Canada Highway, having just crossed the Kicking Horse River and climbing a long hill, the engine started acting just like Pete Peterson's Toyota had with water in the gas. Before the trip, I had installed two-way radios in both vehicles, so I radioed Evelyne and told her the truck was kicking like a horse. At the top of the hill, I pulled over and emptied the sediment bowl and repeated that at Lake Louise, but the problem wouldn't go away. After staying overnight in Calgary, we had only a hundred and eighty miles, fingers crossed, to reach Edmonton. Fifteen miles up the road, the skies opened up and the rain came down in sheets. The truck decided right there and then that it wasn't going any farther in that deluge.

Colin was riding with me at the time, and he quipped, "Hey Dad, your truck's a 'F. O. R. D.—Found On Road Dead.'"

We drove the Honda into Airdrie to a garage where I told Evelyne that I would probably see her the next day at her parents' house. The truck was towed into the garage, and the mechanic got on it right away. In no time I was back on the highway. It turned out that it wasn't water in the gas after all, but a loose connection on the condenser wire causing the engine to miss and eventually quit altogether. The normally reliable Carl Charko, a good friend of mine and a radar tech in labs, had tuned up the truck before we left the valley, but these things happen. And let's face it, the old Ford was no spring chicken.

I arrived in Edmonton at the in-laws' doorstep two hours after Evelyne. Another memory of that trip was that Evelyne's back started giving her grief every time she used the clutch. When she shifted gears, her left leg would be screaming from sciatica. Many painful years later, it was discovered through a MRI that she had spina bifida occulta, a congenital spinal cord defect worsened by helping patients in and out of beds and wheeling around three-hundred-pound patients on stretchers. That '82 Honda was the last standard transmission vehicle we owned. Our next four Hondas were all automatics.

Once we settled into our new home, Evelyne applied for and was hired as Head Nurse at the Mayfield Medicentre in the west end. It was ideal for her because she worked four days a week and never evenings or weekends. In September, Danielle carried on with French Immersion at a Catholic school also in the west end. She had been pestering us for a few years, wanting to take piano lessons, so we bought a huge upright antique piano with a wonderful sound and weighing all of twelve-hundred pounds. The agreement with Danielle was that as long as we didn't have to nag her about practising, the piano could stay. There was no problem on that account. She was a natural on the ivories and eventually completed grade eight in piano, which qualified her to teach the neighbourhood kids years later and helped her financially while she was in university. Colin went to Wellington School in the public system, a school with the programs and resources that met his needs, and where he excelled. We were surprised that he did so well playing the sax in the school band. Like his sister, Colin had a good ear for music.

I had kept every scrap of paper relating to the building of our dream home in Courtenay. There were receipts, bills, workers' wages, any and every building expense involved, big or small. We did okay when we sold and were able to buy the house in Edmonton mortgage free, but I wanted to add up all the numbers to see what the bottom line was. After a few minutes of sorting through the papers I said the hell with it. I didn't want to know the bottom line. The house was no longer ours. It was history, so I just burned all the papers in the fireplace. Those four years were definitely an experience, sometimes enjoyable, sometimes not. Lots of stress, grief, tons of sweat equity, injuries—I broke a chip on my heel falling off the roof—but when it was all said and done, we were happy that we did it. But no more ambitious projects like building a house. Maybe just the odd renovation here or there.

At 440 Squadron, working on the Twin Otters was much different than working on a Hercules aircraft, and it was mainly because of the serviceability. The Twin Otters hardly ever broke down. I loved the hours also: only day shift Monday to Friday. Saturdays and Sundays were handled by the "weekend warriors," the reserve squadron. Quite frankly, the job was a tad boring. In the morning, the aircrew would take off, do some training, a few touch-and-goes, then land midday for lunch. While the aircrew ate lunch, we would refuel. If any problems had been written up, we would de-snag and then relaunch for the afternoon training flights. Boring. The Twin Otter aircraft was ideal for Search and Rescue because it was so reliable, could operate on short runways, fly in extremely cold conditions and could be equipped with wheels, pontoons, or skis. On a few different occasions, Kenn Borek Air of Calgary had installed long-range fuel tanks and snow skis on their Twin Otters and flown all the way to the southern tip of South America to perform medical evacuations in Antarctica in minus sixty degrees Celsius weather. Other aircraft could possibly land there, but in that extreme temperature, they would probably be grounded for months until it warmed up.

I was with 440 Squadron for about ten months, and in that period, there wasn't a single search mission other than an emergency locator transmitter signal (ELT) that turned out to be a false alarm. A private aircraft inadvertently transmitted the emergency signal while it was parked overnight. Not that I was specifically hoping for air disasters, but anything other than starts, parks, and refuelling would break the monotony of our daily existence.

In 1987, I would have twenty-four years of service in the military, and I was forty-three years old. Time for a second career. A few of my air force buddies had been hired by Dow Chemical in Fort Saskatchewan, and they were bringing home pretty decent pay cheques every two weeks. Dennis Coughlin thought it was a great place to work and encouraged me to apply although I wondered about working in a chemical plant all day long with an emergency respirator strapped to my belt. As it turned out, Dow Chemical wasn't hiring at the time, so I applied at North-West Industries (NWI) at Edmonton International Airport. For years, NWI had contracts with the Canadian military for support work on the Tudor, T-33, CF-104 and Hercules aircraft, and in the fall of '87, the company had taken another contract to perform all the Hercules major inspections that were previously done by the airforce technicians. I went in for an interview and was accepted, so I submitted my release from the military, carefully calculating that my official release date was into my twenty-fifth year so that my pension wouldn't be reduced. We called that the "twenty-four years plus one plan." As long as you served twenty-four years and at least one more day into your twenty-fifth, you weren't penalized five percent on your monthly pension.

So that was it. I closed that chapter of my life and wasn't sad about it, nor did I regret joining in the first place. Joining the airforce was my ticket out of Ocean Falls, I saw much of the world, met and married a wonderful woman, was trained as a technician and was paid a half decent wage, albeit not very well in those early years. I had a lot to be thankful for.

When my termination date was finalized, I was talking with Pete Peterson, and he was all excited, telling me that he, along with his brother-in-law, Marcel Bertrand, were retiring in late June. They didn't know what I had been up to, so I burst his bubble when I told him that I had them beat by two weeks. That weekend, they and their wives Brenda and Freda came to our house for a uniform burning ceremony. We each threw a work dress shirt into the fireplace and found out that they were indeed flame resistant. I had to produce my dress uniform shirt so that we could have a toast to our careers. Marcel was hired on with a company doing non-destructive testing of oil pipelines, and Pete and Brenda moved out to Maple Ridge, B. C. where Pete worked with his brother insulating commercial parking garage ceilings. And he thought that working on Hercs as an airframe tech was a dirty job!

CIVVY STREET

1987 - Present

BACK ON THE HERC

I spent my first six weeks at NWI working on T-Birds and Tudors, doing functional power checks and trouble-shooting, and then the company wanted me to attend a month-long comm/radar Herc course in Trenton, even though I'd already taken the course back in 1969 while in the military. The company insisted, so I had to go. Evelyne wasn't too pleased, but I promised her that it would be the one and only work-related trip that I'd ever have to take for NWI. The course was a piece of cake. I wouldn't say I could have taught it, but it certainly wasn't very difficult. I was put up in a decent motel downtown with a meal allowance, so I didn't have to rely on mess hall grub. Halfway through the course, Evelyne flew down for a weekend. We rented a car and drove down to Toronto to see the big city. We were walking up and down Yonge Street, taking in all the street activities, and it was getting really hot, so I hauled Evelyne into a pub for a cool one. I ordered a beer and she a coke that came without ice and in a dirty glass. While she was complaining about this, I noticed that she was the only woman in the pub, and when I glanced around and saw that the pub was called CHAPS, it dawned on me that it was a gay bar. Perhaps that was the reason the waiter was a bit surly with Evelyne. He didn't get much of a tip from me that day.

When the first Hercules arrived for the major overhaul, the learning curve wasn't too steep because many of us in 4 Hangar had prior Hercules experience. It seemed that half of the workforce were sheet metal technicians—tin rats—so there was a constant noise from the endless riveting. When we first started the program, all the air force Hercules were "E" model C-130s

C-130E Hercules Transport

with high airframe hours, which meant replacing fuselage skins in some cases and splicing in new floor beams because of corrosion. The tin rats banked many, many hours of overtime to stay on schedule. They were mostly younger guys with mortgages, so they didn't mind working three weeks straight with time and a half overtime and double on Sunday.

Initially, there were two of us in my trade in the Herc program, but after a year, Tony and his wife separated and he took a job with Air Canada in Vancouver. A recent grad from the tech school in Edmonton, Darren, was hired on to help me out. This was quite a contrast to the years when I worked in Hercules maintenance in the air force. We had more than enough guys back then and plenty of slack time or days when we just stayed home. It was a rude awakening. Sometimes the aircraft electricians or the integral systems tech would help me out, or a tech from 5 Hangar would come over for a day or two if I was really swamped. The integral systems tech, Dave, had been a neighbour of the Petersons in St. Albert before they moved to British Columbia. I had to laugh when Pete told me that Dave was a bit of a drinker. It was like the pot calling the kettle black. A year and a half into the program, Dave dropped his wife off at the airport so she could visit relatives back east, and then he went on a bender. When he picked her up two weeks later, she was none the wiser that he'd fallen off the wagon and was no longer employed. In that whole period, he never made it to work, never even phoned in. We don't know if he was fired or just quit, but either way he was history. I worked for eleven years at NWI and can only recall one other person who was canned, and that was alcohol-related also. The company terminated a technician once for carelessly damaging aircraft equipment, but the union paid a lawyer a tidy sum to have him reinstated with ten months back pay. My father was a union man and for good reason, but sometimes unions are just too powerful for their own good.

My biggest beef was how the smokers abused the system. Since smoking wasn't allowed in the hangar, many of these guys would nip outside for a puff just before the fifteen-minute coffee break and then stay outside after the break for another cigarette, in effect doubling their coffee break. I take that all back. The smoking issue was just damned annoying. It was the working conditions due to the air that we were breathing that was a major bone of contention. Sometimes, in the confined cargo area where we were working, the aircraft refinishers, the painting crew, used paint removers and spray paints that were highly carcinogenic. They donned respirators, but in my position, it was impractical or impossible to use a respirator due to the cramped quarters and the nature of the work. When they were spray painting the fuselage, clouds of the cancer-causing fumes floated about the hangers. Our safety rep, being a smoker, wasn't too concerned about what we were inhaling. A few times I complained to the foreman, but he was more concerned with being on schedule than with a little old safety issue. There was an opening for a shop steward in our hangar, so I ran for election, and much to my surprise I was voted in. Surprised, because I wasn't too popular with the refinishers. The shop steward was basically there to help settle petty grievances between union members and management, which in most cases were even less than petty, more like silly. I was talking to the safety representative one day, and he had always wanted to be a shop steward, so I suggested we should switch jobs even though the members should have voted on it. We would just inform the union president a few weeks later, after the fact, and that's what we did. Better to ask for forgiveness than permission.

It wasn't long after the switch that the union sent me to Montreal for a four-day safety convention. I knew that I had promised Evelyne no more trips, but this one was short and unavoidable. Our union belonged to the International Association of Machinists (IAM) and Aerospace Workers, with the majority of the membership being U.S. based. It seemed that a good portion of the time at the convention was spent honouring the long-time president of the IAM whom I'd never heard of, but I did come away from Montreal with a greater understanding of carcinogens in the workplace, knowledge which I put to good use at NWI. It wasn't too long before any significant aircraft paint spraying had to be carried out on the evening and midnight shifts when the bulk of the workforce wasn't there. I was even less popular with the refinishers when that happened.

MARITIMES REDUX

A year after moving back to Edmonton, Evelyne and I and the kids flew to Montreal where we rented a car to tour the Maritimes. We regretfully missed out on Cape Breton and Newfoundland due to time constraints, but we had a wonderful time, and the weather co-operated for the entire trip.

We stayed in Montreal an extra day so that Evelyne could re-connect with Laurence, a girl she met during a bus trip to Expo 67 with thirty other francophone students. Laurence wanted us to meet her elderly mother who lived on a small acreage south of the city with her significant other, Daniel. The mother looked old enough to be Laurence's grandmother, and it seemed to me that she had mild dementia. This was before Alzheimer's was such a common term, but thinking back, I'm sure she was in the early stages. When we arrived at her house in the afternoon, the old guy was still in bed. I could hear Laurence's mother in the bedroom yelling at Daniel in French. Evelyne translated for me. She was telling the "lazy old bugger" to get up because they had company and he shouldn't be sleeping all day. Finally, he emerged from the bedroom and walked bow-legged and in obvious discomfort to the backyard where we were sitting. Daniel's hobby was handcrafting wooden axe handles that he would sell. He showed me a finished product and then proceeded to forcefully juggle it from one hand to the other, repeating in English, "I'm going to kill her.

I'm going to kill that woman."

Later, Laurence filled in the blanks for us. The old couple had a forty-five-gallon metal barrel that was used for burning garbage, and at one point it had been crawling with maggots. Daniel turned the barrel on its side and while he was spraying in aerosol to kill the maggots, Laurence's mother came along with a better idea. Without warning poor old Daniel, she threw in a match which resulted in one badly scorched scrotum and one very pissed off significant other. There was no homicide that day while we were there because, for one thing, it would be weeks before he could move fast enough to catch her. It was painful just to see him walk.

We spent some time on Prince Edward Island where Evelyne and Danielle took in an *Anne of Green Gables* play, and Colin and I went cod fishing on a fishing boat. The east coast fishery was quite depleted by that time, but we did manage to land enough cod for a few meals. PEI was probably the highlight of our vacation that year. It's such a beautiful little province with a small and friendly capital city. We bumped into the Premier of the province, Joe Ghiz, while touring the Legislative Building, and the next day bumped into him again in a restaurant. That's a prime example of how small PEI is. After shaking his hand, we mentioned that we hoped the Confederation Bridge, due to be completed in the '90s, wouldn't change the Island in a negative way. Joe would never know because he died at an early age in 1996, a year before the eight-mile-long toll bridge was operational.

We really enjoyed Nova Scotia as well. All I could remember of my first visit there back in the mid '60s was overcast skies, snow, rain and more rain. This time, I saw the southern tip of the province and drove up the East Coast, through Lunenburg, Bridgewater, Halifax and, of course, Peggy's Cove where my camera got a real workout. In Bridgewater, we popped into the bike shop/taxi stand to have a visit with my old pal Charlie Horstman and family. Not much was happening that evening, taxi-wise. I think his wife was the dispatcher and Charlie and his two sons, eighteen and nineteen years old, were likely the drivers as well as the bike mechanics. It appeared that marriage had slowed down the "Bridgewater Bomber!" It happens to most of us, thank God. Both of Charlie's sons were thinking about enrolling in the U.S. Navy because, at that time, decent jobs were scarce in their hometown. Years later, I tried to connect with Charlie but had no success.

ROLLING STONES AND THE HIGH ARTIC

When our integral systems tech had either quit or was fired (I was leaning towards fired), the company hired a young francophone who had taken his release after only six years with the military. Carol Grenier was, hands down, the best technician that I had the pleasure of working with. Over the years, I had run into smart technicians, but in many cases, they hardly ever got their hands dirty because they were just plain lazy. Carol wasn't afraid to handle any problem and sometimes it involved my trade, comm/radar, but more frequently it involved electrical snags with the turbo engines. After two years at NWI, he probably knew as much or more than the aircraft electricians. In 1994, the British rock and roll band, the Rolling Stones, stopped over in Edmonton for their "Voodoo Lounge" tour. These boys knew how to tour. They had a leased Boeing 747 jumbo jet that had all the comforts of home and then some. The aircraft crew chief arranged for some maintenance support with NWI, so Carol was seconded to clear up a list of snags for the 747. He had never worked on a Boeing before—the Hercules was built by Lockheed Martin—but it didn't take him long to rectify all the problems. I spent a few hours assisting Carol, and I was just amazed how the leasing company had configured that jumbo jet to suit "The Greatest Rock and Roll Band in the World." Nothing but the best for Mick and his mates. He had a bedroom right behind the cockpit, complete with a king-sized bed and a built-in TV and VCR. Down below on the main deck were numerous couches, coffee tables, TVs and, of course, the standard bar set-up for refreshments and such.

I worked at NWI for eleven years, and normally we were quite busy. At that time, the air force was buying the newer updated Hercules, the C-130H model. Five of these were converted to air-to-air refuelling tankers to support the CF-18 Hornet fighter jets. They also purchased two used C-130H-73s and a few stretched Hercs with fifteen feet added to the fuselage. NWI was heavily involved with them before the air force took them over. The H-73s were parked for a couple of years on a damp, rainy island overseas before the RCAF purchased them, so the tin rats had a lot of extra work dealing with serious corrosion.

On October 30, 1991, a Hercules that we had just recently overhauled was involved in a tragic accident in the High Arctic. Tail number 322 crashed about ten miles short of the runway at Canadian Forces Station Alert, Ellesmere Island, on a re-supply mission. Even though the aircraft was a complete write-off, fourteen passengers and crew survived the impact. Sadly, the aircraft pilot, Captain Couch, eventually succumbed to hypothermia and died after unselfishly giving up his parka to a passenger who had lost his either in the fire or because it was soaked in jet fuel. The newspapers were speculating on the cause of the disaster, and many theories were bandied about. One so-called expert opined that a failure of the low-range radar altimeter could be the reason for the crash. I didn't enjoy reading that in the *Edmonton Journal* because I was responsible for that system. Before the aircraft was handed over to the military, I had done complete power checks of all communication, navigation and radar equipment on board, and then the aircrew had performed an extensive test flight. Only when all systems were serviceable had the flight test crew accepted the aircraft and flown it home. I suppose it could have been the radar altimeter, but when it left NWI, it was working well. I don't know if any one factor was attributed to the crash, but it was noted that on approach, the aircraft was on "visual approach" instead of "instrument approach." At that time of the year, it's awfully dark up there. Two years later, in 1993, a made-for-TV movie titled *Ordeal in the Arctic* was released. When 322 met its demise and those five people died, it really put everything into perspective for me. We had a critical job to perform, and hopefully we were up to the task.

In 1994, the air force base at Namao was history. The Search and Rescue Squadron, 440, and their Twin Otters were transferred to Yellowknife, Northwest Territories. I thought that move made sense; however, when the Hercules Transport Squadron 435 ended up in Winnipeg, it had the markings of political maneuverings of the first order. Lloyd Axworthy, Winnipeg Member of Parliament and Cabinet Minister under the Liberal Prime Minister Jean Chrétien, was instrumental in the big move. Bristol Aerospace of Winnipeg, after seventy years of federal contracts with the military, was on its last legs. When the CF-101 Voodoo was retired by the Air Force, Bristol lost the contract they'd held since the early '60s, and then in 1995 they would lose the CF-5 contract due to a phase-out of that aircraft. Their helicopter contracts were finished also. To top it off, the lucrative CF-18 Hornet maintenance and overhaul contract went back east to Canadair in Montreal. Soon, a few of the Bristol sheet metal techs headed west to Edmonton to work at NWI, and a whole squadron of Hercules flew east to Manitoba to roost in their new home. As for Namao, it grew into the largest army base in Canada. They even erected buildings on what was at one time the longest runway in the British Commonwealth and used the huge aircraft hangars to house and service the armoured vehicles and tanks. Now, when the paratroopers wanted to do jump training, they had to be bused down to the Edmonton International Airport where they boarded a Winnipeg Hercules that flew them over Drop Zone Buxton by the army base. Having the comm/radar labs relocated to Winnipeg meant I no longer had the chance to drop in and talk to the bench technicians if I had a really weird or complicated snag.

THE BROKEN CORD, COLLEGE MATHIEU AND EVELYNE'S NEW CAREERS

Back home, Colin continued to struggle with his disabilities in spite of being very intelligent. He found it difficult to learn using conventional methods. The doctors never did clue in about fetal alcohol spectrum disorder, but many years after Colin was out of school, Evelyne was in the public library and in her words, "A book titled *The Broken Cord* just fell off the shelf in front of me." The more she read, the more she realized that this could have been Colin's story. Michael Dorris had written a heartfelt and powerful story of his family's experience with their adopted son who lived with FASD. It was unfortunate that the experts hadn't come up with a proper diagnosis for our son when he was young.

After Danielle finished grade nine, we enrolled her in Collège Mathieu, a private francophone boarding school in Gravelbourg, southeast of Swift Current, Sask. Evelyne's father, Marcel, was born in Gravelbourg and his father was buried there. One of Danielle's classmates at Collège Mathieu turned out to be a third cousin of Marcel's, Natalie, who lived on a farm close by. When we drove down in September to get Danielle settled in, we discovered that students were four to a room. I took the house mother aside and advised her in no uncertain terms that Danielle would not be rooming in with a particulor student, who had been a classmate of hers in Edmonton and was quite a troublemaker. Sure enough, by the spring, that student was permanently expelled for conduct unbecoming.

Danielle really excelled during her three years there. She was also involved in music, playing the keyboards for the school band, and in her final year, toured as far as Vancouver with her bandmates. Twice a year, at Christmas and Easter, she would take the bus home for an extended break, and during that time she would pound non-stop on the old upright. She said that the electric piano came in a poor second in the tone department compared to the antique, old faithful. Around the same time, I was enjoying my own musical instrument. I was spending three hours a week attending an acoustic guitar building course. It took me approximately two years to build one, but once finished, it had beautiful sound and that was verified by Norm McNeil, who was a guitar aficionado. With my previously mentioned musical talents, this beautiful hand-crafted guitar was wasted on me, so Danielle ended up with it.

Acoustic Guitar

Due to a wonky back that never improved, Evelyne had to finally resign from her position at the private clinic. She had been there for seven years doing what she loved, but it was now too much, so she made the decision to step back. After five years of forced retirement, an opportunity came up for her to ease her way back into nursing when the University of Alberta offered a one-year speciality in Parish Nursing for the first time. After graduating, Evelyne was the first parish nurse to be hired by a faith community in western Canada. It was an independent practice with an office at Mount Zion Lutheran Church in Edmonton. With an elderly congregation, many of the seniors were falling through the cracks and Evelyne was there to support them and help them navigate the healthcare system. Her days were filled with home visits, health counselling, referrals and teaching. She loved it, and her patients loved her. The following year, she completed a clinical pastoral education course (chaplaincy training) at the Royal Alexandra Hospital, a portion of which was spent working on call as chaplain on weekends. It wasn't unusual for her to be called into the hospital in the middle of the night to support patients or their families in crisis, usually in the emergency department.

Over the years, Evelyne had been involved with a group supporting victims of sexual abuse by clergy in the Catholic Church. When she and the Lutheran Bishop had a conversation at a conference sponsored by the Lutheran Church and dealing with that subject, he was surprised to learn that she was well versed on the topic. There had been a resignation at the synod, and the position of adviser to the Bishop on matters of abuse by clergy was open. She was offered the position. She was there to support victims, but as it turned out the position morphed into raising awareness, teaching and presenting at synod conferences. Eventually, she ended up planning, participating in, and presenting at several conferences in Chicago and San Antonio sponsored by the Evangelical Lutheran Church of America and the Commission for Women. Planning for each conference meant several trips to Chicago. Lutheran women from all over the world participated. Rewarding and eye-opening experiences. Eventually, however, Evelyne realized that change would come at a snail's pace, if at all, and she became disillusioned. She felt that the Bishop might have paid lip service but was unlikely to act in any meaningful way, so she resigned.

The Evangelical Lutheran Church of Canada had a strong emphasis on healthcare, and every year the Canadian Healthcare Association Conference was held in Banff, Alberta. One year, Evelyne was nominated and, much to her surprise, was elected president. This was a precedent for the association—there had never been a woman nor a lay person in that position. Eventually, she ended up serving on the Board of the Good Samaritan Society, a Lutheran non-profit that managed many assisted living residences in Alberta and British Columbia. All of these conferences/presentations involved travelling, and with back problems continuing to plague her, I was nominated her unofficial chauffeur. It was easier for her to ride as a passenger and be able to shift positions frequently than to drive, so I would take books along to catch up on my reading as well as go sightseeing while the conferences were in session. Banff isn't such a bad place to spend a few days. I even had a chance to ski the slopes at Sunshine a few times.

RENOVATION BLUES

For my forty-ninth birthday, Evelyne bought me a two-year-old Toyota truck in excellent condition. Three years previously, I had sold the old '68 Ford at a garage sale because it was a regular gas guzzler and starting to show and act its age. That summer, I figured out why I was now driving a truck. Evelyne saw an older house that was for sale just a block south of our very first house on 127 Street. She fell in love. This house, circa 1926, had tons of character along with a multitude of problems, hence the need for a truck to carry out all the renovation projects if we purchased. I liked our present house although it had its faults. The yard was too small and the one-car garage had major problems with the footings that caused the building to shift, affecting the garage door to no end. We also weren't too thrilled with the three break-and-enters in the six years we lived there. Evelyne's major beefs with the house were that it was too big and too dark. The little house on 127 Street was smaller, had more windows to let in the light, a much nicer yard and a decent two-car garage. All this offset the fact that it was a serious fixer-upper. Our bid was accepted, but we wouldn't move in until the house was half-way habitable, almost eight months later.

The first problem I tackled was the heat, or lack thereof, on the top floor where the three bedrooms were located. Neil Spellman, a sheet metal technician from NWI, came to have a look and declared that the

Ensuite renos

amount of heat coming up the duct work to the master bedroom could be equated to the family dog breathing up your pant leg, so he recommended a new furnace and an upgrade to the ducting, which we did with his help. The new gas furnace was half the size of the original but twice as efficient, always a good thing for surviving Alberta winters.

The previous owner must have thought that he was a decorating guru because in the master bedroom, he had flung bright blue drywall mud in huge globs all over the walls and the ceiling. It was so thick that my only option was to remove all the drywall sheets that were "decorated." Man was it ugly. With my brother-in-law Gilles' help, we soon filled up a dumpster bin in the back alley—more than a few times, I might add. The ensuite bathroom was bare bones. All it had was a non-working toilet and one copper pipe for cold water. The floor had four inches of slope, and the door was non-existent. I spent many weeks in that sorry excuse for a bathroom before it was functional. An old beat-up clawfoot bathtub had been left behind in the garage, so we sent it out to be re-finished, and I installed it once I had dealt with the tilting floor. We were lucky that there was a cavity alongside the brick chimney coming up from the basement to the roof, passing through the ensuite. This cavity allowed us to feed up new water lines, furnace ducts and electrical wires quite easily without having to cut through floors and ceilings.

The basement was another headache. First of all, the basement doorway and stairway were much too narrow for all practical purposes, so I enlarged the opening and then installed a wider set of stairs. I don't know why the main floor didn't collapse into the basement because some of the two by eight floor joists had up to six inches of wood cut away to accommodate heating ducts and pipes. I beefed those up with steel box beams where possible. In order to operate my table saw and thickness planer, I had to remove a good number of the supporting posts in the basement. I installed a heavy eight-inch steel I-beam spanning the basement from foundation wall to foundation wall and augmented that with two screw jacks, mid-section. Now I was satisfied that we could at least survive a medium-sized earthquake.

I couldn't believe some of the obvious faults that I encountered in that house after we bought it. Much of the wiring wasn't done with the electrical code in mind, so I had to straighten that out as well as run additional circuits to the upper level. I beefed up the attic insulation, and while I was up there, I noticed that the main floor bathroom exhaust fan vented into the attic instead of to the outside. Even the dryer vent in the basement wasn't vented outside. Scary, scary, scary. Some do-it-yourselfers give the rest of us a bad name.

It took us longer than expected to sell our other house because the housing market in Edmonton was down, but that was okay because it took me longer than expected to make our "fixer-upper" livable. When it finally sold, we hired a small moving company that did only local moves in Edmonton and the surrounding area. Because it was winter and a slack period, the company sent two leadhands and one helper. For the entire time of the move, the two leadhands bickered and argued every step of the way. The small wiry guy believed in a technical approach for the art of moving heavy objects; whereas, the big strapping leadhand employed brute strength. I thought it was quite humorous until I watched the twelve hundred-pound antique piano sliding down the front yard slope in the snow. There were a few anxious moments, but somehow the piano survived the trip. Our good friends across the back lane, Chuck and Lori Samis, had agreed to store it—and play it—in their house until we could find a buyer. Danielle was sorry to see her beautiful upright go, but it was soon replaced by an electronic keyboard, purchased from Joe Glidden, a young comm tech that I knew in Comox who was now stationed in Cold Lake. Danielle would need it to teach the neighbourhood kids piano lessons on Tuesdays.

Around the time that we moved, Colin was on the move also. After he finished with school, he was at loose ends and he was always talking about going back to BC. He and a friend pulled up stakes one day and just left. We didn't know if they drove or hitchhiked. All we knew for sure at the time was that he was no longer in Edmonton. The whole family was in flux. Danielle had aspirations of becoming a veterinarian, and so she enrolled at the University of Alberta in the Faculty of Science. This was quite a shock after having spent her high school years in residence in a small town with few amenities and where supervision by a "house mother" was evident at all times. The emphasis had been on scholarship and comradeship. Living at home again, and hopefully more mature, Danielle had a taste of freedom as the reigns were slackened. Halfway through her first semester, Danielle got a phone call from one of her classmates one evening, and shortly thereafter a whole car full of girls showed up at the house. They were going out to do a bit of partying, and Danielle assured us that they wouldn't be late because some of them, Danielle included, had exams in the morning. We thought that was a dumb idea, but off they went anyway.

By two in the morning she wasn't home yet and we were getting worried. No one had cell phones at that time. I decided to drive to a popular club on the south side. No luck there, so I headed over to West Edmonton Mall where I spotted her. The club was wall-to-wall with teenagers, standing room only. It was so loud in there that you couldn't talk, so I motioned that she should follow me outside. Danielle was really concerned, thinking that something serious had happened, like a death in the family, and when I said, "No, just an exam you have to write in the morning," she was none too happy with me. She stayed in the garage for the rest of the night, refusing to come in. A month later, she moved into an apartment with three other girls, one of them her cousin Natalie who had moved up from Gravelbourg. That was the first of many moves where my truck came in handy for relocation during her university years. We told her room and board was free at 127 Street, but she was determined to be independent. We had been paying into a registered educational savings plan for years, so with that and a part-time job in the University Animal Research Lab, she could scrape by. No doubt student loans were involved, but we didn't want to know about that. And, of course, the four or five piano students a week and weekly housekeeping for Mom all helped to pay the rent. She was not totally out of our lives, but that's how we found ourselves as empty nesters. Years later, she told me that she was never so embarrassed as that night at West Edmonton Mall.

Our house had all the original windows from 1926. Single pane with storm windows and in many cases with rotting frames. After a few winters in the house, we decided to replace most of the windows with double-pane vinyl units, windows that you could actually open in the summer versus the current ones that were permanently painted shut. I didn't touch the living room and dining room windows because of their size and expense in replacing. They also had slight imperfections in the glass which added to the character of the house. I couldn't believe how easy and how inexpensive it was to install the new windows. My final big project was to scrape, sand and paint the wood siding. That would prove to be very difficult and time-consuming.

Around that time, NWI was gearing up to do some major modifications to the C-130 Hercules fleet, so they hired a number of recent avionic graduates from Northern Alberta Institute of Technology (NAIT). When the mod program was delayed, the company started laying off some of these young techs, which was a shame because eventually they would likely be snapped up by the competition, and NWI would lose them forever. By the late '90s, I had the most seniority in the company in my trade after two of the older guys who had been there since the '50s finally retired.

I approached Human Resources and offered to take a layoff that summer so that at least one of these new techs wouldn't be going down the road, and more importantly, I could slop some paint on the house. H.R. went for it although my foreman in the hangar wasn't too sold on the idea. It took all of two months to paint the house what with sleeping in every morning and, of course, our annual two-week vacation on the west coast. We normally drove out to B. C. in the middle of the summer when NWI shut down for a two-week period. Once the kids no longer came with us on summer holidays, we found it much faster and easier if I drove solo to the coast and then picked up Evelyne at the airport. She couldn't sit in the car for long periods. My back wasn't all that great either after a lengthy trip, but I would rebound much faster than she would.

NORMALIZATION

Evelyne and I attended the 1998 Ocean Falls Reunion on July 4th in Campbell River. There was a decent turnout of eight hundred people although the numbers were decreasing over the years, partly due to waning interest, but mainly because some of the older folks were dying. One of the reunions in the '80s drew approximately fourteen hundred "Rain People." I had a good visit with John and Pat Riley, Roy and Marlene Chernishenko and Bozena Watroba whom I hadn't seen in thirty-five years. After the picnic on Sunday, we drove up to Port Hardy where we boarded the plane to Ocean Falls. While flying north, Evelyne was amazed by the spectacular views of the coastline and again by the beautiful setting as we came in for a landing on Cousins' Inlet. Had we been flying under the clouds in December, she might have had a much different impression. The airline terminal was two properties over from our old house, formerly Tom Mudie's place. The terminal was run by Jimmy Owens, the only person in Ocean Falls who was actually born there. He also ran a small store that carried the essentials and not much more. We had booked a room at Inge's B&B across the bridge in south Martin Valley. Due to a recent flood, the room had a musty smell, but we couldn't afford to be too picky because that's pretty well all there was for accommodation. The huge hotel, the Martin Inn, was now locked up, and the town itself was history.

Crown Zellerbach had shut down the mill due to operating losses, obsolete equipment and its isolated geographical location. The beginning of the end came in 1968 when the kraft and sulphite operations were shut down, resulting in a hundred job losses. In 1972 and 1973 the groundwood operation, sawmill and three remaining paper machines closed, costing another three hundred jobs, but in 1972 there was a glimmer of hope when the NDP won the provincial election. The B. C. Government bought the mill and the town site from Crown Zellerbach for one million dollars, formed the Ocean Falls Corporation and declared the mill back in business. For awhile, the corporation was successful, but not for long. Factors like weak markets, labour unrest and rising costs didn't help matters, but the real killer was that the mill didn't have enough timber rights to operate at a profit. When the Social Credit Party won the provincial election in 1975, they tried to keep the mill running, but it was like flogging a dead horse. On May 31,1980, the mill became a footnote in history. In most cases, the workers had had no problem finding jobs during the twelve years of the slow death. Some transferred to Crown Zellerbach's two other B. C. locations in Campbell River and Fraser Mills. The new mills at Kitimat, Kamloops, Quesnel and MacKenzie benefited also, scooping up many of the skilled mill workers.

When Evelyne and I walked into town, I couldn't believe what I was seeing—or not seeing. Most of the houses and the wooden plank roads had been bulldozed and burned. The corporation had carried out a "Normalization Procedure," which is a fancy term for demolition. Thirteen years later, the hillside had filled in with trees and bush where a town, my hometown, had nestled. There's no stopping nature in a rain forest. A few of the remaining residents staged sit-ins to stop the destruction, but it was hopeless. However the government did agree to leave some of the houses for heritage reasons. They even allowed part of Fifth Street, what we called the "School Hill," to remain untouched. Out of all the wooden plank roads that added so much to Ocean Fall's character, it was the only stretch to survive the onslaught. When we walked up past the hydro dam to the ball park, we discovered that a logging company was now using the field as a dry land log sorting area. A few years previously, the logging company employees had been staying in the hotel annex. When they left, no one thought to turn off the water, which resulted in burst water pipes and major damage when the temperature dropped in the winter months.

Last of wooden roads 'School Hill'

Come winter, the population drops to maybe fifty people, and they all live in the private houses in Martin Valley. In summer, the numbers explode to upwards of a hundred and fifty folks. The sole industry there year-round is the Central Coast Power hydro plant that supplies power to Martin Valley and Bella Bella via underwater transmission lines. A fishing charter outfit operates during the summer. I found the mile-and-a-half road between Ocean Falls to Martin Valley had been much improved. It was widened, and the more dangerous curves had been straightened. I was pleasantly surprised to see that the long wooden bridge was no more. At what must have been great expense, tons of rock had been blasted from the mountainside, so the vehicles could now drive on solid ground. In the late '50s, our neighbour, Allan Mudie, with two other teenagers, had crashed his father's pick-up truck through the guard rail and ended up in the salt chuck. Both passengers survived, but Allan was not so lucky. A twenty-minute walk past the former bridge were the pathetic remains of the Fairy Rock. It was also known as the Penny Rock when I was growing up. All that remains is a plain old boulder about two feet high with a sign stating, "This is the location of the original Fairy Rock." Before the road crew got carried away with dynamite and heavy equipment, the rock was massive, at least twelve feet high with more than a few crevices and cavities where adults would hide money. When a group of kids walked the Valley road, it was always a race to get to the rock first and pocket the coins. Early one Sunday morning years ago, I was walking with my mother into town for church when I hit the jackpot. Fourteen dollars. And who said religion doesn't pay? I wanted to show Evelyne one of my favourite haunts, the sand bar, but the trail was so overgrown that we soon gave up because we couldn't even find it. Twin Lakes was also out of the question because we only had two days.

My childhood home was now owned by a man called Darrell Saggo, and he had also purchased the house next door, which had been formerly owned by George McRae, the Standard Oil agent. Darrell Saggo turned that house into a bar. Saggo's Saloon was a cozy little place where you could enjoy a beer and mingle with the local characters, which we did. The locals were only too happy to talk to an original "Rain Person." The sign read: "Open Monday, Wednesday, Friday, 4 p. m. until the crowd disperses." When I told Darrell who I was, he remarked that my father had sure built a solid house. Some of the houses in the Valley were really beginning to show their age. He also said that I was more than welcome to walk through our old home, and I took him up on the offer. Downstairs, looking out my former bedroom window to the ocean, a flood of memories came rushing back.

Forbes house in Martin Valley

In the mid-to-late '50s, an old fisherman came into town with a large litter of Irish Water Spaniel pups for sale. Mary-Lynne got wind of this and asked Dad if he would buy one.

Dad happened to know that the litter was completely sold out, so he said, "Yes, of course."

However, my sister heard that one of the pups had been returned, so she went down to the wharf and picked up the last pup. This was like a chess match, and my sister had the upper hand. When she marched into the house with "Lucky," she told Dad that he had to pay the fisherman.

"What!" he said. "Do you think I'm going to pay forty dollars for that little mutt?" But he did because he had given his word, even though forty dollars back then wasn't chicken feed. Lucky turned out to be a great pet, and he was more or less my dog. You couldn't keep him out of the water. He used to pester the ducks out on the salt chuck in front of our house. When he got too close, the ducks would dive, and then Lucky would dunk his head under the surface to see where they went. It was unfortunate that up in our neck of the woods we didn't have the luxury of a veterinarian. When Lucky was about four years old, it was obvious that he was quite sick. One day after school, I searched high and low for him without success. Finally, after dark, I thought maybe, just maybe, he could be down by the ocean that he so loved. I grabbed a flashlight, and sure enough, there was my faithful companion lying on the beach, staring out over the water. The tide was coming in and the waves were just beginning to lap at his front paws. I carried him home and put him in the basement where he died during the night. I was grief-stricken.

Mom tried to console me, and Dad, being Dad, just said, "He was a good dog."

We were told, after the fact of course, that purebred dogs required distemper shots if they were to have a long and happy life.

Another story involving my sister was an incident that happened when she was in her early teens. She told me this story many, many years after she left the Falls, when she was a grandmother a few times over. Her best friend, Patsy Beggs, Johnny's sister, wasn't too happy at home, and she confessed to Mary-Lynne that she wanted to run away. My sister, being a supportive friend who was up for the challenge and also a bit of a shit disturber, told Pat that she would go with her. More easily said than done when you consider that the nearest road to freedom was sixty miles away by water in the Bella Coola Valley. Bucky Robertson had tried it once. He got hold of a boat and made it as far as King Island, about twelve miles south on Cousins' Inlet, where he camped for two weeks. It's pure speculation on my part, but he probably ran out of canned beans and had to return home to face the consequences.

The girls hatched a plan that was both unique and bold but, in retrospect, also quite foolhardy. First, they told their respective parents that they were going to hike up to Lost Lake. This was a small lake just past the ball park that was popular for skating during the winter if it ever froze over. It would be poetic. When they didn't come home in the evening, they would be considered "lost" at Lost Lake. Step two would be to swim from our property to the Standard Oil dock and sneak on board the tanker that was pumping gas and oil into the fuel tanks at the station. Then they would stow away in one of the covered life boats on the deck, disembark at the Vancouver harbour, find a drug store, buy a hair dye kit, then dye their hair. That was it. That was the plan. It was ill-conceived and poorly executed. I wonder if they ever gave serious thought to the possibility that the tanker could have more ports of call before docking in Vancouver. If so, they would be getting a little hungry. Step two was to be their downfall. Mary-Lynne swam over first, holding her dry clothes over her head. After climbing onto the dock, she motioned for Pat to follow.

She kept waving, and finally Pat blurted out, "I can't, my typewriter will get wet." She had a brand new portable typewriter, her pride and joy, and there was no way she was leaving town without it. Who knows, perhaps she was a budding author and was going to write a teenage *On the Road* best seller.

When I was sixteen I was trying, without much success, to sleep in on a Saturday morning. At seven a.m., a couple of ravens were being quite vocal, probably scrapping over mussels or whatever else they ate on the beach. I owned a 22 rifle, and I loaded it with a 22 "short" bullet. Those weren't as loud as the regular bullets, and they didn't have much in the way of velocity or power. I opened the bedroom window and drew a bead on the largest bird, aimed two or three inches over its head and squeezed the trigger. Much to my surprise, I nailed it. Surprised because I was far from being a marksman, as I had proven as a junior member of the Ocean Falls Shooting Club. I hit it but didn't kill it. I could see it flopping around amongst the rocks on the beach, so I dressed quickly and ran out there where I could see blood squirting out of its breast. I felt terrible for the raven. I put it out of its misery with a large rock. After that I didn't have the stomach to kill any other creatures except for fish and the odd rodent.

Back in Edmonton, we would buy bulk peanuts in the shell to feed the blue jays and squirrels. I was busy one day woodworking in the basement when I heard a rustling noise on the storage shelves against the wall. I crept over and sure enough it was a cute little mouse inside the plastic bag, nibbling away on the peanuts. I quickly grabbed the bag and headed out to the back lane, picking up a shovel on the way. I was intending to send it to rodent heaven but had a change of heart. When I set the bag down, the mouse escaped and made a beeline back towards the house. That's when I took the shovel and played "whack-a-mole" in the back lane. At least I had given him a chance. He made the wrong choice that day.

When I was about thirteen years old, I was sitting on my bed puffing away on a big cigar that a friend had "borrowed" from his father's stash and given me. In no time at all, I became light-headed and nauseated. Don wasn't too happy when I spewed all over the floor. He paid Barbara a quarter to clean up the mess, and the only saving grace was that our bedroom had a hardwood floor, not carpet. I was glad that Grandpa Forbes wasn't staying with us that summer like he had the other two previous years. That incident, along with the fact that Mom had a smoker's cough, was a deciding factor for me becoming a lifetime non-smoker.

Don and Granpa Forbes '54 Martin Valley

Sometime after Grandma Forbes died in the late '40s, Grandpa sold his house in Regina and moved to Vancouver. Twice he came to Ocean Falls to spend the summer with us, bunking in with Don and me downstairs. What I remember of him was that he always wore a heavy tweed suit, always seemed to have a pipe going, and had numerous drugstore reading glasses scattered throughout the house. Grandpa was a quiet little man, and for his age, at that time eighty-three, he was in remarkably good health. He spent hours everyday across the road with a buck saw cutting up alder logs for firewood. That was the only time that we saw him without his suit jacket on. At the end of the day, Don and I would haul the firewood home in a wheelbarrow. Grandpa moved back to Regina in 1959 and moved in with his son Ian and family, but unfortunately was evicted for smoking his pipe in the house. Uncle Archie took him in. That winter, he had a bad fall on the icy streets of Regina and saw a doctor for the first time in his entire life. Within weeks, he passed away. Grandpa was eighty-seven years old.

Once in my mid-teens, Mom told me that she would bake a blueberry pie if I could pick enough berries, so I was busy picking away on a large bush about a block from our house. I had the bucket half full when I noticed some movement on the other side of the blueberry patch. Damned if it wasn't a black bear happily feeding away. He didn't bother me and I didn't bother him, but Don Hart got wind of this, and he rushed home and returned with 30-30 rifle. He shot the bear right then and there, but I couldn't see the point. Maybe he thought that he was protecting the women and children of the village.

Before we knew it, our two-day jaunt in Ocean Falls was over. I was glad that we visited my hometown, but on the other hand, I was quite sad to have witnessed the "Normalization" close up. Not only was Ocean Falls now a shell of its former self, but even in Martin Valley the unoccupied houses were rapidly declining. Moss on the roofs was bad enough, but I could just imagine how much mold was inside those unheated houses. When we boarded the aircraft for the flight to Port Hardy, all eight seats were occupied and there was a large load of frozen fish on board. The other six passengers were tourists from Washington State who weren't going home-empty handed after their charter fishing excursion. I'm sure that we must have been close to the maximum take-off weight because the Grumman Goose amphibious aircraft needed a good one hundred percent from both engines and over half a mile before it could lift off from Cousins Inlet. Before takeoff, when she noticed that the water was at the level of the portholes, Evelyne was convinced that we would crash into the mountainside. Once airborne, we were treated to another aerial panoramic view of the West Coast, which helped to dissipate some of the bad vibes that I had experienced in Ocean Falls on that trip.

FLARES AND THE FINAL STRAW

After about ten years working at NWI, I was getting tired of the rat race. The union had negotiated with the company so that we had the option of taking time off in lieu of overtime pay, which suited me just fine. With my military pension added to overtime pay, I would be taxed in a higher bracket anyway, so given the choice, I usually opted for the time off. In view of the C-130s flying in the war zones in the Middle East at the time, NWI had been contracted to install a missile defence system on the fleet. It was a rather elaborate way of dispensing flares and chaff because the bad guys now had heat-seeking missiles that could fly up the tailpipe of a turbojet engine—not a pretty sight. Due to the lack of hanger space at the International Airport, the modification program was carried out at the Edmonton Industrial Airport, minutes from our home. Here was my chance for a change of pace and the added bonus of a five-minute commute versus my present thirty. The crew consisted of eight techs and a foreman who was well-liked, but unfortunately after three aircraft, the project came to an end, so we were all transferred back to the International where NWI was gearing up for a huge project.

The entire fleet of E model Hercules, the older ones, would be re-wired and updated with solid-state equipment. I started out working in the harness shop building the wiring harnesses, and that's when it hit me that the scope of this project was mind-boggling. NWI was hiring the

NAIT graduates as well as recently retired air force techs. On the hangar floor, there were two shifts going. First the easy part, ripping out all the old wiring, and then the not-so-easy part, clamping in the new harnesses. What a nightmare. I was regretting transferring out of the C-130 inspection program. The final straw for me was the evening shift just a few days before Evelyne and I were due to leave on our summer holiday. All the wiring harnesses terminated at plugs that were eventually attached to control boxes or electronic equipment throughout the aircraft. It was a simple matter of crimping a pin onto the wire and then inserting the pin into the plug with a special tool, but for some unknown reason the intercom boxes had the older low-tech solder-type plugs. When I climbed into the cockpit at three thirty p.m. to start my shift, I couldn't believe what I was seeing. This young kid had just about finished soldering all the wires—thirty-five plus—on the co-pilot's position intercom plug. It was in a terrible state. Blobs of solder were shorting out every second pin. I asked him what the hell he was doing. He thought it was okay. It turned out that the tech school didn't teach him any of these low-tech soldering techniques. I couldn't really blame him, but I could certainly point a finger at the supervision, or lack thereof. It was going to be a steep learning curve. And there were at least nine intercom stations on the C-130 aircraft that had to be soldered. For the co-pilot's position, I just cut off all the wires and re-soldered them on to a new plug, throwing the old one in the garbage.

Wilson Chew and Carol Grenier in harness shop in '96

FREEDOM 54 AND THE HANDYMAN

Just a few days later, we were heading west for our summer vacation. Evelyne was travelling with me because we were planning to visit Joanne and Brian Wiseman who now lived in Penticton. Just as were leaving the city, I turned to Evelyne and said, "God, I hate the thought of going back to work in two weeks." She replied that I should just quit. We were mortgage free, she was working part-time as a parish nurse, and I had my air force pension. We wouldn't starve. It took her all of thirty seconds to convince me. You've heard of impulsive shoppers. I must be an impulsive quitter because at the next town, Spruce Grove, I pulled over and faxed the company, telling them I'd be back in two weeks to pick up my final pay cheque and my tool box. That made our vacation much better. Eleven years in the rat race was enough.

A funny thing happened while we were touring Vancouver Island. After spending a week in Tofino on the west side of the island, we drove over to the Comox Valley to look up old friends. We knocked on Teasdales' door, and Sue answered with a phone at her ear.

"Where's Scott?"

"Right here," Sue replied as she handed me the phone.

Scott blurted out, "What are you doing there? You're supposed to be here, in Edmonton." It turned out that Scott was hired on at NWI for the massive re-wiring job.

I just laughed and said, "You poor bastard, good luck."

He retired as a warrant officer, so he hadn't done much physical labour in several years other than mowing his lawn and splitting firewood. He lasted just a few short months.

During those years, a financial institution was always advertising its plan, "Freedom 55." When I left NWI I was fifty-four years old, so I told all my friends that I took the "Freedom 54" plan, one better. I didn't miss getting up at six a.m. five days a week to face a long commute and a job I no longer cared for. The first thing I did was to take out a trial membership at a gym downtown, but I soon grew tired of that. Then I caught the golfing bug and took out a membership at Lancaster Park, the former air base that is now an army base. My brother Don had been bugging me for years to take up the sport. At the time, he was working at the pulp and paper mill in Peace River, three hundred and ten miles northwest of Edmonton. Don had worked as a mechanical engineer for seventeen years in the mill at Kitimat, B.C., but due to the declining price of paper, the Engineering Department was reduced and he was handed his walking papers. He was bitter about what happened there. Don had seniority, but the company kept the younger, less experienced engineer, probably because the man had a wife and kids to support and Don was single. He eventually found employment at a mill in Red Rock, Northern Ontario. He worked there for four years and then landed in Peace River when that mill cut back.

Don was also a curling nut, and he was slowly wearing me down, so I thought, what the heck. I have lots of spare time now. I'll give that a shot also. That summer, I spoke to the famous Hec Gervais, winner of the World Championship curling title in 1961, now manager of the Avonair Curling Club on Kingsway Avenue. Hec had a corner on the nickname market. He was known as the "Potato Farmer from St. Albert," the "Friendly Giant," and the "Gentle Giant." He weighed in at two hundred and seventy pounds. Hec told me to come back in October and that he would find a team for me. I did that, but never saw Hec again because he died of a heart attack at the age of sixty-one, just a few weeks after I had spoken with him. That winter, I discovered that curling wasn't as easy as it looked, but it was a wonderful sport. After that, when Don and I had our weekly phone call, the conversation would get around to sports. It could be golf, curling, basketball, football, tennis or baseball, my favourite, but I drew the line at bowling. I said to him, "Look Don, I don't care if it's my nickel or your nickel, we're not talking bowling on the phone."

It would be an understatement to say that Don was serious about golf. Sometimes playing together wasn't all that enjoyable because of his quirks on the course. Normally Don came to Edmonton where we had a multitude of courses to choose from and where he could sample Evelyne's home cooking, but one weekend, I drove to Peace River, and we played two different courses. I had to watch where I stood on the T- box while he swung because if he could see any part of me in this back swing, he would stop and have me move. Once Don was attempting a hundred and sixty-five yard lay-up where a large pond guarded the green. He took a mighty swing with a five iron, hit it fat and consequently advanced the ball only forty yards.

I quipped, "Nice lay-up, Don."

To which he replied, "Any damn fool can see that wasn't a lay-up. I just duffed the shot."

"Hey, I'm just joking," I said.

He answered, "Golf is no laughing matter."

End of discussion.

So, there I was, all set for life with my curling and exercise bike in winter and golfing in summer with a bit of cycling thrown in for good measure. If only. I soon became bored and realized that I was too young to be doing virtually nothing constructive. One typical winter day, I was getting a haircut at a salon two blocks from our home when the stylist asked if I could shovel her sidewalk that day and for the remainder of the snow season. That would get me out of bed in the morning, maybe earlier than I wanted, but it was exercise at least, so I took it on as well as her neighbour's, a small publishing company that supplied Canadian schools with history books. Soon, at minimum wage (which I thought was a bit of an insult) I was hired on by the company to come in once a week to package and ship books across Canada. After three months, I asked for a pay raise and was turned down, so I gave them two weeks' notice. I was back to square one—no job and now no snow to shovel because it was spring.

When Evelyne mentioned that I should have saved some of those home renovation jobs for my retirement, a light bulb went on. I could do renovation/handyman stuff. She even thought up a name for this new enterprise: "John's Job Jar." Not wanting to join the rat race again with forty plus hours of work a week, I didn't advertise but rather relied on word-of-mouth through friends. My favourite client was a widow, a good friend of my in-laws, who lived in a large house in south Edmonton. Sheila and her husband raised seven kids who were all very successful as lawyers, engineers, teachers, even a fire chief in the mix. With twenty-one grand-children to entertain at Christmas and Easter, she didn't want to give up her house after her husband died, so I always had lots of projects on the go, from yard work, electrical, plumbing and painting to hanging doors. In her mid-sixties, Sheila was such a lively, upbeat character. Even with her bad knees, she never turned down a backyard ball hockey game with her grandkids, and she always made a point of sitting down at the end of the day to have a beer with me. One project she had for me was installing an exhaust fan in her basement bathroom. First, I ran a new wire from the circuit breaker box to the bathroom ceiling, and as I was moving some of the acoustic ceiling tiles, the end of the wire touched a hot water copper pipe. I was standing on a stepladder, and when the one hundred and ten volts shorted out on the pipe, it sounded like a gunshot, and I went flying off the ladder. Talk about getting your heart rate up. I had water spraying all over the cedar walls, and I didn't know where the main water shut-off valve was, so I yelled up the stairs for Ross to come down to help me, and to make it quick. Ross was a professional engineer I had met on my guitar-building course, and he was unemployed at the time. I had recruited him to help me paint some of the top floor bedrooms. We found the shut-off valve and mopped up the water. Thankfully, Sheila was out shopping at the time—probably buying beer for us. I had to drive back across the river to pick up my propane torch in order to splice in a new section of copper pipe. When I got back, Sheila was home. I showed her the water-stained wall and told her about the ladder, the loud bang, etc. And she almost burst a gut she was laughing so hard. Most people would have been madder than hell, but not Sheila. She thought that was the funniest thing going. How could you not like this woman!

Even after I stopped doing handyman work, I always found time to do various jobs for Sheila. I also did some work for her friend Helen who lived in an older high-rise in downtown Edmonton. Her bathroom had one of those old electrical shaver outlets which couldn't handle a hair blower, so I installed a ground fault interrupter outlet for her. One job led to another because Helen now wanted a new kitchen countertop with a new sink and taps. When I shut off the kitchen water supply, one of the valves was still dripping, so I thought, no problem, I'll just close the main shut-off for the apartment and replace the leaky valve. Much to my surprise, I discovered that the individual apartments didn't have main shut-off valves, and the building manager wasn't about to shut off the water in a fifteen-story apartment building with a restaurant and a beauty salon on the ground floor just, to accommodate me and my plumbing woes. I had to catch the drips in pots and leave it overnight, giving Helen strict instructions to check it every few hours. I didn't sleep very soundly that night. I had visions of water damage in the nine apartments directly below Helen's, and me being sued to within an inch of my life. And that's why plumbing isn't one of my favourite pastimes. A real plumber has the knowledge, training and experience as well as a van full of every tool known to man; whereas, I had none of the above. Plumbing isn't for the amateur unless he wants to live on the edge.

Some of the other jobs I took on were landscaping and yard clean-ups, small dry-walling jobs, eaves trough cleaning, electrical wiring, painting, door hanging, attic insulation, small siding jobs, baseboard installation and even a squeaky floor repair. My ex-air force friend, Dennis Coughlin, helped me with the siding and insulation jobs. Sometimes when I didn't have any jobs on the go, I volunteered at Habitat for Humanity with Dennis. My speciality was door and window trim, baseboards and hanging doors. Once we were on a job for a single guy who had a disc jockey entertainment business. He had two different plumbing leaks—not again—and he complained that in the winter his furnace would run for hours on end. In total, there were seven different problems we had to address, and we spent three days there. Dennis and I beefed up the attic insulation as well as the attic access hatch, a major fault present since the house was built. For years the heat had escaped through the flimsy plywood uninsulated hatch. The owner was a typical single guy, not too keen in the housekeeping department. Lunch in the kitchen meant clearing off the table first. That's when we noticed all the uncashed cheques from his DJ business lying all over the table and attached to the fridge door with magnets. When we added up the total, it came to eight thousand dollars. Either this guy had a great business and this was just chicken feed or else he was a slob. I suspect the latter. We should have jacked up our rates and stretched out the job.

I didn't mind painting although one lady really tried my patience. It was a thirty-minute drive out of town to paint two bedrooms and a bathroom. She was picky. When she came home at four p.m., she could spot a flaw as small as a pinhole at thirty paces. And, naturally, at that point, all my brushes, rollers and trays were cleaned up and I was ready to head out the door. When I completed that job, I said never again, but a month later she wanted me to paint two more bedrooms. I told her that I'd increased my hourly rate by twenty percent.

But she said, "That's okay. Can you start next week?"

I operated "John's Job Jar" for about two years. It was okay but still restricting, and it was interfering with my "Freedom 54" plan and retirement. Clients didn't seem to appreciate it when I quit a job early to go golfing or curling. Except Sheila, of course.

PRAIRIE SENTINALS

I would soon get into something that I really enjoyed. My friend, Dennis Coughlin, was quite a versatile person. Not only was he an excellent artist, but he had a picture framing business in his basement, and he was a talented woodworker. He was the one who got me interested in restoring antique furniture as a hobby. One Christmas, he gave us wooden Christmas tree ornaments that were miniature sleds. This gave me an idea. I had always been intrigued by the grain elevators that graced the skyline of every town, village and hamlet of the three prairie provinces—and even a few in B.C. Now, I wanted to build some as ornaments. I mulled over my plans for a few months, wondering how to do it economically and easily. If I started out with a block of wood and then cut out the various roof angles, it would be not only very tricky, but also very time-consuming. Evelyne must have been thinking it over also because she came up with a solution. Basically, I was to cut the roof lines first, clamp and glue them to the centre section that was the cupola and then glue the shed onto the front. It might sound complicated on paper, but really, it was quite simple. When my finished product turned out satisfactorily, I figured that with a bit of research and fine-tuning I could probably find a market for my elevators. I visited the Provincial Museum of Alberta first, where the curator really helped me get a grasp of the various elevator companies that had evolved over the years.

It was at that time, Christmas of 1999, that we flew to Hawaii for two weeks. We had no problems with accommodations and flights because many people refused to travel, afraid that all the computers in the world would crash when the new millennium rolled over on January 1, 2000. As we would discover, absolutely nothing happened. It was just fear mongering at its worst, and we had a wonderful time in Maui. Didn't miss shovelling snow. What did elevators and Hawaii have in common? Many a night in those two weeks I would be lying awake, my mind in overdrive, thinking of all the different models that I could build. Those hours proved quite productive. Within a year, it was full steam ahead with seventeen models on the go. I was able to procure decals for nine different companies and I had a print shop run off decal copies for model sizes from two to twelve inches in height. Some of the models were clocks—wall and mantel—pen holders, napkin holders, salt and pepper holders, steak knife holders, bookends, Christmas tree ornaments, plain elevators and business card holders. The most popular were the toothpick holders and the fridge magnets. As far as favourite companies went, not surprisingly, Alberta Wheat Pool was number one with Saskatchewan Pool a close second. Pioneer and United Grain Growers were also popular along with Searle and Federal even though the latter two were no longer in existence. I had found a source for kiln-dried wood at a sawmill on the Yellowhead Highway by Spruce Grove, Alberta for a very reasonable price: free. The wood consisted of cut ends that were destined for the burn pile.

Our unfinished basement became my workshop, with benches, power tools, a multitude of hand tools, a painting table and a dust extraction system that I built to keep my spouse happy. Brother Don drove down from Peace River one weekend, and after inspecting the basement, he remarked that it looked like Santa's workshop. During a visit

Pair of 'Book Ends'

from Mary-Lynne and her husband Tony, she asked me why I had "UGG" decals on the white elevators. I had to explain that it stood for United Grain Growers. She should have known better, having been born a stubble-jumper in Regina.

Up until the mid '60s, all the grain elevators were painted the same rusty red colour known as CPR red, as were the railroad grain cars and, in many cases, the elevator operator's house, fence and outhouse. Every Thursday, I rented a table at the farmers' market in the Westmount Shopping Centre close to where we lived. What the customers appreciated was that I printed the name of their town on the front and both sides of their selected model while they waited. At a market just before Christmas, I sold six Saskatchewan Pool fridge magnets to an older lady with the name of the hamlet where she was originally from. An hour later she was back because she realized that she had given me the wrong spelling, so I had to label six more and print the correctly spelled name. Then, of course, it meant re-sanding and repainting the originals.

My timing was perfect for selling the handcrafted miniatures of those Canadian prairie landmarks. People wanted something that reminded them of "the good old days" because the elevators were fast disappearing in the Canadian West. Unprofitable rail lines were removed, and grain companies merged and then centralized their terminals. The traditional elevators morphed into concrete super structures with ten times the capacity. The old wooden elevators would be bulldozed over and burned. In many cases, this resulted in the smaller prairie towns and hamlets just withering away and dying. At their peak, there were approximately fifty-eight hundred of these prairie giants out west, and today, I don't believe there are any left that are handling grain. The bulldozers were busy. A precious few survived, hauled away to a farmer's barnyard or converted into museums. Not only did this new reality create ghost towns, but the grain farmer now had to drive sixty to eighty miles to sell his crop instead of the previous eight to ten miles. To keep these trips economical, he had to either buy a much larger truck or else pay a trucking company to haul the grain. As if those farmers didn't have enough overhead as it was. And the heavier traffic was hell on the road surfaces. It was a win-win situation for the grain companies and the railroads but not for the little guy.

When I started flogging my wares at the farmers' market, I was soon known as "The Elevator Guy," and then some of the other craft shows started to recruit me. It was a good way to experience rural Alberta. One of my favourite events was the Smoky Lake Great White North Pumpkin Weigh-Off and Fair in early October. Some of the pumpkins were over twelve hundred pounds, and what the growers fed those pumpkins was a closely guarded secret. Some of the shoppers were intrigued with the construction of my models. I recall one elderly man who scrutinized my steak knife holder on the table. He kept turning it over, trying to see how I cut the slots to house the knives. He was either too cheap to buy it, only thirty-five dollars including the knives, or too proud or embarrassed to ask me. I would have told him had he asked, but he walked away empty-handed and more puzzled than ever. I especially enjoyed talking to the old timers who came by my table. Occasionally, I would strike up a conversation with a retired elevator operator, but most times it would be the operator's widow, because the job wasn't conducive to good health. Not only was grain dust highly combustible and could burn down the wooden elevators if ignited, but the grain dust played havoc with the respiratory system.

Without a doubt, the most interesting character I came across was Gordon, a quiet eccentric in his late twenties who was very focused. Focused on elevators. He had an encyclopedic and uncanny knowledge of grain elevators. Name a small hamlet on the prairies, and right off the top of his head he could tell you the current status of the elevators located there. When they were built, burned down, bulldozed over, sold or merged, he knew it all. He was simply amazing. As far as I knew, he didn't have a job and he lived with his parents in Fort Saskatchewan. His mode of transportation was an old three-speed bike equipped with panniers to haul his camping gear. Gordon would pedal around Alberta and Saskatchewan during the summer months to photograph his beloved elevators and to write up a log called *Super Gems* that he would email to anyone who showed an interest. He sent me a copy dated June of 2001 that contained fifty-nine pages. The Super Gems were rated from one star to a five star classic. A five star would have to be very photogenic, in good condition, with no power poles or steel bins to spoil the view. The lowest of the low was NR—no rating. He even informed the reader where the better camera views were and at what time of the day to shoot the best photo. Some of the Super Gems also had a symbol: two upside-down V's indicated if the elevator and rural setting would be ideal for aerial photography.

Once, when Gordon ventured into Manitoba on his trusty old bike, he talked his way into the Canadian Wheat Board archives in Winnipeg and was allowed to photocopy the complete record of every grain elevator, which included the location, the company and the capacity in bushels, for 1961. He made me a copy that proved to be invaluable when my customers needed help in deciding what company decal they wanted on their purchase. In many cases they couldn't remember exactly what was in their hometown. In exchange for the records, I made Gordon a few six-inch elevators of older companies, and of course they had to be the classic CPR red. He didn't want a tricked-out model like a mantle clock or a pencil holder—just a plain model elevator, thank you. With the demolishing of so many of the iconic buildings, Gordon rapidly became disillusioned and bitter. At first the newspapers and news outlets would report and record the death of another elevator, but it became so common that another tear-down was no longer newsworthy. Time marches on. It was inevitable that Gordon would have to focus on his other interest, a distant second, which was old vinyl records.

Before elevators started disappearing from the landscape, a prairie traveller looking for a "cool one" to wet his whistle could count on finding a licensed hotel in a three-elevator town. He would be out of luck in a two-elevator town. And when aviation was in its early days, if a pilot was lost he could always find his way by flying close to an elevator, because the name of the town was painted in bold letters on the front and two sides. I was in the model elevator business for two plus years and thoroughly enjoyed it. I could work as hard as I wanted or I could slack off if I felt like it.

COMOX VALLEY REDUX

In the summer of 2002, we drove to Tofino for four days and then spent two days visiting friends in the Comox Valley. After doing the rounds and playing a round of golf with Scott Teasdale, we were heading to Victoria when Evelyne remarked that she sure missed Vancouver Island. I agreed wholeheartedly. What was there not to like? Beaches, mountains, valleys, rivers, mild winters and best of all, no mosquitoes. By the time we reached Victoria, we had debated all the pros and cons at least six times. Evelyne pointed out that Westjet now had a direct flight from Edmonton to the air base in Comox, which would make it so convenient for us to visit family and friends. I was being very stubborn, expressing concerns with real estate, cost of living, moving expenses and a number of other excuses why we couldn't make the move.

So back to Edmonton we went, and within two days I said, "To hell with it. We're going."

Maybe it was the mosquitoes eating us alive that evening and the thought that in less than four months the snow-shovelling season would soon be upon us. This decision was another perfect example of our partnership: I lead, but Evelyne pushes. Or gives me a gentle shove anyway.

We didn't have to do too much to the house to attract potential buyers. It was in a good location in a nice neighbourhood, curb appeal and plenty of character. All I had to do was clean up the basement workshop. We avoided paying real estate commissions by going the DIY route. Two firm offers were presented after our second open house; the successful buyers were a young couple who were flexible on the possession date.

In late November, we were back in the Comox Valley on a house hunting trip. It was quite a chore just getting there. We flew to Calgary for a connection to the Island and ended up sitting in the terminal for six hours due to serious fog on the west coast. Once boarded, the pilot announced that there might be a small window of opportunity to land in Comox, so off we went. He would make two attempts and if he couldn't land, we would be spending the night back in Calgary. On the second attempt, we landed safely amid loud clapping and cheers from the relieved passengers. The next morning, our agent, Rosemary, who Evelyne knew from having worked with her at the local hospital years prior, showed up at our motel with a compass in hand. We wanted a view of the famous Comox Glacier. We needed that compass because the entire Valley remained completely fogged in and would remain so for the entire trip. At that time, there were few houses on the market with our "must haves," but Rosemary kept plugging away and we finally found a suitable house at the highest point in east Courtenay. We checked with the neighbours who assured us that we had our desired view, confirming what our compass was telling us. I was happy with the dedicated workshop on the ground level even though it was much smaller than my previous workshop. Another bonus was the location. Less than three blocks away was a pretty decent golf course, Crown Isle. Crown Zellerbach used to own that land, hence the name.

Back in Alberta, we hired a small family-owned moving company in Leduc for a very reasonable price because it was off-season. We shipped the car with our furniture. Our very good friends from Saskatoon, Phil and Margot, were there helping us with terminal cleaning and touch ups, such welcome support at a stressful time. Meanwhile, I loaded up all the paints, stains and houseplants that the moving company wouldn't take into my truck and left Edmonton on February 12, 2003. What a trip. Not a flake of snow the entire way. In Kamloops, I chose a hotel for its underground parkade so that my cargo wouldn't freeze. The parkade was closed for renovations, but after begging and pleading with the desk clerk that my wife would be very disappointed if her houseplants didn't survive, he agreed to let me park inside.

We moved into our house on Valentine's Day. How romantic is that. I told Evelyne that as long as I lived I would never have to buy her another Valentine's gift, but I'll admit that I have weakened since. Danielle and her boyfriend Tim at the time, had also helped us with the move, and they flew out to help us settle in. We put them to work again. It was nice to move into a house where I didn't have major renovations to carry out. All I needed were shelves to showcase my antique radios and more shelves for all my tools in the workshop. It came complete with a work bench and cabinets. The backyard was another matter. It was bare bones, one shrub and one tree, but my friend Rex showed up with his expertise and muscle to help me transform the yard. After his twenty years in the RCAF, Rex had taken a two-year arborist course and then started a landscaping business that he ran until his knees gave out. I knew that with Rex running the show, the work would be done right. Typical of the yards of many spec homes, I was lucky to have two inches of top soil before hitting rocks, boulders, hard pan and blue clay. I hauled many a load to the dump in Cumberland.

On one trip, I was just heading out of Courtenay when I pulled over to pick up a hitchhiker. He asked me if I was going to Dodge. The locals in Cumberland, a village not far from Courtenay, called their little town Dodge City, like the Wild West, I guess. When he saw my load of clay and rocks, he asked if I could dump it off in his yard. I was only too happy to accommodate and it saved me a few miles on rough road. Over the next week, I delivered three more loads, and five years later when I drove by this house, the pile was still there, untouched. Why he wanted it I have no idea, but whatever it was he was in no hurry to use it. By the time we finished landscaping, there were plenty of trees, bushes, shrubs, beautiful roses, a tomato patch, a raspberry patch and even a two-section compost bin that the rats soon discovered. I eventually had to go to a sealed compost before my neighbours lynched me. That was one advantage Alberta had over BC. The only rats we knew of in Edmonton were the two-legged variety that hung out at the legislature.

Once we were settled into our new home, I signed up at the golf course as a volunteer. My five or six hours of unpaid labour entitled me to more free golf than my body could handle. I know a good thing when I see it, so I'm still volunteering. Evelyne soon found opportunities to contribute to the community by volunteering at the hospital in the Pastoral Care Department and later by working part-time at Hospice as a bereavement counselor. When she learned about the important work of the Community Justice Centre, an alternative to the court system, she started volunteering with them as a panel member and has been there ever since. It didn't take long to establish roots in the community again.

Later on that summer we drove up to Port Hardy to visit Roy Chernishenko. He had lived there for 25 years, working in the power plant at the local hospital. Roy had noticed that while swimming he had little stamina which was really concerning because he had always been a strong swimmer. He was diagnosed with mesothelioma, a rare type of cancer affecting his lungs. This was caused by exposure to asbestos in his work environment. His prognosis was poor. Roy was involved in a class action lawsuit for job-related asbestos victims but he passed away October 28, 2004, before the lawsuit was settled. Marlene, you lost a wonderful husband and lifelong companion and I lost a great and loyal friend.

'92 Ocean Falls Reunion in Kamploops. L-R - Me, Mel Gribble, Roy Chernishenko

DON

My brother Don retired from the pulp mill in Peace River in 1999 at the age of fifty-nine. He was considering moving to Edmonton because there was a great selection of apartments to rent. I pointed out that the golfing season was six months at best and suggested Chilliwack in the Fraser Valley. There had to be a surplus of apartments there because the federal government was closing the army base and transferring the three major units to Edmonton, AB, St. Jean, P.Q. and Gagetown, N.B. Our cousin and the best man at our wedding, Neil Gourlie, had retired there after twenty years as a soldier and twenty more working for customs on the Canada/US border. There would be an instant golf partner and lots of family, including two sisters living in the Vancouver area. So, after working in seven different pulp and paper mills, Don called it a career and looked forward to a life of leisure, which to him meant golfing and curling. He certainly deserved it. He had enjoyed his work even though it could be quite stressful at times. He got at most three years of retirement before his body quit on him, physically and mentally. One knee started acting up from an old ski injury, which affected his gait, which affected his hip and in turn gave his lower back nothing but grief. By 2002, he couldn't swing a golf club or even slide a curling rock down a sheet of ice.

For years and years Don hid from us the fact that he suffered from bi-polar depression. It wasn't until he moved to Alberta that he was

Don in '82

comfortable enough to tell us. We often wondered, but it wasn't a subject easily discussed unless he brought it up. In early spring, after we moved back to the Comox Valley, Don drove over for a visit. He was in obvious pain, and could hardly walk around the block even with a cane. He had aged, turning into an old man in a matter of a few years. There was nothing left for him in Chilliwack, so he moved to Surrey to be closer to family. In retrospect, I realized that when he paid us that visit, he was basically saying his good-byes. I also learned later that he re-wrote his last will and testament in February of the same year.

We were keeping in touch frequently by phone, and it was obvious that he was sinking into depression. After our call on a Friday night, I had a bad feeling and so decided to ring the next day. With no success after many attempts, I contacted Lynne (she had dropped the "Mary" in her name) who was also quite concerned. She asked her oldest daughter, Debbie, who was probably Don's favourite niece and who lived close by, to check up on him. The landlord gave her access to the apartment, but it was too late. He had ended his life with an overdose of medications. Don was two months short of his sixty-third birthday. It was shocking but not surprising. He was considerate enough to leave a note apologizing to the family and explaining that over the last two years his mood swings had been so severe that he couldn't take it any longer, and that he loved us all. Don had accomplished a lot in spite of his serious health problems. An intelligent man, he was acutely aware of the stigma of mental illness, and he lived with his painful beliefs that people would think he was crazy. The last few years of his life seemed to be one long round of treatments, medications, and hospitalizations. We could not blame him for wanting to end it all.

Evelyne and I drove to Surrey to attend the celebration of life that took place eight days after Don's passing. We helped clear out this apartment. I was given the task of going through his filing cabinet which contained basically thirty-five years of his engineering projects. I had no idea what the scope of his work entailed. It was mind-boggling to say the least. As we were doing our thing in the apartment, a couple of vultures from the building showed up looking for handouts. We gave them a few items, but the majority went to nieces and nephews. Later on, we were happy to hear that Don included all nine of his nieces and nephews in a share of his estate. Lynne, who was executor of Don's will, asked me to drive his 2001 Honda Accord back to Courtenay and find a buyer for it. That buyer turned out to be me when I realized that it was a good opportunity to upgrade.

Don's celebration of life was held at a Memorial Centre in Surrey, with Dan Hare officiating. Dan, an ordained minister in the Baptist Church, was married to Lynne's youngest daughter Lynette. He was a professional musician managing his popular show band, March Hare, full time. Before the service began, Dan noticed a big man, a stranger, pacing back and forth in the reception area, so he approached him.

He said, "Hi, I'm Dan. What's your name?"

The man looked at him and replied in a deep voice, "It doesn't matter what my name is."

He turned out to be Johnny Beggs who had bused out from Vancouver after reading Don's obituary in the newspaper. Many old friends came to pay their respects, including one couple that Don had known in Peace River. The family historian, that would be me, wrote the eulogy and Evelyne read it. We were all so grateful for Dan who facilitated a memorable and poignant celebration. Afterwards, Lynne and Tony hosted a wake at their home. Some of us shared a few stories about Don, downing a few beers in the process.

I've never forgotten my brother-in-law Tony and his huge Rottweiler named Daisy. On that day she was no Daisy. We were enjoying a wonderful feast prepared by Lynne when Tony picked up a BBQ chicken leg which he waved around while making a point. Daisy jumped up and bit the thigh off, devouring it in two seconds flat. Tony, still gesturing, didn't even notice that he was left with the drumstick only. Everyone was concerned that Daisy's life expectancy would be considerably shorter after ingesting those chicken bones, but I knew better. Chicken bones, pebbles, prescription sunglasses, all good roughage for that mutt.

Johnny Beggs and my Uncle Pete hit it off at the wake. What they had in common were their experiences on the northwest coast of B. C. Both of them knew a character I had never had the pleasure of meeting, Highline Shorty, who earned his living as a fisherman and sometimes as a hand logger. Fact or fiction, but the B. S. was flowing fast and furious that day. Johnny so charmed my uncle that he conned him into driving him to his apartment in Vancouver, quite a distance from Fran and Pete's home in Burnaby. Johnny was the building manager of the apartment block in exchange for a greatly reduced rent. He called himself "The Lord of the Manor." He was a diabetic and he didn't look after himself. Johnny's best friend, Rick White, told me that the "Lord of the Manor" had died in his apartment in 2004, and that his body wasn't discovered for a few days after his passing. R. I. P. John Francis Beggs. You were an unforgettable character.

At my brother's wake, our cousin Neil was given Don's expensive putter in appreciation for having been such a good friend and golfing partner. A few years later, Neil was to develop his own serious health issues. He ended up with a rare cancer and a poor prognosis. Here was a guy who really looked after himself, unlike Johnny Beggs. Not an ounce of fat on his body, a jogger, a golfer who never used a power cart, and Neil was on the brink. His daughter-in-law called me with the bad news, so I drove to Chilliwack with my friend Rex to say my goodbyes. After dropping Rex off at a coffee shop—Rex loves his coffee—I drove to Neil's home. He was in such bad shape that I was limited to a scant two minutes with him. I don't know how he did it, but he pulled through that bad bout and lived another year and a half. The following summer, Evelyne and I looked him up and he was a shell of his former self but in good spirits. Eventually, the cancer won out. Neil was my favourite cousin, he was best man at our wedding and he had remained a good friend. Sometimes life isn't fair.

BARBARA SUN

I've been negligent in not mentioning my younger sister Barbara and her family. I'll fill in the blanks. After high school, Barbara left the Falls to take nurses' training, but that didn't take, so she toured England, worked there for awhile and then returned to Vancouver where she worked for various banks.

Barb married an architect who had come from Hong Kong to study in Canada. One day when Cheng Yuen Sun, age seventeen, was walking in downtown Chicoutimi, Québec, with his friends, they urged him to adopt a first name that was easier on the Canadian tongue.

As they walked past the Roxy theatre he said, "That's it. That's my new name, Roxy."

And it stuck. Luckily he wasn't passing by the Woodward's Department Store on Hastings Street in Vancouver at the time or he might be known as Woody Sun today.

When Barbara gave birth to Elayne, the first of their four children, Evelyne sent a gift and a card addressed to Mr. and Mrs. Moon. Oops. We didn't clue-in until our Christmas card arrived later that year, signed and underlined, Roxy and Barbara SUN.

When Barb and Roxy came to Comox to visit us in our first house on Hillside Avenue, Elayne was just a toddler. Barb was helping Evelyne with supper, so she gave Roxy strict instructions to watch Elayne in the living room. A few minutes later, Barb walked in to see Elayne stripping the fern by the window.

"Roxy, I told you to watch Elayne."

He replied, "I am watching her." Watching her strip Evelyne's prize fern.

Before we built our dream home on Stafford Avenue in Courtenay, we contemplated purchasing a non-conforming building lot in Comox. On a cul-de-sac, the lot was pie-shaped, but the main problem was the underground pipeline in the backyard which would dictate the footprint. Roxy, an experienced architect, put pencil to paper and came up with some unconventional designs. I recall one was a group of round modules, held together on the exterior with steel cables. Now, wouldn't that be a drywaller's nightmare. Needless to say, we passed on that lot and chose a more traditional one.

Roxy is quite talented in various fields. He can sketch, paint, write poetry, play the guitar, but where he really excels is languages, mainly Chinese dialects. He is fluent in Mandarin and Cantonese and has a working knowledge of Shanghainese and Taishanese. After his retirement, he worked as a translator for the law courts and in hospitals in the Vancouver area.

Barbara and Roxy have one daughter and three sons, all wonderful people, all getting established.

STRAIGHT GRAIN

Shortly after moving back to Vancouver Island, I was getting some exercise on my mountain bike when I came across an old barn that was being re-sided just outside of Courtenay on Condensory Road. It was originally a milking barn, circa 1895, with straight grain Douglas Fir siding that was beautiful and in surprisingly decent condition. You were hard-pressed to find a knot in the entire lot. The story was that Comox Logging Company had been granted a right-of-way to lay railway tracks across the farmer's land, provided the company built the farmer a barn. A portable sawmill was hauled in and the thirty-two-foot siding was milled on the site. The logging company gained access to some of the finest timber on Vancouver Island and the farmer became the proud owner of a huge barn that lasted for well over a century. The present owner was in the process of applying cedar siding which looks nice for about two years before it weathers to an unattractive grey. It was fortunate that I showed up when I did because the fir siding was destined for the burn pile the next day. The owner was only too glad to give it away, so I spent hours trucking it home. I set up saw horses in my driveway, donned coveralls and a dust mask, and using a nylon flap wheel on an electric drill, I cleaned all the mud, manure and loose paint on the wood. What a mess. When I came in from "sanding," I was absolutely filthy, head to toe.

Everyone, including friends, neighbours, and my dear wife, thought

I was crazy, but in the end, I had a huge stash of premium wood for building furniture. At one time, the barn was painted red, but depending on the exposure and weathering and fading, there was a beautiful patina with five different colours—red, orange, purple, brown and black. The fun part was building the various pieces of furniture from a bedroom suite to a coffee table, among others. I originally intended to build just a few items for our home, but Danielle requested two bedside tables, Rex ordered three, and even Arch, our carpet-cleaning guy, wanted one. Evelyne's favourite was a dresser with a curved top. I built a number of serving trays that came in handy as gifts for special occasions. None of the pieces were stained. I just applied urethane to bring out the grain and the colour. Even the numerous nail holes added character. The hand-forged square nails left a rectangular hole in the wood giving it a rustic look.

EXPANDING FAMILIES

Danielle and Tim were married in June of 2005 at a golf course southeast of Edmonton, outside and under umbrellas because of a slight drizzle. Apparently, rain is a good luck sign on a wedding day. They were a striking couple, and it was a lovely ceremony followed by dinner and the usual speeches and a dance. As father of the bride, it was my opportunity to embarrass her.

My speech went like this: "I suppose that it's my duty to say a few kind words about my favourite daughter, Danielle. From an early age, she seemed like a shoo-in for a nursing career. My earliest inkling came when she was four or five years old and she wouldn't eat because she had 'a headache in her tummy.' And she wasn't too fond of hospital gowns either. After she woke up from her tonsillectomy at the age of four, Danielle was whimpering quite a bit, more than was expected, so Evelyne asked her what was wrong, thinking that she must have been in a lot of pain.

Tim and Danielle Homeniuk June 25, 2005

'Whimper whimper'—

'Tell us sweetheart'—

'Whimper whimper'—Finally she blurted out, 'I don't got no pants on!'"

Friends and relatives came to the blessed event from Saskatchewan, B. C. and of course Alberta, so we had a good reunion with those folks.

The newlyweds drove out to Tofino and Ucluelet for their honeymoon, where Danielle had a not-so-enjoyable reunion with the ice cream bucket. She and her new husband went out on a day-long deep-sea fishing charter. Even before the boat left the sheltered harbour, she lost her breakfast. Out on the open seas with those huge rollers, it got even worse. She was sick for the entire trip, all eight hours. That girl always had an issue with motion sickness, even as a young kid. Whenever we drove up to Mt. Washington to ski, if Danielle was in the back seat, she was always armed with an ice cream bucket just in case. But Tim had a great time, landing a thirty-pound halibut which they had frozen and brought back to Edmonton.

You never stop worrying about your kids even if they've been long gone and married. In October of 2006, Evelyne received a call from Danielle who announced calmly that she was sitting in an ambulance, but not to worry because she was fine but her car was totalled. Not what you want to hear from your daughter, especially when she is eight-and-a-half months pregnant with a long-awaited grandchild. A seventeen-year-old kid driving a company pick-up truck hit Danielle's Honda head on, and the truck won. She and the baby were extremely lucky. Danielle was battered and bruised, but she was reassured that the baby was fine. A month later, with this baby now two weeks overdue and after twenty-four hours of labour, she had an emergency C-section because the baby was in distress.

Kaylie and Shayla 2014

Of course, Evelyne had already been in Edmonton for a few weeks to await the blessed event and to help out. When all the problems started, I took the next plane out and just missed the birth by a few hours. Shayla was a healthy little baby in spite of a very difficult birth, and I was soon retrained in diaper changing. The skill came back quickly. Just like riding a bike. When another sweet baby, Kaylie, made her grand entrance on April 15, 2009, Danielle opted for an elective C-section as a precaution. Less stress for everyone, including the grandparents.

We are finding out firsthand that grandparenthood can be a lot of fun. I see the kids a couple of times a year when they come out to the Island, and Evelyne more often due to her trips to Edmonton to see her elderly mother. Two different characters and both talented. Shayla is the reserved one and her younger sister Kaylie is the bubbly one. I have mentioned the Fairy Rock back on the Martin Valley road a lifetime ago. We have a similar version here for any kids who come to visit. It's a three-foot log that Evelyne uses as flower basket stand by the front door. I found the log on the beach. In its former life, it was part of a boom stick and had a large hole drilled at the end where the boom chain would be inserted. For years now, our nieces and nephews would pocket the change they found in the hole of the "magic log." Now it's our granddaughters' turn. The "fairies" don't care how Shayla and Kaylie split up the loot, as long as it's fifty-fifty.

A few years prior to Shayla's birth, the Alberta adoption agency decided to lighten up on their confidentiality policy and unseal their records. Through the agency, Danielle found her birth mother's name. A cross reference could be done, and if the mother also requested contact, then it could be arranged. In this instance, the mother had not requested a contact, so Danielle put her quest on the back burner. After Shayla's birth, she asked Evelyne to help her search. Armed with a name and approximate age, Evelyne placed over a hundred calls to all of those listed with that surname and living in Alberta, before she hit pay dirt. The surname was a fairly common Ukrainian name, but we found it astounding that there were five women in the province of Alberta with the same first, middle and last name and approximately the same birth date. Evelyne eventually found a birth uncle and through him the birth mother, who claimed that she had been searching as well and was anxious to meet her daughter.

The experts say that for adopted children, reconnecting with their birth parents is sometimes a good experience and sometimes not. Danielle proved that. Although her birth mother was delighted to be reunited, to meet her granddaughter and to introduce Danielle's much younger half brother, she had serious mental health issues, which quickly became a nightmare for Danielle. After six months of disappointments and realizations that this relationship was doomed and unhealthy, Danielle cut off all communications.

The only positive that came of this meeting was finding out who her birth father was and his probable location. When Danielle called him, he was astounded to learn that he had a third daughter. It was a joyful reunion with him and his parents. His parents were ecstatic to find out that they had another grandchild and another great-granddaughter. They were welcomed with open arms.

Danielle's grandparents were both eighty-five and still lived on their farm north of Stony Plain. Grandma still planted a large garden every year, and Grandpa was well known throughout the district as a harness maker for working horses. We were invited to their farm a few times, and we couldn't have met a finer couple. They treated us like royalty, with Grandma literally serving a banquet which she prepared herself, and Grandpa giving us a tour of the farm on his quad.

The strange thing about this adoption story is that Danielle had never liked her name. All of her friends called her Dani. While still a young child, maybe five or six, she announced to the world that she wished her name was Shannon. Years later when the adoption records were opened, we discovered that her mother had named her Shannon Lee prior to putting her up for adoption.

Evelyne had had an easier time finding Colin's birth mother, making a mere seventy-five or so calls before locating her. She still lived in Alberta, and Colin gained five new half siblings although he was never that interested in connecting. He was more interested in his medical history. As he put it, "I already have a family." We did meet with his birth mother, a good person who was raised in a dysfunctional family, and whose boyfriend at the time of her pregnancy had disappeared when he found out she was pregnant. She was sixteen at the time and living a very unhealthy lifestyle which led to her child's developmental disabilities.

CARE-A-VAN

In 2007, Evelyne and I started to volunteer with Dawn to Dawn, an action group that is non-profit and focused on ending homelessness in the Comox Valley. Both of us helped with fund-raising for the program, and I also helped with building maintenance and furniture moving when clients were handed keys to an apartment. It's a wonderful program.

Helen Boyd, a nurse and mental health therapist in the Comox Valley, saw the need for better access to healthcare for the homeless or those at risk of homelessness. Many people were falling through the cracks. Helen is very charismatic and very focused. She had a vision, and it was difficult to say no to her. She spoke to many service groups about her vision for a mobile healthcare clinic in the Comox Valley, and in 2009 her brainchild was launched with the help of many service groups. It was the only program west of Calgary at that time that offered such a service.

Care-A-Van

The local VW Dealership and Sunwest RV Centre owner, Barry Willis, donated a twenty-seven-foot motorhome, and his employees donated many extra hours of labour to make it happen. The vehicle was gutted and then rebuilt with new windows, floor, cabinets and examining table, everything that a regular medical office would have. Rick Pizzey, a local sawmill owner, provided his barn to shelter the van. Helen recruited two physicians, nine nurses and a few drivers to make the rounds in Courtenay three times a week. The volunteers handed out donated clothing, especially in the cold and rainy season. In some cases, tents were given to needy clients. The Care-A-Van was an instant success and eventually other practitioners were added: optometrist, dentist, denturist, audiologist, chiropractor, pharmacist and counsellor.

From 2010 to 2016, I was the driver for the "dental run." Once again, Barry Willis stepped forward and loaned us a VW van to transport up to sixteen patients throughout the day on a monthly basis to Dr. Bill Armstrong's Dental Clinic in Cumberland. Bill was a Godsend for the program. He put the smiles back on many grateful patients.

For several years, Evelyne helped with patient assessments two days prior to the actual dental day every month, and she eventually took over from Helen, riding in the van with the patients. Helen was just too busy with all of the other programs. When Bill sold his clinic, Dr. Chris Becir took right over, not missing a beat, and continues to serve those who cannot afford dental care.

In 2012, the Comox Bay Care Society was formed to focus solely on all the services provided by the Care-A-Van. The Care-A-Van is now completely separate from Dawn to Dawn. It is remarkable that it operates with no government funding but with the generous donations of service groups, churches, individuals, and of course volunteer fund-raising events. The difference that a few good people can make in a community is amazing. We can thank Helen Boyd for her vision and her drive to make it all possible.

In the six years I was involved, I can only recall one person among hundreds who was not satisfied with his dental treatment. Can't beat those odds. I quite enjoyed meeting these folks. In many cases, through no fault of their own, the people we helped were victims of circumstance. It might have been growing up in disadvantaged families, having a brain injury, mental illness, FASD, or just plain bad luck.

TRANSITIONS, SNOW-BIRDING AND RED ROCKS

Evelyne's parents were getting on in years. They sold their house in 2008 and moved into St. Thomas, a seniors' residence with three levels of care. It was ideal for them because it catered to French-speaking residents. A Catholic church was next door, and they were able to maintain their independence. Marcel had some vascular dementia due to minor strokes that he suffered over the years, which meant that Germaine was his caregiver, a 24/7 commitment which she managed herself, never wanting or accepting respite.

After five years at St. Thomas, Germaine was admitted to hospital with pneumonia and nearly died. When she was discharged, it seemed that she had lost her short-term memory, and independent living became more and more difficult, even with support. Family members searched for an appropriate placement where she and Marcel could stay together, and finally they moved into an assisted living suite in Canterbury Court. They were happy there for a few months, but as Marcel's dementia progressed, he had to be admitted to hospital. He died in July of 2015 at the age of ninety, after only two months in hospital.

Marcel had been retired from the railroad for thirty-one years. I always got along well with him. He and Germaine never interfered in our lives, and he was always ready and able to lend a hand. In short, he was everything that you could possibly hope for in a father-in-law.

A few years after moving back to the Island, we started "snowbirding" every year in late fall for six to eight weeks to Indio in Southern California. Our good friends, the Wisemans, had just bought a park model trailer at an RV park, and they hooked us up with a rental unit. I must say that we really enjoyed the weather down there in November and December. We always came home in the middle of the rainy season on the "Wet" Coast.

The first time, Evelyne flew to Palm Springs and I drove alone, but on the return trip, she decided to ride with me, which, as it turned out, would be the first and last time. Driving north on Interstate 5 was a nightmare with heavy rain storms and then snow in the high mountain passes. The state troopers at the Oregon border even made everybody chain up because there was half an inch of slush on the highway. Evelyne's back couldn't take the drive, so after that I went solo both ways.

After eight years of holidaying in Indio, we had enough of "fun in the sun." Sure, I liked the golf and the restaurants, but I'm not one for sitting around the pool half the day. If it hadn't been for the mountain bike that I brought down, I would have died of boredom. Then there were three incidents that did it for me.

Once, while driving down, I was in the city of Lancaster just north of L. A. and maybe three hours from Indio when I was rear-ended by a pick-up while stopped at a red light. As I got out of the car, the light tuned green. The truck pulled around me and roared off. It was dark by then, so I didn't get his licence plate number. Then I noticed the two patrol cars that were parked across the avenue, so I drove over and asked the cops, who were just standing there shooting the breeze, if they'd witnessed the hit and run. "Sorry buddy, can't help you," they said, "We're California Highway Police," CHIPS. They told me to turn left, then go straight north for seven miles to the city police station. I did that and found myself waiting at least an hour before the desk sergeant could clear up the drunks and common criminals to deal with me. He told me that it would be better if I got a motel for the night and then phoned in the complaint. At one a.m., a patrol car showed up at my motel to take my statement. He told me that at best there was a five percent chance of solving this hit and run. In the collision, the truck drove my bike's front forks into the trunk lid. The front wheel looked like a pretzel, but at least the car was drivable.

The second incident happened on the pickleball court at the RV park. As I reached for a ball, my sneaker slipped and I went down. When I tried to stand, my right foot wasn't co-operating. It was just dangling there like a half-dead fish out of water. I hopped on my good leg back to our unit where Evelyne and her friend Joanne, another retired nurse, thought that it was looking a lot like an Achilles injury. It was ice and elevation that day, but the next morning, Evelyne drove me to the ER at the Eisenhower Hospital, the best hospital in the Coachella Valley, where the doctor ordered an X-ray. We couldn't figure out what good an X-ray would do, but who were we to argue. The doctor informed me that I had a partial tear of the Achilles tendon, and I was given a removable boot cast and crutches and sent on my way. I asked if I should fly home and have surgery.

He said, "No, you'll be okay. Stay here in the sun and enjoy your holiday."

There wasn't much enjoying for the final three weeks, on crutches or in a wheelchair. For some reason, the insurance company wouldn't fly me with Evelyne via Westjet, which was a direct flight from Palm Springs to Vancouver. Instead, I had to fly through L. A. to Vancouver. The poor kid in the L. A. International had to push me in a wheelchair and drag my luggage for a good half mile in order for me to make my connection.

Unfortunately, the insurance company wouldn't pay for the return of my car, so I paid a trucker to haul it to the Canadian border. Dealing with insurance can be annoying. The previous year, when the pick-up truck rear-ended me in Lancaster, I couldn't claim for the damage to the bike even though it was a direct result of the accident. I was fortunate that it was just the front wheel that was hit and not the rear wheel where all the gears are located. I was also fortunate that Lynne lived within ten miles of the US border because she was able to pick up my car and drive it to Courtenay.

When I saw the orthopedic specialist at St. Joseph's hospital in Comox, he ordered a CAT scan and then just shook his head when he saw the results. My Achilles tendon was completely severed, and in his opinion, it should have been operated on within two days of the injury. They gave me a boot cast with a cork wedge that I wore for months to allow the scar tissue to eventually fuse the tendon. It healed just fine and the only lasting effect is that my right calf is atrophied and much smaller, as if I'd had polio. I've never felt any pain, and I can walk, hike and cycle just as I did before, but I don't dare try any racket sports. What a shame because I really enjoyed the little time I spent playing pickleball.

The third incident—three strikes and you're out—involved my bike once again. I pedalled three miles over to the huge Winco grocery store in Indio to pick up a few items one day. I chained up the bike to a bike rack in front of the entrance and went in. Unbeknownst to me, Brian and Joanne Wiseman had driven over to do some shopping also.

As they were walking into the store, Joanne said to Brian, "Isn't that nice. That guy's picking up John's bike, it must have fallen over."

It fell over because the guy cut the chain with bolt cutters. When I came out the only thing left lying by the bike rack was an old beater bike that the culprit rode in on when he was looking for an upgrade. I checked with the store security guy and he showed me his video tapes. The outside cameras took terrible pictures, very grainy and blurred—totally useless; however, the video tapes covering the meat department were top grade, almost Hollywood quality. The security guy said the bike was either on a truck with a bunch of other bikes headed for Mexico, or else it was in a homeless camp in the desert somewhere. With all its bells and whistles that bike was worth a thousand dollars.

I asked Brian what this thief looked like and he said. "You know, John, I'm not sure if it was a man or a woman. He/she was wearing a woollen tuque."

For years I razzed him about that. "What kind of eye witness are you anyway, Brian?"

We had once visited Sedona, Arizona for three days and really enjoyed it, so the following year we booked a casita at a par-3 golf course in the Village of Oak Creek, four miles southeast of Sedona. I golfed with the old guys in the morning, and after lunch, Evelyne and I would normally go for a hike. One of the characters there, Boots, is still out on the course every day at the age of ninety-seven. We have to tee up the ball for him

Bell Rock Sedona Nov. 2010

and tie his shoe laces, but he's determined to carry on until he reaches the century mark.

At an elevation of forty-five hundred feet, Sedona never gets as hot as Indio, and being a small town, the traffic noise is negligible. The best features that Sedona has to offer are the fantastic scenery of the red rocks and the many hiking and biking trails. Many of the cowboy movies filmed in the '50s were shot amongst those red rocks. Sedona is a very laid-back, easygoing, artsy town with a lot of metaphysical events happening. It attracts many psychics, healers, mediums and artists of all descriptions. It is a very peaceful place with a corresponding low crime rate even though Arizona prides itself on being the Wild West. That is quite apparent in the state gun laws that we Canadians find quite surprising. The State Constitutional Provision, Article 2, Section 26, allows citizens to own rifles, shotguns and handguns without permits, licensing or registration providing they are twenty-one years or older and not a prohibited possessor. Handguns in Arizona can be carried openly or concealed, even in restaurants.

Once at a yard sale in the Village of Oak Creek, I could have purchased an assault rifle, complete with ammunition. You have to be wary of road rage incidents down there because some of these folks could be packing a firearm. Also, on the highways, chances are if a Harley Davidson passes you, it's highly likely that the biker won't be wearing a helmet. He'll be wearing a doo rag, unlike the Honda bikers who normally have helmets. In the Wild West, it's your constitutional right to die anyway you want.

That said, we'll continue to holiday in Sedona because of the great scenery, the good friends that we have come to know there, and as Evelyne puts it, the powerful energy in those red rocks.

FOR THE RECORD

If I want to end this, it's best to tell you how it began. About a year and a half ago, we were in Victoria for the celebration of life for Ron Houle, Evelyne's cousin. His widow, Irm, read four pages that she had written about their life together. It was a moving tribute, but it was also interesting, funny and important for his children, grandchildren and even other family members and friends.

As we were driving home, Evelyne turned to me and said, "You could do that John, document some of your stories for your kids and grandkids."

I replied, "Ya, I imagine I could manage four pages."

"Actually, how about writing about your life even before you met me?" she said.

I thought that she was out of her mind at that point, but being the diplomat that I am, I just said, "I don't think so," and forgot about it.

However, because of the typical wet, rainy winter weather and the fact that I can't sit around the house day and night vegetating on the couch reading books and watching TV, I thought maybe I should do something constructive, like write my story.

Over the years, Evelyne and many others heard about some of my funny and not so funny experiences. Some of these people wondered how I managed to survive my teen years, and they just got the sanitized version. Well, I survived, and here I am.

My father led a very interesting and adventurous life for a number of years, but, unfortunately, there is virtually no written record of it. When, or if, my memory leaves me, I want the luxury of this book to fall back on, not only for me but for my descendants and friends. It has been a good life with more ups than downs, but then again, nothing is perfect. Except for my soul mate. When I met and married Evelyne, it made my life complete.Our meeting must have been more than the simple act of flipping a coin over my left shoulder into the Trevi Fountain in Rome.

And now I'm finished. It's time to go golfing.

ACKNOWLEDGMENTS

I would like to start by acknowledging Katherine Gibson. When I showed her one of my chapters, "Travels with Charlie," she encouraged me to continue because she thought it was engaging and that it had promise. With that, and with her offer of guidance and her expertise with writing books, I decided to jump in with both feet and complete my autobiography.

I thank my editors Marlet Ashley and Linda Graceffo, who spun their magic helping me turn those chapters into a book.

And a special mention to Evelyne's good friend Carol Muirhead who went above and beyond the call of duty in carrying out the important final reading and edit.

I would like to mention my boyhood friends: Lyle Green, Jack Cronin, John Riley and Ray Chernishenko, two of them already deceased. We shared so many adventures and so much fun. Without them, this book would have been much shorter. I also thank Ray's widow, Marlene, who bequeathed Roy's high school yearbooks (so handy for research) and his Ocean Falls photo albums to me.

And into the mix I'll include my air force buddies: Charlie Horestman, Dave Clarke, Rex Rexin (who lives nearby and has a wonderful memory), Pete Peterson (the guy who dragged me to the nurses' dance), Rick Foreman and Dennis Coughlin.

As far as my academic world is concerned, my grade-six teacher,

Don Little, comes to mind. He introduced me to my very first woodworking project, and it was his spiel about the air force that provided direction for me. And of course, my high school principal, Bob Scott, who believed in me, which still surprises me.

Over the years we've had great neighbours who became life-long friends and with whom we shared so many good times: Brian and Joanne Wiseman and Chuck and Lorie Samis. More recently, our Wisconsin friends Torkel and Janet Modahl have contributed to our enjoyment of Sedona, Arizona.

I mustn't forget my sister Lynne who was an excellent resource while I researched our journey in the early years.

And of course my golfing partner Bill Penner who was my go-to guy for our computer problems that were more numerous than I care to remember.

Last but certainly not least, the love of my life, my wife Evelyne, who contributed both the idea and the push (gentle!) to get this done. I owe Evelyne my gratitude for her unfailing support and for providing a sounding board for my story.

I thank you all.

-John Forbes